Digital Marketing

by Ryan Deiss and
Russ Henneberry

for
dummies®
A Wiley Brand

Digital Marketing For Dummies®

Published by: **John Wiley & Sons, Inc.,** 111 River Street, Hoboken, NJ 07030-5774, www.wiley.com

Copyright © 2017 by John Wiley & Sons, Inc., Hoboken, New Jersey

Media and software compilation copyright © 2016 by John Wiley & Sons, Inc. All rights reserved.

Published simultaneously in Canada

No part of this publication may be reproduced, stored in a retrieval system or transmitted in any form or by any means, electronic, mechanical, photocopying, recording, scanning or otherwise, except as permitted under Sections 107 or 108 of the 1976 United States Copyright Act, without the prior written permission of the Publisher. Requests to the Publisher for permission should be addressed to the Permissions Department, John Wiley & Sons, Inc., 111 River Street, Hoboken, NJ 07030, (201) 748-6011, fax (201) 748-6008, or online at http://www.wiley.com/go/permissions.

Trademarks: Wiley, For Dummies, the Dummies Man logo, Dummies.com, Making Everything Easier, and related trade dress are trademarks or registered trademarks of John Wiley & Sons, Inc. and may not be used without written permission. All other trademarks are the property of their respective owners. John Wiley & Sons, Inc. is not associated with any product or vendor mentioned in this book.

LIMIT OF LIABILITY/DISCLAIMER OF WARRANTY: THE PUBLISHER AND THE AUTHOR MAKE NO REPRESENTATIONS OR WARRANTIES WITH RESPECT TO THE ACCURACY OR COMPLETENESS OF THE CONTENTS OF THIS WORK AND SPECIFICALLY DISCLAIM ALL WARRANTIES, INCLUDING WITHOUT LIMITATION WARRANTIES OF FITNESS FOR A PARTICULAR PURPOSE. NO WARRANTY MAY BE CREATED OR EXTENDED BY SALES OR PROMOTIONAL MATERIALS. THE ADVICE AND STRATEGIES CONTAINED HEREIN MAY NOT BE SUITABLE FOR EVERY SITUATION. THIS WORK IS SOLD WITH THE UNDERSTANDING THAT THE PUBLISHER IS NOT ENGAGED IN RENDERING LEGAL, ACCOUNTING, OR OTHER PROFESSIONAL SERVICES. IF PROFESSIONAL ASSISTANCE IS REQUIRED, THE SERVICES OF A COMPETENT PROFESSIONAL PERSON SHOULD BE SOUGHT. NEITHER THE PUBLISHER NOR THE AUTHOR SHALL BE LIABLE FOR DAMAGES ARISING HEREFROM. THE FACT THAT AN ORGANIZATION OR WEBSITE IS REFERRED TO IN THIS WORK AS A CITATION AND/OR A POTENTIAL SOURCE OF FURTHER INFORMATION DOES NOT MEAN THAT THE AUTHOR OR THE PUBLISHER ENDORSES THE INFORMATION THE ORGANIZATION OR WEBSITE MAY PROVIDE OR RECOMMENDATIONS IT MAY MAKE. FURTHER, READERS SHOULD BE AWARE THAT INTERNET WEBSITES LISTED IN THIS WORK MAY HAVE CHANGED OR DISAPPEARED BETWEEN WHEN THIS WORK WAS WRITTEN AND WHEN IT IS READ.

For general information on our other products and services, please contact our Customer Care Department within the U.S. at 877-762-2974, outside the U.S. at 317-572-3993, or fax 317-572-4002. For technical support, please visit https://hub.wiley.com/community/support/dummies.

Wiley publishes in a variety of print and electronic formats and by print-on-demand. Some material included with standard print versions of this book may not be included in e-books or in print-on-demand. If this book refers to media such as a CD or DVD that is not included in the version you purchased, you may download this material at http://booksupport.wiley.com. For more information about Wiley products, visit www.wiley.com.

Library of Congress Control Number: 2016957570

ISBN: 978-1-119-23559-0

ISBN 978-1-119-23561-3 (ebk); ISBN ePDF 978-1-119-23565-1 (ebk)

Manufactured in the United States of America

10 9 8 7 6 5 4 3 2 1

Contents at a Glance

Table of Contents

Introduction

Congratulations! With the purchase of this book, you've taken a big step toward generating engagement, leads, and sales for your company by using digital marketing.

This book is full of insights and strategy tips for anyone starting a new business or hoping to take an existing business online. Or if you're just looking to hone your current digital marketing skills and get up to speed on the latest in digital marketing tactics and resources, this book is for you as well.

The online marketing scene moves fast, no question about it. Tools and applications rise (and fall) every month. Blogs declare a marketing tactic hot one week and dead the next. So how does a book about digital marketing avoid becoming outdated before the ink is dry? Simple. Today, digital marketing is less about *digital* and more about *marketing*.

Sure, the Internet has disrupted every industry, from retail clothing to taxi services — but, over time, fundamental disciplines have emerged as the staples of marketing any organization in a digital world. As you see in this book, these timeless fundamentals of digital marketing remain pertinent, regardless of the tool, tactic, or application.

About This Book

There's nothing magical or tricky about properly executed digital marketing, and you don't need to be overly technical to succeed at it. If you offer a product or service that the market desires, you can find success online by applying the techniques that you learn in this book.

Digital Marketing For Dummies doesn't present hype about the latest flashy tactics in marketing, digital or otherwise. Instead, the book covers foundational disciplines such as content marketing, social media marketing, and email marketing, always in the context of the goals that businesses care about. These goals include acquiring new leads and customers, monetizing the leads and customers you already have, and creating communities of brand advocates and promoters.

To help you absorb the concepts, this book uses the following conventions:

>> Text that you're meant to type just as it appears in the book is in **bold**.

>> If we provide an example of how to say something, we use *italics* to indicate a placeholder, as in *your company name,* which means that you need to replace the italics with your own information.

>> We also use *italics* for terms that we define.

>> Web addresses appear in monofont. If you're reading a digital version of this book on a device connected to the Internet, you can click the live link to visit a website, like this: http://www.dummies.com.

Foolish Assumptions

We made a few assumptions about you as we wrote this book:

>> **You have a great product:** Remember that even the most brilliant marketer can't sell a poor product or service over the long run. This caveat is particularly true in a digital landscape, where word of mouth can spread to the four corners of the earth in the blink of an eye.

>> **You aren't overly technical:** Digital marketing can be as technical as you want to make it. If you want to learn how a web server works or how to write in PHP code, feel free. However, to succeed in the marketing field, you need to understand marketing, not code. Feel free to leave the technical side to someone who understands code, but not marketing.

>> **You're willing to implement and adjust:** To get results, you need to act on the knowledge you gain. In contrast to print, television, and radio marketing, digital marketing can go from idea to execution in a matter of minutes. And because your marketing campaigns live in a digital format, you can change virtually everything you do on the fly.

Icons Used in This Book

This book wouldn't be a *For Dummies* book without the familiar icons in the margin of the book. Keep a sharp eye out for these icons alerting you to important information:

TIP

The Tip icon marks tips (duh!) and shortcuts that will put you on the fast track to digital marketing success.

REMEMBER

This icon points out the fundamentals of digital marketing. If foundational principles are what you're after, skim each chapter looking for this icon.

WARNING

Avoid these digital marketing mistakes to stay on the path to digital marketing success.

Beyond the Book

We have written a lot of extra content that you won't find in this book. Go online to find the following:

>> **Customer Avatar Worksheet:**

Download and complete this worksheet to determine who your ideal customers are, where they are, and what they're likely to buy. Use what you learn about your ideal customer to drive everything from your content and search marketing to your digital ads and email promotions. The customer avatar is truly the Swiss Army Knife of marketing tools.

>> **Customer Journey Worksheet:**

Download and complete the customer journey worksheet to clarify the path your customers will follow in moving from total unawareness of your business to being an avid promoter of your brand, products, and services.

>> **The Cheat Sheet:**

The Cheat Sheet contains additional at-a-glance guidance on developing and executing successful digital marketing campaigns. To find this book's Cheat Sheet, go to www.dummies.com and search for *Digital Marketing For Dummies Cheat Sheet.*

>> **Updates to this book, if we have any, are at**

www.dummies.com

Where to Go from Here

In true *For Dummies* fashion, you don't have to start this book at Chapter 1 and read it all in order. Each part of this book stands on its own, so keep it within arm's reach and reference it often as you execute your digital marketing campaigns. That said, however, if you have the time, we'd like nothing more than for you to read it from cover to cover.

If you're struggling to get results from your digital marketing efforts, or you're new to digital marketing, use Part 1 to ensure that the marketing tactics you use positively impact your business goals. In Part 2, we explore content marketing, a fundamental discipline that affects every digital marketing campaign you execute. If generating more website traffic is what you're after, flip to Part 3 for insights on search and social media marketing, email marketing, and digital advertising. In Part 4, you learn to tackle the measurement and optimization of your digital marketing campaigns. In Part 5, we show you how to avoid the ten most common mistakes in digital marketing so you can stay on the path to success. You also learn about the hottest skills in digital marketing, and the tools you need to execute digital marketing campaigns.

If you have a specific issue, browse through the Table of Contents and Index to pinpoint the section that can solve your problem.

Here's to your digital marketing success!

1

Getting Started with Digital Marketing

Chapter **1**

Understanding the Customer Journey

Think about the last important purchase you made. Perhaps you bought a car, hired a babysitter, or switched coffee suppliers at your office. Chances are, you consulted the Internet to read reviews, get recommendations from friends and family on social sites like Facebook, and boned up on the features, options, and price of the product or service before you made your choice. Today, purchases and purchasing decisions are increasingly made online. Therefore, regardless of what you sell, an online presence is necessary to capitalize on this trend.

This new digital landscape is impacting organizations in more than just the lead and sales generation departments, though. Savvy companies use the Internet to drive awareness and interest in what they offer, but also to convert casual buyers into brand advocates who buy more and encourage members of their network to do the same.

In many ways, nothing in marketing has changed. Marketing is still about developing a mutually beneficial relationship with prospects, leads, and customers. We call the development of this relationship the customer journey. In this chapter, you learn to create a customer journey for your organization and the role digital marketing plays in that journey. The rest of this book helps you to create and execute offers and marketing campaigns that intentionally move customers through the stages of this customer journey.

REMEMBER

The role of your digital marketing is to assist in moving a prospect, lead, or customer from one stage of the customer journey to the next.

Creating a Customer Avatar

Because the role of your marketing is to move people through a series of stages from cold prospects to rabid fans and promoters, you must first attain clarity on the characteristics of your ideal customers. You want to get clear on their goals, the challenges they face meeting those goals, and where they spend time consuming information and entertainment. Creating a customer avatar will give you this clarity. Other terms for *customer avatar* are *buyer persona*, *marketing persona*, and *target audience*, but *customer avatar* is the term we use throughout this book.

A *customer avatar* is the fictional, generalized representation of your ideal customer. Realistically, unless your product or service fits within a narrow niche, you will have multiple customer avatars for each campaign. People are so much more than their age, gender, ethnicity, religious background, profession, and so on. People don't fit neatly into boxes, which is why broad, generic marketing campaigns generally don't convert well; they don't resonate with your audience. It is absolutely crucial that you understand and make your customer avatar as specific as possible so that you can craft personalized content, offers, and marketing campaigns that interest members of your audience or solve their problems. In fact, the exercise of creating a customer avatar impacts virtually every aspect of your marketing, including:

>> **Content marketing:** What blog posts, videos, podcasts, and so on should you create to attract and convert your avatar?

>> **Search marketing:** What solutions is your avatar searching for on search engines like Google, YouTube (yes, YouTube is a search engine), and Bing?

>> **Social media marketing:** What social media sites is your avatar spending time on? What topics does your avatar like to discuss?

>> **Email marketing:** Which avatar should receive a specific email marketing campaign?

>> **Paid traffic:** Which ad platforms should you buy traffic from and how will you target your avatar?

>> **Product creation:** What problems is your avatar trying to solve?

>> **Copywriting:** How should you describe offers in your email marketing, ads, and sales letters in a way that compels your avatar to buy?

Any part of the marketing and sales process that touches the customer (which is pretty much everything) improves when you get clear on your customer avatar. After all, you're aiming toward a real person — one who buys your products and services. It pays to get clear on the characteristics of that person so that you can find and present him or her with a message that moves this person to action.

What to include in your customer avatar

The customer avatar possesses five major components:

» **Goals and values:** Determine what the avatar is trying to achieve. What values does he or she hold dear?

» **Sources of information:** Figure out what books, magazines, blogs, news stations, and other resources the avatar references for information.

» **Demographics:** Establish the age, gender, marital status, ethnicity, income, employment status, nationality, and political preference of the avatar.

» **Challenges and pain points:** What is holding the avatar back from achieving his or her goals?

» **Objections:** Why would the avatar choose not to buy your product or service?

In some cases, you need to survey or have conversations with existing customers to accurately flesh out your customer avatar. In other cases, you may already be intimately familiar with the characteristics of your ideal customer. In any case, move forward. Don't wait for surveys or interviews to be conducted to create your first draft of an avatar. Instead, go ahead and make assumptions despite having no data or feedback, and put completing your research on your short list of to-do's. In the meantime, you can begin benefiting from the avatar you've created.

TIP

Giving a customer avatar an actual name assists in bringing this fictional character to life. In addition, your team members have a way to refer to each avatar among themselves.

Using the five elements described in this section, we created a worksheet that we complete each time we create a new customer avatar. The worksheet helps you hone in on the ideal customer and pair him or her with the right message. In the following sections, we go into more detail about this worksheet so that you can use it in your own business.

Introducing Agency Eric: A customer avatar example

In April 2015, DigitalMarketer introduced a new offer. We began selling a new type of digital marketing training product: Certification Classes. These new trainings include exams, certificates, and badges, and they appeal to a new ideal customer. Of course, having a new ideal customer means that a new customer avatar must be built.

As a result, we defined four distinct buyer personas who would be interested in certifications and training from our company:

» **The marketing freelancer:** Wants to distinguish herself from the other freelancers she is competing with in the marketplace.

» **The marketing agency owner:** Wants to add to the services he can offer his clients and to sharpen the marketing skills of his employees.

» **The employee:** Wants to distinguish himself at his place of employment or to secure a new job or promotion within his existing job.

» **The business owner:** Wants to sharpen her own marketing skills and the skills of her internal marketing team members.

From the buyer personas, four new customer avatars were born. We call one of these new avatars, pictured in Figure 1-1, Agency Eric.

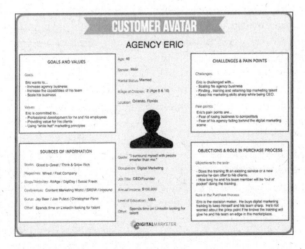

FIGURE 1-1: Agency Eric is a customer avatar who purchases the certification product from DigitalMarketer.

The next section describes the approach to filling out each section of the customer avatar worksheet so that you can define your customer avatars.

Getting clear on goals and values

The customer avatar creation process begins with identifying the goals and values of one of your ideal customers. Make note of the goals and values that are relevant to the products and services you offer.

Being aware of your customer avatar's goals and values drives decisions that you make about

>> **Product creation:** What products or services can you develop to assist the avatar in meeting his or her goals?

>> **Advertising:** How can you describe these offers in your ads and sales copy?

>> **Content marketing:** What blog posts, podcasts, newsletters, and other content vehicles might your avatar respond to?

>> **Email marketing:** How can you tailor your email subject lines and body copy to be consistent with the avatar's goals?

At DigitalMarketer, our Agency Eric avatar owns a digital marketing agency and manages a team of marketers providing services to clients. One of Agency Eric's goals (shown in Figure 1-2) is to increase the capabilities of his team. Agency Eric knows that a more capable team will result in satisfied customers.

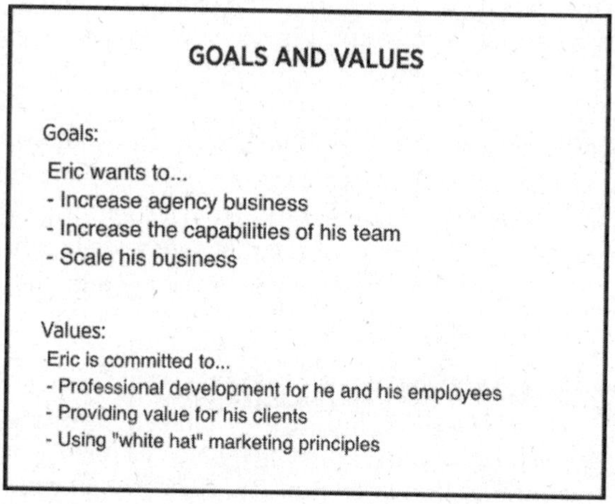

GOALS AND VALUES

Goals:

Eric wants to...
- Increase agency business
- Increase the capabilities of his team
- Scale his business

Values:

Eric is committed to...
- Professional development for he and his employees
- Providing value for his clients
- Using "white hat" marketing principles

FIGURE 1-2: Understanding the goals and values of your avatar is important.

Because Agency Eric has this goal, he is likely to open and respond to an email that promotes our company's Content Marketing Certification with the following subject line:

Need Content Marketing training?

Finding sources of information and entertainment

This section of the customer avatar worksheet is critical to determining where your customer avatar is spending his time on and offline. What books does he read? What celebrities does he follow? What blogs does he read? This is vital information when considering where you will advertise and how you will target those advertisements. We cover digital advertising and ad targeting in Chapter 10 of this book.

TIP

The key to truly understanding where your customer is getting information and entertainment is in identifying niche sources. Identifying these niches is fairly simple using the "But No One Else Would" Trick. To use this trick, you simply complete sentences like:

>> My ideal customer would read [*book*], but no one else would.

>> My ideal customer would subscribe to [*magazine*], but no one else would.

>> My ideal customer would attend [*conference*], but no one else would.

The idea is to find the niche books, magazines, blogs, conferences, celebrities, and other interests that your ideal customer would be attracted to — but no one else would. For example, if you sell golf products, you wouldn't assign Tiger Woods as a celebrity. Tiger Woods is a celebrity your customer avatar would follow, but a large percentage of people interested in Tiger Woods are not golfers and aren't likely to buy your golf products.

Instead, choosing a more niche golfer like Rory McIlroy allows you to hone in on your ideal customer and exclude people who wouldn't find value in your product. If you find these niches when buying traffic from ad platforms like Facebook (covered in Chapter 10), you can often laser-target your audience by focusing on prospects who have these niche interests, while excluding less-than-ideal prospects.

Honing in on demographics

Applying demographic information brings your customer avatar to life. In this section, you add information to your avatar such as age, gender, marital status, and location.

TIP

Although the usual demographics are critical, the exercise of filling in the "Quote" field (shown in Figure 1-3) can be particularly helpful to get inside the head of your ideal customer. The Quote field is how this avatar might define himself or herself in one sentence, or it's the motto the avatar lives by. For instance, our quote for Agency Eric is "I surround myself with people smarter than I."

This sentence says a lot about this avatar's character and motivation to purchase our marketing training products. Brainstorm ideas for your avatar's quote with your team or someone who knows your business well.

FIGURE 1-3:
Demographics
bring the
customer
avatar to life.

Age: 40	**Quote:** "I surround myself with people smarter than I."
Gender: Male	**Occupation:** Digital Marketing
Marital Status: Married	**Job Title:** CEO/Founder
#/Age of Children: 2 (Age 8 & 10)	**Annual Income:** $150,000
Location: Orlando, Florida	**Level of Education:** College Graduate
	Other: Spends time on LinkedIn looking for talent.

Demographic information for your customer avatar is also useful for choosing targeting options in ad platforms like Facebook. Bring your avatar to "life" as much as possible, even by visualizing the person if you can, because when you're writing content, email, or sales copy, it can be beneficial to write as though your avatar were sitting across the table from you. Demographic information like age, gender, and location gives your persona a look and feel.

Adding challenges and pain points

This section of the worksheet can help drive new product or service development. It can also help inspire the copy and ad creative you will use to compel your ideal customer to action. *Copy* is any written word that makes up your ad, email, web page, social media post, or blog post. *Ad creative* is an object that communicates information in visual form, such as an image, a GIF (graphics interchange format), a video, an infographic, a meme, or another form of artwork that you use to convey your message. You use copy and ad creatives to call out to your audience, capture people's attention, and address how your product or service adds value to their lives by solving a pain point or a challenge they face.

When selling certifications to Agency Eric, for example, our company would do well to build solutions to his challenges and pain points and use language that addresses them in our marketing messages. For example, this avatar would respond to sales copy like the following:

Are you tired of losing proposals simply because you don't offer content marketing services to your clients? Certify your team with DigitalMarketer's Content Marketing Mastery Course and Certification.

Copy like this receives a response from Agency Eric because it is specific to one of his pain points, which is the fear of losing business to competitors (see Figure 1-4).

CHALLENGES & PAIN POINTS

Challenges:

Eric is challenged with...
- Scaling his agency business
- Finding, training, and retaining top marketing talent
- Keeping his marketing skills sharp while being CEO

Pain points:
Eric's pain points are...
- Fear of losing business to competitors
- Fear of his agency falling behind the digital marketing scene

FIGURE 1-4: Understanding the challenges and pain points of your customer informs your marketing efforts.

Preparing for objections

In the final section of the customer avatar worksheet, answer why your customer avatar might choose to decline the offer to buy your product or service. The reasons your avatar doesn't buy are called objections, and you must address them in your marketing. For example, if we know that Agency Eric is concerned with the amount of time his team members will be out of the office or unable to work while getting trained, we can send an email that overcomes that objection with a subject line like this:

Get Content Marketing Certified (in one business day).

You can prepare your own customer avatar as we discuss with the help of a resource from DigitalMarketer. Find it at www.digitalmarketer.com/customer-avatar.

TIP

Getting Clear on the Value You Provide

An important part of planning for digital marketing success is understanding the value your organization brings to the marketplace. The value your company provides is far greater than the products or services it sells. In fact, people don't buy products or services at all; instead, they buy outcomes.

Imagine a group of people who are discontent for one reason or another. This group of people are in what we call the "Before" state (see Figure 1-5). No matter what you're selling, you're trying to reach a group of prospective customers who are in this Before state. To gain some insight, write the adjectives that describe your prospective customer before she has experienced your product or service. Is she sad? Out of shape? Bored?

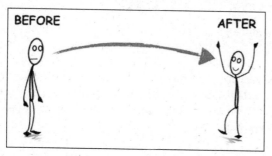

FIGURE 1-5: Businesses provide value by moving prospects from a "Before" state to an "After" state.

Source: https://www.digitalmarketer.com/customer-value-optimization/

Now, leap forward into the future, to the point after your prospective customer has experienced your product or service. What is her "After" state? How has this person changed? In the same place where you took notes about her Before state, describe her After state. Is she happier? Healthier? More excited?

The shift from the Before state to the After state is what your customer is buying. This shift (or outcome) is the value that your business brings to the marketplace. Furthermore, the role of your marketing is to articulate this move from the Before state to the After state.

The understanding of this transition from Before to After is what allows you to craft what is called a Statement of Value. This statement is important because it sums up the value of your product or service. To craft your Statement of Value, simply fill in the blanks on the sentence shown in Figure 1-6.

STATEMENT OF VALUE

_____ enables
(Product Name)

_____ to experience
(Customer)

_____

_____

FIGURE 1-6: Fill in the blanks on your Statement of Value.

Source: http://www.digitalmarketer.com/launching-a-business/

The role of your marketing is to assist in moving a prospect, lead, or customer from one stage of the customer journey to the next. At the beginning of this journey, your customer is in the Before state. By the end, you will have taken your customer on a journey to that customer's ideal After state.

Knowing the Stages of the Customer Journey

If your business has acquired even a single customer, some kind of customer journey is in place. Perhaps this customer journey was not created intentionally, but it does exist. Or perhaps you call it something else in your organization, such as a marketing or sales pipeline.

Regardless of what you call it, becoming intentional about the movement of cold prospects, leads, and existing customers through the stages of this journey is the purpose of your marketing. When you've properly charted your ideal customer journey, you quickly find the bottlenecks that are restricting the flow of prospect to lead, lead to customer, and customer to raving fan.

We can't overstate the importance of sequence in marketing, and particularly in digital marketing. Moving cold prospects from one stage of the customer journey to the next must be done seamlessly and subtly. You're not likely to convert a complete stranger into a brand advocate overnight. But you can gradually move the prospect from one stage of the relationship to the next. To move people through the stages of the customer journey, go through the following eight steps. A worksheet, Figure 1-12, that visualizes the steps of the customer journey is provided in the final section of this chapter.

Step 1: Generating awareness

Every repeat customer and raving fan of your business was, at one time, a complete stranger to your company. She had no idea what problem you solve, what products you sell, or what your brand stands for. The first step on her journey from cold prospect to raving fan is awareness. We go into more detail about tactics later in this book, but if awareness is your issue, you should employ the following digital marketing tactics:

>> **Advertising:** Advertising, both online and offline, is a reliable and effective method of raising awareness.

>> **Social media marketing:** Billions of people access social media sites such as Facebook, Twitter, and LinkedIn every day. Social media marketing is an inexpensive method of raising awareness.

>> **Search marketing:** Billions of web searches on sites such as Google and Bing are processed every day. Basic search marketing techniques direct some of that traffic to your website.

Figure 1-7 shows an awareness campaign from TransferWise, a company that was created by the same people who built Skype. TransferWise is a relatively new company in the money transfer business, and it uses the Facebook advertising platform to raise awareness of the service. Notice how the language used in this ad focuses on teaching what TransferWise is and how you benefit from using the service.

Source: http://www.digitalmarketer.com/launching-a-business/

Step 2: Driving engagement

It's not enough to simply make a cold prospect aware of your business, products, and brand. You must engineer your marketing to capture the attention of your prospect and engage him. For a digital marketer, that engagement almost always takes the form of valuable content made freely available in the form of

>> Blog posts

>> Podcasts

>> Online videos

For example, the grocery store Whole Foods prides itself in selling fresh, organic foods from its hundreds of brick-and-mortar locations. The supermarket chain's online strategy includes its Whole Story blog, which engages its ideal customer with content relevant to the products the company sells. Blog articles with titles such as "9 Refreshing Summer Drinks You Need to Try Right Now" (see Figure 1-8) show existing and prospective customers how to use the products sold at Whole Foods.

9 Refreshing Summer Drinks You Need To Try Right Now

👍 Like 0 🐦 Tweet
G+1 3

By Kate Rowe, July 12, 2016 | Meet the Blogger | More Posts by Kate

The summer heat is now upon us, but you can stay cool with refreshing, family-friendly drinks right now. We're all about using unexpected ingredients, making juice in the blender, and finding shortcuts to delicious summer sippers.

Source: https://www.wholefoodsmarket.com/blog/9-refreshing-summer-drinks-you-need-try-right-now

FIGURE 1-8:
An engaging blog post from the Whole Foods blog.

REMEMBER

A prospect, lead, or customer may spend anywhere from a few minutes to a few years at any one of the stages in this customer journey. For example, a prospect might become aware of your blog and engage with it for a year or more before moving to the next phase of the journey. Others will sprint through multiple stages of the journey in the space of a few minutes. A healthy business has groups of people at all stages of the journey at all times.

Step 3: Building subscribers

The next step in the customer journey is to graduate a prospect from the "merely aware and engaged" stage into the stage of being a subscriber or lead. A subscriber is anyone who has given you permission to have a conversation with him. Savvy digital marketers create lists of subscribers by building social media connections on sites such as Facebook and Twitter, attracting podcast subscribers on services such as iTunes and Stitcher, or generating subscribers from webinar registrations.

Offline companies might build subscription online by offering aware and engaged prospects the ability to receive physical mail or request a consultative sales call or product demo.

But the Holy Grail of lead generation in the digital marketing realm is email subscription. Email is, by far, the cheapest and highest-converting method of moving a prospect through the rest of the stages of this customer journey. We tell you more about email marketing in Chapter 11, but for now, take a look at an example of an effective email marketing campaign from one of the world's largest furniture retailers, IKEA.

IKEA builds social media subscribers on Facebook, Twitter, Pinterest, and more, but acquiring email subscribers is clearly the focal point of IKEA's digital marketing efforts. Upon visiting the IKEA website, you're asked in multiple locations to join IKEA's email list. Figure 1-9 shows an email opt-in form from the IKEA website.

FIGURE 1-9:
An email subscription offer from furniture retailer IKEA.

Source: http://www.ikea.com/us/en/

Step 4: Increasing conversions

At this stage, the goal is to elevate the commitment level of the prospect by asking him or her to give you a small amount of time or money. Low-dollar products or services, webinars, and product demos are all good offers to make during this stage.

Up to this point, the relationship with this prospect through the first three stages of the customer journey has been passive. The goal of Stage 4 is not profitability, but rather an increased level of connection between the prospect and your business. One company that achieves this increased connection is GoDaddy, which allows you to, among other things, register a domain name for a website as well as host and design one for your business. GoDaddy uses a low-dollar domain registration offer with a two-year purchase (see Figure 1-10) to acquire customers and ramp up the commitment level.

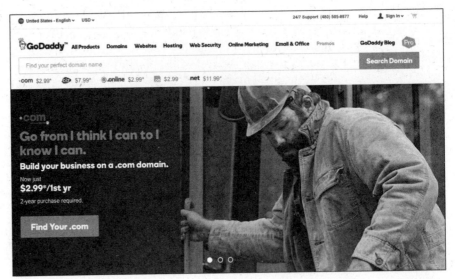

FIGURE 1-10:
A low-dollar offer
from domain
registration
company
GoDaddy.

Source: https://www.godaddy.com/?isc=gofd2001sa&ci=

Step 5: Building excitement

Your marketing should intentionally encourage your customer to use the offer that your lead or customer accepted in Step 4. The business term for getting your prospect to take advantage of an offer is *customer onboarding*. Regardless of whether the conversion in Step 4 was a commitment of time or money, the relationship with this customer or prospect has a much greater chance of success if she received value from the transaction.

At DigitalMarketer, we have a community called DigitalMarketer Lab made up of thousands of entrepreneurs, freelancers, and small business owners. Each new DigitalMarketer Lab member receives an onboarding packet (see Figure 1-11) from our company through post mail that teaches Lab members how to get the most out of their new purchase. This packet builds excitement by explaining all the benefits of being a member, and it shows members exactly how to get started receiving those benefits. By building excitement and teaching our customers to be successful, we've seen dramatically lower cancellation rates.

REMEMBER

The value of the offers you make should far outweigh the price paid by your customer. Deliver great products and services and create marketing campaigns that encourage the use of those products and services. After all, your customers aren't likely to continue buying or promoting your brand to others if they aren't using the product or service themselves.

FIGURE 1-11: This onboarding packet builds excitement and teaches the customer how to be successful with our product.

Step 6: Making the core offer sale and more

At this stage, prospects have developed a relationship with your brand. They may have invested a bit of time or money with you. People who develop this rapport with your company are much more likely to buy a more complex, expensive, or risky product or service from you. We call this jump from passive prospect to buyer *ascension*.

Unfortunately, this is where most businesses start and end their marketing. Some ask cold prospects to make risky investments of time and money with a company they know nothing about. This is the equivalent of proposing marriage to someone on a first date: The success rate is low. Other brands stop marketing to a customer after that particular customer has converted (made a purchase) instead of staying in touch with and converting that person into a repeat buyer.

In the ascension stage, customers or prospects purchase high-ticket products or services, sign up for subscriptions that bill them monthly, or become loyal, repeat buyers. Assuming that you have done the hard work in Stages 1–5 of the customer journey, you should find that some of your leads and customers are ready to buy more, and buy repeatedly. That's because you've built a relationship with them and effectively communicated the value you can bring to their lives. When you market to your customers in this sequence, they're on the path to becoming brand advocates and promoters (see the upcoming sections about Steps 7 and 8). We discuss different strategies for selling more to your existing customers in Chapter 3 when we cover profit maximizers.

Step 7: Developing brand advocates

Brand advocates give you testimonials about the fabulous experience they've had with your brand. They are fans of your company and defend your brand on social media channels and, if asked, leave great reviews for your products or services on sites such as Yelp or Amazon.

Your ability to create brand advocates depends on the relationship you have with these leads and buyers. When you've reached this step, your customer and your company are like close friends in the sense that developing the relationship to this level took time and effort, and maintaining that relationship — one that is mutually beneficial to both parties — will take time and effort also.

You build this relationship by adding value, delivering on the promise of your product (meaning that it actually does what you claim it will do), and with responsive customer service. By consistently delivering quality products and services, you can turn people into brand advocates and ultimately move them into the final step: brand promoter.

Step 8: Growing brand promoters

Brand promoters go beyond advocacy and do everything from tattooing your logo across their chest (think Harley Davidson) to dedicating hours of their free time blogging and using social media to spread their love of your brand online. The difference between an advocate (Step 7) and a brand promoter is that the promoter actively spreads the word about your business, whereas the advocate is more passive.

For brand promoters, your company has become part of their life. They know that your brand is one that they can trust and depend on. Brand promoters believe in you because your brand and your products have delivered exceptional value again and again. They have committed not only their money but also their time to you.

Preparing Your Customer Journey Road Map

For successful businesses, the customer journey doesn't happen by accident. Smart digital marketers engineer marketing campaigns that intentionally move prospects, leads, and customers from one stage to the next. After you become aware of your ideal customer journey, the tactics (taught in the remaining chapters of this book) that should be employed become clear.

For example, if you determine that you have an issue building subscribers (Step 3 of the customer journey), you want to deploy tactics that generate email leads (covered in Chapters 3 and 11) and social media connections (discussed in Chapter 9) to move customers through this part of the customer journey.

Creating a customer journey road map that clearly delineates the eight stages that we cover in the previous section of this chapter (see Figure 1-12 for just such a road map) is a fantastic way to plan and visualize the path that an ideal customer will take from cold prospect to brand promoter. Gather the stakeholders in your company and complete a customer journey road map for at least one of your major products or services. Brainstorm which campaigns and offers (covered in Chapters 2 and 3) to use at each step of the customer journey to make people aware of your product and move them from awareness to their desired "After" state onto the path of a brand promoter.

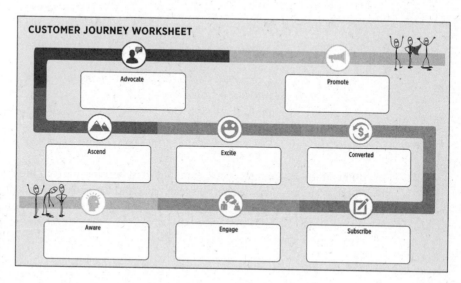

FIGURE 1-12: Create a customer journey road map for at least one of your core offers.

TIP

You can create your own customer journey road map with a resource from DigitalMarketer by going to www.digitalmarkter.com/customer-journey.

Chapter **2**

Choosing the Right Marketing Campaign

Digital marketing is a broad term that can mean anything from posting an image of your product on Facebook to crafting an email subject line to optimizing a blog post for search engine traffic. Digital marketing involves many seemingly disconnected tactics, and that's what makes this chapter so important.

This chapter helps you understand what a marketing campaign is. We explain the three different types of campaigns and how and when to use them so that you can use these strategies effectively in your digital marketing campaigns.

Every business is interested in generating leads, making sales, retaining the customers they have, and selling them more of the company's products or services. Achieving each of these goals requires a different approach, however. In this chapter, we help you decide what you want your digital marketing to accomplish by identifying your business objectives, because those objectives are what should dictate the campaigns you construct and, ultimately, the tactics you employ.

Establishing Marketing Objectives

Before you start a blog, open a Pinterest account, or start gathering email addresses, you need to choose your business goals. When you know what you want to accomplish, you'll be able to direct your energy into the right marketing campaigns and employ marketing tactics that move the needle on the right business metrics.

Here are six common goals that your digital marketing strategy can affect:

» **Increasing problem and solution awareness:** Your online marketing can help prospective customers become aware of something they need, an effect called *problem awareness*. Your marketing can also make prospective customers aware that your company provides a solution to a problem — called *solution awareness*. Your objective is to help people realize that you can take them from the "Before" state, in which they have a problem, to the desired "After" state, in which they have obtained a positive solution. (We cover this idea in greater detail in Chapter 1.)

» **Acquiring new leads and customers:** Gaining more leads and customers is a primary objective of most businesses. Without generating new leads and customers, your business will never grow beyond what it is now. You need to bring in new blood in order to scale your business.

» **Activating leads and customers:** If you've been in business for more than a few months, you likely have leads and customers who have yet to buy or haven't bought in a while. You can use your digital marketing campaigns to encourage people to buy from you for the first time, as well as to remind past customers who haven't purchased from you lately of the value you bring and why they should buy from you again. Your digital marketing campaigns can activate these dormant leads and customers and help keep your business in mind.

» **Monetizing existing leads and customers:** Acquiring new leads and customers is expensive and time consuming. Don't forget to create digital campaigns intended to sell more products and services to those new leads and customers. Monetization campaigns make upsell, cross-sell, and other types of offers to sell more to your best leads and customers

» **Onboarding new leads and customers:** New leads and customers deserve special treatment simply because they are new. They need to be taught who you are and how to be successful with what they've purchased. To achieve this goal, create content such as welcome emails or welcome packets that tell people how to use your product or service, what they can expect, and where they can go if they need help with their purchase.

>> **Building community and advocacy:** To move prospects, leads, and customers beyond a shallow, transactional relationship, you need to build campaigns that create communities of advocates and brand promoters. One of the most effective ways to achieve this advocacy is through social media, such as through a Facebook group or a Twitter page. Here, people can reach out if they have praise for or questions about your product or service. By creating an outlet, you help to cultivate a sense of community for your customer base, which leads to increased satisfaction and loyalty. Find more on social media tactics in Chapter 9.

Defining a Digital Marketing Campaign

Meeting your business objectives and moving a customer through the customer journey (discussed in Chapter 1) from ice-cold prospect to raving fan requires actions. Those actions, if coordinated properly, are called *campaigns*. Digital marketing campaigns, as we define them in this book, have a set of specific characteristics. Digital marketing campaigns are

>> **Objective based:** Digital marketing campaigns are coordinated actions intended to achieve a specific business goal.

>> **Multiparted:** Every digital marketing campaign requires assets like content and landing pages, as well as tools like email software or web forms. But those assets aren't enough to ensure the success of your campaign; you need the ability to make those assets visible. In other words, you need traffic. Yet another part of every campaign is the measurements you track so that you can determine how it is performing.

>> **Seamless and subtle:** It's worth pointing out that these multistep, multipart campaigns are most successful if you walk the prospect gradually through the customer journey (for more about the customer journey, see Chapter 1). To help move people through the customer journey, you need to include a call to action (CTA) within your campaign. A CTA is an instruction to your audience designed to provoke an immediate response. Usually, a CTA includes an imperative verb to convey urgency, such as "buy now," "click here," "shop today," "watch this video," "give us a call," or "visit a store near you." Next, a well-oiled marketing campaign removes the friction between the prospect and the action you want that prospect to take. An extreme example is to ask an ice-cold prospect to buy a $10,000 product or service. Such a tactic would be neither seamless nor subtle. In the coming chapters, you find out how to

structure your campaigns in a way that moves your cold prospects to become repeat buyers and purchasers of high-ticket items.

>> **In flux:** The word *campaign* often refers to an initiative with a short life span, but as it is defined in this book, a campaign can be something your business runs for as little as a day or as long as several years. The advantage of digital campaigns over physical ones (such as direct-mail campaigns) is that small tweaks and even wholesale pivots are much simpler in a digital environment. As a result, you can optimize digital marketing campaigns on the fly to achieve the best results.

The most important takeaway from this section is that a campaign is a process, not a single event that is made up of numerous steps and parts. Digital marketing campaigns might seem complicated to you now, but rest assured that campaigns can be extremely simple, and we cover everything from asset creation to traffic and measurement in this book.

PUTTING TOGETHER A GOOD-LOOKING DIGITAL MARKETING CAMPAIGN

Consider the digital marketing campaign of a company like LasikPlus, which offers the Lasik corrective surgery for eyesight. As are most companies, LasikPlus is interested in acquiring new leads and customers for the procedure.

In this company's marketing campaign, a prospect might first encounter an advertisement, such as the banner ad shown in the following figure.

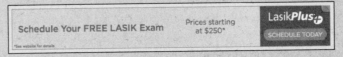

Source: http://www.menshealth.com/sex-women/boyfriend-voice?
utm_source=t.co&utm_medium=Social&utm_term=
593110700&utm_campaign=Men%27s%20Health

Clicking the ad shown in the first figure takes the prospective customer to a landing page, shown in the next figure, that explains the benefits of doing business with LasikPlus and makes a call to action to schedule a consultation.

Source: http://www.lasikplus.com/lasik-affordable-250_quiz

Selecting the call to action to schedule an appointment takes the prospect to a page where the prospect chooses the most convenient LasikPlus location for his or her consultation. After that location is chosen, the prospect is taken to a calendar page where a time for the consultation can be chosen, as shown in the final figure in this sidebar. The last step in setting the appointment is the entering of name, email, phone number, and birth date to confirm the appointment.

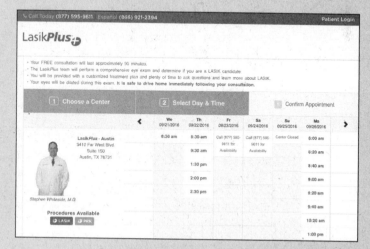

Source: https://www.lasikplus.com/am/#/Austin/schedule?
latitude=30.352204&longitude=-97.7504

(continued)

(continued)

But it doesn't stop there. The LasikPlus campaign continues via email. Separate emails are sent to confirm the consultation appointment, teach the prospective Lasik candidate a bit about the procedure, and to remind the prospect of his upcoming appointment. Also, notice that LasikPlus graduates the prospect from a cold lead to a consultation rather than asking the person to pay for the procedure immediately after seeing the ad. This campaign moves the prospect seamlessly and subtly toward the conversion.

Understanding the Three Major Types of Campaigns

Although you may have many business goals that you want to affect through your digital marketing, you'll find that you can meet most objectives with three broad categories of digital marketing campaign: Acquisition, Monetization, and Engagement.

Each of these types of digital marketing campaign has a very specific role to play in your business, as follows:

>> Acquisition campaigns acquire new prospects and customers.

>> Monetization campaigns generate revenue from existing leads and customers.

>> Engagement campaigns create communities of brand advocates and promoters.

The following sections explain these types of campaigns in much more detail.

Campaigns that generate new leads and customers

If your goal is to raise awareness for the problems you solve or the solutions you provide, or if you're just looking to acquire new leads and customers, you need an Acquisition campaign.

The role of your marketing is to help move a prospect, lead, or customer from the awareness stage of the customer journey to brand promoter. You deploy Acquisition campaigns to do the work on the front end of this journey, taking the prospect from Aware to Converted (see Figure 2-1).

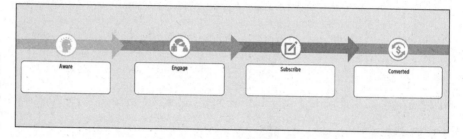

FIGURE 2-1: Acquisition campaigns move prospects from the Aware to Converted stages.

The stages of the customer journey that Acquisition campaigns complete are the following:

>> **Make Aware:** To bring in new leads and customers, you need to reach out to what amounts to complete strangers. You should structure Acquisition campaigns to reach prospects who are completely unaware of the problem you solve or the solutions you provide.

>> **Engage:** The movement from Make Aware to Engage is often accomplished by providing value to the prospect, usually in the form of entertainment, inspiration, or educational content, before asking her to buy something or commit a significant amount of time. This is known as *content marketing,* a strategic marketing method focused on creating and distributing valuable, relevant, and consistent material designed to attract, retain, and ultimately drive a customer to a profitable action. Content marketing consists of a broad spectrum of activities and types of content, including blogging, videos, social media updates, images, and more. We cover content marketing in more detail in Chapter 4.

>> **Subscribe:** At this stage, the prospect has given you permission to market to him. At the very least, he has connected with you on social channels (Facebook, LinkedIn, and others) or, ideally, has become an email subscriber. The Subscribe state is a critical stage to reach in the relationship because you can now continue the conversation with more content and offers.

>> **Convert:** The transformation of a prospect from being merely interested and subscribed to converted is the final stage of an Acquisition campaign. At this point, the prospect has placed trust in your organization by giving you either money or a significant amount of her time. Don't forget that your marketing should be gradual and seamless, particularly online, where you must often

build trust with someone you've never actually met. If this final stage of your Acquisition campaign involves a sale, it shouldn't be a risky (think expensive or complex) purchase. The goal here is to simply transform the relationship from prospect to customer.

Note that Acquisition campaigns are not about profit. Although you might be making sales at the Convert stage, the goal of those sales is not return on investment (ROI) but on acquiring leads and buyers. This idea can seem counterintuitive, but keep in mind that customer and lead acquisition is different from monetization. These two campaign types have different goals, tactics, and metrics.

TIP

Most of the campaigns that you create to acquire new leads and customers can also work to activate leads and buyers who have never purchased from you, or haven't purchased from you in a while. We refer to campaigns like this as *Activation campaigns*. A healthy business has a large number of recent and, if applicable, frequent buyers. Deploying campaigns to activate dormant subscribers and buyers is a good use of time and effort. We tell you more about the types of offers that can activate these leads and buyers in Chapter 3.

Campaigns that monetize existing leads and customers

If your business objective is to sell more to the customers you already have or to sell high-dollar, more complex products and services and profit maximizers (as described in Chapter 3), you need a Monetization campaign. In short, the goal of a Monetization campaign is to make profitable sales offers to the leads and customers you acquired with your Acquisition campaigns.

WARNING

Don't build a Monetization campaign first if your business has no leads, subscribers, or existing customers. Monetization campaigns are meant to sell more, or more often, to those who already know, like, and trust your business.

The stages of the customer journey completed by Monetization campaigns and shown in Figure 2-2 are the following:

>> **Excite:** You target Monetization campaigns at customers who have already spent time learning something from you, or have already purchased something from your business. Savvy digital marketers build campaigns that encourage prospects or customers to get value from the interactions they've already had with your business.

>> **Cause customers to ascend:** For every group of people who purchase something, some percentage of them would have bought more, or more often, if given the chance. For example, for every buyer of a Rolex watch, some

percentage would buy a second (or third or fourth!) watch, or would buy the most expensive Rolex watch if presented with the opportunity. This concept is critical not only to digital marketing but also to your business goals. Your Monetization campaigns should capitalize on this concept by making offers that increase the value of your existing leads and customers.

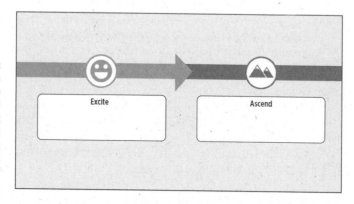

FIGURE 2-2:
Monetization
campaigns create
excitement and
cause existing
leads and
customers to
ascend to a
higher level of
purchasing.

Campaigns that build engagement

If your business objective is to successfully get new customers on board and move new leads and customers from being prospects to fans of your brand, or to build a community around your company, brand, or offers, you need an Engagement campaign. The most beloved companies create online opportunities for customers and prospects to interact with each other and with the brand. Companies that build engagement into their marketing enjoy the benefits of customer interactions that go beyond the simple transaction of buying goods and services.

The stages of the customer journey completed by Engagement campaigns and shown in Figure 2-3 are the following:

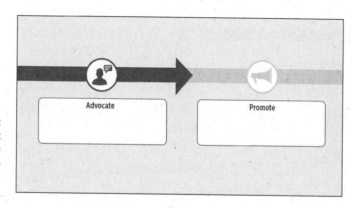

FIGURE 2-3:
Engagement
campaigns create
brand advocates
and brand
promoters.

- **Advocate:** You can create marketing campaigns to give your best customers the ability to recommend your business through testimonials and customer stories. These advocates defend your brand on social media and recommend your products and services to their friends and family when prompted.

- **Promote:** Customers who actively seek to promote your business are worth their weight in gold. These are the customers who create blogs and YouTube videos about your products and services. They tell the story of your brand and their success with it on social channels, and do everything they can to spread the good word about the value you provide. These people are your brand advocates.

WARNING

Creating brand advocates and promoters begins with having a superior product or service, coupled with a customer service experience to match. Word travels fast in the digital world, and if you aren't providing value, you find that your marketing creates the exact opposite of advocates and promoters. Instead, your marketing only speeds the spread of information about the poor experiences your customers have had. Before attempting to build engagement and community, optimize the amount of value you bring to your customer.

When done right, Acquisition, Monetization, and Engagement campaigns seamlessly move people through the customer journey. These three strategies help people go from their "Before" state in which they have a problem to their desired "After" state of having gained a positive outcome through your product or service. (We discuss the customer journey in greater detail in Chapter 1.) Figure 2-4 shows all the stages a person goes through, ideally, in the customer journey. Use the Acquisition, Monetization, and Engagement tactics discussed in this chapter to help move people down this path.

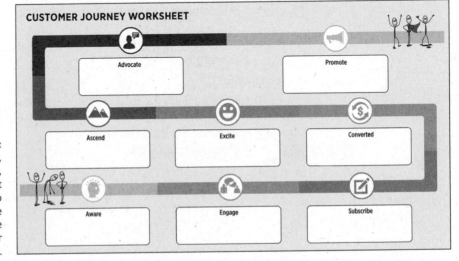

FIGURE 2-4: Use Acquisition, Monetization, and Engagement campaigns to move people through the customer journey.

Balancing Your Marketing Campaign Calendar

You may be thinking, "Which campaign should I be using in my business?" This is the wrong question, however. The right question is, "Which campaign should I be using in my business right now?" Every business should deploy each campaign type at different times to different people. So consider a few questions:

» Do you want more leads and customers for your business?

» Do you want to sell more to the customers you have or activate customers and leads who haven't purchased in a while?

» Do you want to turn customers into raving fans willing to buy anything you offer, and give you testimonials and referrals?

The answer, of course, is yes on all accounts.

But this point is critical to understand: One campaign can't replace or do the job of another. An Acquisition campaign can't do the job of a Monetization campaign. Likewise, a Monetization campaign can't do the job of an Engagement campaign. Each campaign excels at meeting one particular goal. To maintain a healthy, sustainable business, you need to allocate time on your calendar for all three major campaign types.

If you run nothing but Acquisition campaigns, you'll never be profitable. If you run nothing but Monetization campaigns, you'll never add new leads and customers and, as a result, you won't grow. If you run nothing but Engagement campaigns, you'll have a loyal audience, but you'll never convert your audience into customers.

TIP

If you have no sales but do have a massive following on social media, a popular blog, or podcast with lots of subscribers or downloads, you have mastered the art of creating Engagement campaigns. The good news is that you have accomplished one of the most difficult tasks in digital marketing: building an audience. By adding Acquisition and Monetization campaigns to your marketing mix, you can transform that audience into a profitable business.

Choosing the Campaign You Need Now

In this chapter, we make the point that your business needs all three campaign types: Acquisition, Monetization, and Engagement. To run a sustainable, healthy business, you need to be acquiring new leads and customers, monetizing them, and engaging customers who advocate and promote your brand. That said, if you're new to creating digital marketing campaigns, you should focus on building a single campaign first:

>> If you're starting a brand new business or have no existing leads or subscribers, build an Acquisition campaign.

>> If you have existing leads and customers, but they aren't buying as much as you would like, build a Monetization campaign.

>> If you're happy with the number of leads and subscribers and the monetization of those leads and customers, build an Engagement campaign.

If you simply don't know where to start, begin by building an Acquisition campaign, because every business needs to understand how to acquire fresh leads and convert new buyers. In the subsequent chapters of this book, we offer a number of ways to develop awareness for your brand, products, and services and convert that awareness into leads and customers.

Viewing Your Digital Marketing through the Campaign Lens

From this point forward, plan your digital marketing strategy and tactics by aligning them with the goals of the three major types of campaigns: Acquisition, Monetization, and Engagement. Never again will you decide to open a new social media account without knowing the ultimate goal behind it. Most entrepreneurs and marketers who are frustrated by digital marketing don't see the big picture.

Frustrated digital marketers don't understand, for example, that blogging is an outstanding tactic for growing awareness but utterly useless for monetization. They don't realize that posting and communicating with customers on a business Facebook page can create an engaged community, but better, more effective ways to generate leads and customers are available.

As we cover specific digital marketing tactics through the remainder of this book, we frequently return to the idea of keeping your business objectives, and the campaigns that meet those objectives, in mind. As you continue on your quest to master the art and science of digital marketing, stay focused on what really matters: growing the business.

Chapter **3**

Crafting Winning Offers

Whether you're asking people to buy something, give you their contact information, or spend time reading your blog, you're making an offer. The way in which you make your offers — and perhaps more important, the sequence in which you make them — will make or break you online.

You should think of creating and nurturing relationships with your customers in the same way that you develop relationships with your friends and family. Your business might sell business to business (B2B) or business to consumer (B2C), but all businesses sell human to human (H2H). Real, individual people are buying your products and services.

Consider how perfect strangers become a married couple. The marriage proposal is an offer that is made after a sequence of other offers are made and deemed successful by both parties. Sure, the occasional marriage proposal on the first date occurs, but most relationships begin with a series of positive interactions over a period of time.

Although most people aren't likely to propose marriage on a first date, many businesses do the equivalent of that with their prospects. They ask cold prospects to buy high-ticket, complex, and otherwise risky products and services before the relationship is ready for that offer. On the other hand, a customer who has received tremendous value from your company over a period of time is much more likely to make a high-dollar, complex, or otherwise risky purchase.

In this chapter, we unpack the different types of offers you can make, the goals of those offers, and the order in which you should present them to prospective, new, and loyal customers. The offers explained in this chapter focus on Acquisition and Monetization campaigns (discussed in Chapter 2).

Offering Value in Advance

Doing business online is different from doing business in person or even over the phone. In many cases, the prospective customer has no further information about your business than what is presented to her online. To acquire new leads and customers, you need to build trust and *lead with value* to build a relationship with your prospects or customers.

A successful relationship is a two-way street. Both sides of the relationship must benefit from the relationship, and because your company wants to begin this new relationship with a prospect, it makes sense for you to provide value first. Prospects won't become loyal customers if you don't first provide some value that builds trust in advance of asking them to buy. The good news is that you can provide this value with something as simple as an insightful, informative blog post or podcast that helps them solve a problem. You offer this value for free and with no strings attached to begin a healthy and mutually beneficial relationship.

We call acquisition offers that lead with value *entry point offers*, or EPOs. An EPO in a dating relationship equates to offering to buy someone a cup of coffee. This coffee offer, which has begun many healthy dating relationships, is a relatively risk-free proposition that provides value upfront. When your goal is to acquire a customer (and not a spouse), the EPO is a way of allowing large amounts of prospective customers to get to know, like, and trust your business without much risk.

There are three types of EPOs:

>> **Ungated:** You usually present this type of offer in the form of a blog post, video, or podcast, and it does not require contact information or a purchase to get value.

>> **Gated:** A gated offer requires contact information (name, email address, and so on) to get value.

>> **Deep discount:** This offer requires a purchase but at an extreme discount, usually 50 percent or greater.

TIP

It pays to provide tremendous value to your prospective customers when you're trying to gain their trust. This idea can seem counterintuitive to some people because they don't see the immediate return on this investment.

REMEMBER

The goal of your marketing is to transform people from being completely unaware of your products or services to being raving fans who promote your products and services to anyone who will listen. The foundation of the relationships you build with your customers is built on offers that provide value in advance of the purchase.

Designing an Ungated Offer

Offers that require no risk on the part of prospective customers are the most powerful way to begin to cultivate strong relationships with customers. An *ungated offer* such as an informative article, video, or podcast gives value without asking for contact information or a purchase. That said, these are still offers. You are offering value to prospects in exchange for their time. And for many people, no other resource is more precious than time.

The value provided by the business is generally made available to prospects using content such as blog posts, social media updates, or videos. Successful digital marketers make free content available that provides one of the following values:

>> **Entertainment:** People pay a lot of money to be entertained, and content that makes a person laugh is content that is likely to be remembered. It's why commercials try to make you laugh (think the gecko from Geico or Flo from Progressive); they have only 30 to 60 seconds to cut through all the noise and get you to remember their product or service. Poo-Pourri's video advertisements on YouTube and Friskies' and Buzzfeed's "Dear Kitten" campaigns are prime examples of marketers providing entertaining content that gets their message across.

>> **Inspiration:** People are highly moved by content that makes them feel something. The sports and fitness industry taps into this sentiment with taglines like "Just do it," by Nike, or Fitbit campaigns showing everyday people (as opposed to celebrities and professional athletes) achieving their goals using Fitbit. Weight-loss businesses also use inspirational content by using successful customer testimonials and "before" and "after" images.

>> **Education:** Ever go to YouTube to watch a how-to video? From DIY projects to how to rebuild a car engine, you can easily find educational content online. People want knowledge, and providing it helps build trust. Entire blogs, sites, YouTube channels, and businesses are built around educating people, to great success. That's why Wikipedia gets roughly 16 billion page views a month.

The first two value propositions (entertainment and inspiration) can be difficult to execute. But the third is within the grasp of every company. In Chapters 4 and 5, we go into more detail about the form and function of the various types of ungated content that can be produced.

REMEMBER

The production of content by brands is at an all-time high. An absolute glut of content is produced on blogs, YouTube channels, and social media sites every day. That said, an insatiable demand still exists for great ungated content. Don't make the mistake of thinking that because this content is free, it does not deserve the time and energy of your other offers. An ungated offer is, in many cases, the first transaction that a prospective customer will have with your company, and you should make it a successful one.

Designing a Gated Offer

To graduate someone from the stage of prospect to lead, you need a gated offer that requires prospects to submit their contact information to receive value. A *gated offer* provides a small chunk of value that solves a *specific* problem for a *specific* market and is offered in exchange for the prospects' contact information. That contact information is typically an email address, at a minimum. Returning to the dating relationship analogy earlier in the chapter, a gated offer is the equivalent of a first date. A gated offer might take the form of a white paper, a case study, or a webinar. For example, Figure 3-1 shows how OpenMarket makes valuable information available in the form of a white paper that requires contact information.

REMEMBER

A gated offer is an exchange in value. No money changes hands; instead, you provide your new lead something of value in exchange for the right to contact the lead in the future. Gated offers are free, and a common notion among digital marketers is that because they're giving the gated offer away for free, the product or service offered doesn't have to be of high quality. That's a mistake. Free does not mean low quality. When someone exchanges his contact information and gives you permission to follow up with him, he has given you value, and a transaction has taken place. This prospect has given you something that's typically private, as well as some of his time and attention. You need to return that value if you hope to build the relationship that is required for lifelong customers. The end goal of a gated offer is to gain leads so that you can nurture them into customers over time.

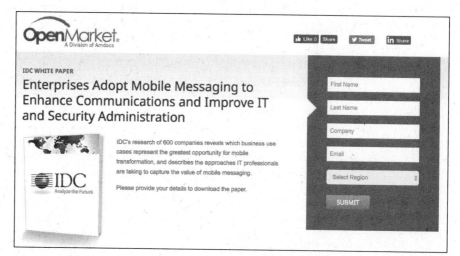

FIGURE 3-1: OpenMarket asks for contact information in exchange for this white paper.

Source: http://www.openmarket.com/download/idc-mobile-security/

Revisit the definition of a gated offer ("a gated offer provides a small chunk of value that solves a *specific* problem for a *specific* market and is offered in exchange for prospects' contact information") — and pay particular attention to the "specific" parts. Specificity is the key to a successful gated offer because it makes your offer more relevant to your audience. A lead form that simply states "Subscribe to our newsletter" is not a gated offer that will get you high conversions because it does not solve a specific problem. In the next section of this chapter, we discuss how to make your gated offer convert prospects by making it specific in terms of problem-solving, which will make your gated offer more relevant to your audience.

Zeroing in on what matters

In the previous section, we establish the idea that a specific and relevant gated offer works best for generating high opt-ins. But what does making the offer specific and relevant entail? High-converting gated offers include one, or a combination, of the following five aspects, in a specific form:

>> A promise

>> An example

>> A shortcut

>> A solution

>> A discount

Including at least one of these five items will help your conversion rates. The following sections take a look at each of these items.

Making a specific promise

Making a specific promise is one of the simplest things you can do to increase the number of leads you receive from a gated offer. Look at the offer that you're delivering and think about how you can make the benefit of the offer more evident. Consider how you can speak to the specific desired end result of your prospect.

Craft a clear promise and then make sure that your promise is in the title of your gated offer. Generic or clever titles generally decrease the conversions on your gated offer. Many marketers are guilty of coming up with cutesy titles or using industry jargon in the title that your market may not understand. In your gated offer's title, talk less about your product and more about your target audience. Specifically communicate, in the gated offer's title, the benefit the gated offer will provide that target audience. Speak to the conversation that is going on inside the mind of your customer, not the one that you're having around the business table. Ask yourself, what are your target audience's concerns, fears, or desires? Think of the desired end result that your customer is seeking, and put that in the title. The gated offer shown in Figure 3-2 delivers a specific promise that resonates with its market.

FIGURE 3-2: Copyblogger's gated offer clearly states what people can expect when they input their contact information.

Source: http://my.copyblogger.com/free-membership/

Giving a specific example

In our experience, the best way to give a specific example in your gated offer is to deliver it in the form of a case study. If you have examples of real customers and prospects who have overcome problems with your product or service, these can work well as gated offers.

For instance, if your company sells surveillance cameras to universities, you might create a case study entitled "How State University Reduced Campus Crime by 73 Percent" that details how the university used surveillance camera technology to reduce acts of crime on the State campus. This headline clearly states the benefit and uses an example to add specificity to the gated offer.

Offering a specific shortcut

A gated offer that can save a person time is appealing and often converts well. For example, a gated offer that delivers a list of healthy snacks a person can eat throughout the day is a useful shortcut for someone looking to eat a more nutritious diet.

Answering a specific question

The fourth way you can make your gated offer more specific is by raising and answering a specific question. If the answer to the question is valuable, your prospects opt in to get the answer to that specific question, and after you've answered the question, you will have delivered on your promise and helped to establish yourself as an authority on the subject, which in turn helps build trust and moves the prospect closer to becoming a customer.

Delivering a specific discount

Price discounts can be a great way to spur sales, and many companies offer coupons that slash prices in the hope of creating a buying frenzy. But instead of handing out discounts, consider asking a prospect to opt in to receive the discount. For instance, your gated offer might say, "Join our Discount Club and receive 10% off any order." This wording is effective because it specifically tells the prospect how much she'll save.

Generating leads with educational content

In this section, we discuss five forms that your gated offer can take. These gated offers offer value by educating the lead on a particular topic related to your brand while also highlighting features of a solution, product, or service you provide.

TIP

Your gated offer does not have to be the length of a Tolstoy novel. Besides being ultraspecific, gated offers should be easy to consume — they should not be a 14-day course or a 300-page book. Rapid consumption of the gated offer is important because you want to provide value to your lead as quickly as possible. The faster your gated offer provides value, the quicker a lead can become a paying customer. Because most gated offers can be sent digitally, they can be delivered instantly, which allows the lead to receive the value of the gated offer quickly. Ideally, prospects receive value from your gated offer within minutes of giving you their contact information. Speedily delivering value helps to build a positive relationship with leads, as well as to quickly move them through the customer journey. (Turn to Chapter 1 for more information on the customer journey.)

Free reports

Reports (also called guides) are among the most common types of gated offers and are usually mostly text and images. Reports usually offer facts, news, and best practices that are relevant to your industry and your target market. If you use a report as your gated offer, however, be careful. Reports can be lengthy and complex, thus they often take more time to be consumed, which means that the report will take longer to deliver on its value. Therefore, whenever possible, keep your reports as succinct and specific as possible so that they can quickly deliver their value and help to establish or reinforce a positive relationship with your lead or customer.

White papers

As is true of a report, a white paper is an authoritative guide that concisely informs readers about a complex issue and aims to help leads understand an issue, solve a problem, or make a decision. Although the white paper helps to educate your prospects, it also helps to promote your business's products or services. White papers can often be very effective at generating business-to-business (B2B) leads.

Primary research

Primary research is research that you or your business collects. It can include interviews and observations. When you take the time to create new research, you're providing a service and saving others from having to do their own primary research, which is why people opt in to a gated offer of this nature.

Webinar training

If you're an expert in your field, or can partner with one, you can host an online training via a webinar that teaches or demonstrates a topic that is relevant to both your brand and to your target audience. You create a gated offer that requires prospects to fill out a registration form for the webinar, thus capturing prospects' contact information and allowing you to follow up with them after the webinar takes place.

Sales material

In some cases, the most desired pieces of information for your market are pricing and descriptions of your products or services. This information helps people who are interested in buying your product or service make informed decisions. The sales material gated offer tends to be longer, in text and content examples such as images or customer testimonial videos, than the other examples in this chapter so far. However, this length is necessary because a person generally needs more information before making a purchase, especially if a big-ticket item is involved. However, this also means that anyone who opts in is more likely to be a qualified lead. A *qualified lead* is someone who is actively seeking more information about your products or services because he or she is interested in buying from you. (An unqualified lead may not have been nurtured enough to make a purchase yet, or isn't sure of what your company does or even what solution he or she seeks.)

IKEA provides a wonderful example of the sales material gated offer. The Scandinavian chain collects contact information in exchange for its catalog, which lists all its products. Figure 3-3 demonstrates IKEA's gated offer, and because IKEA can deliver its catalog digitally, it speeds up the delivery of value to the new lead.

FIGURE 3-3: IKEA's sales catalog is an ideal example of a sales material gated offer.

Source: https://info.ikea-usa.com/signup

Generating leads with tools

Tools make powerful gated offers because they often deliver value *much faster* than the educational gated offers discussed in the previous section. Although white papers, reports, and case studies require someone to invest time in order to receive value, a tool is often immediately useful.

Handout or cheat sheet

Though similar to a free report, both handouts and cheat sheets provide a different value to prospects. A handout or cheat sheet is generally short (one page or so) and cuts straight to an ultraspecific point, making the information easily digestible. You can deliver handouts and cheat sheets as checklists, mind maps, or "blueprints," to name a few examples. Figure 3-4 shows an example of a handout as a gated offer.

FIGURE 3-4: A handout is a prime example of useful content that can be gated.

Source: *https://www.leadpages.net/blog/blogging-for-businesses-should-you-blog/*

Resource list

If people are learning to do something that you're an expert in, chances are they'll want to know what tools you're using to get it done. This type of gated offer makes a list of tools or resources (be it of apps, physical products, hardware, or other items) available to the new lead or prospect. The toolkit or resource aggregates the list so that the lead doesn't have to keep searching for more information.

Template

A template is the perfect example of a proven, well-tested shortcut to better results and can make a tremendous gated offer. A template contains a proven pattern for success that requires less work on the part of the person using it. It might come in the form of a spreadsheet preconfigured to calculate business expenses. Or it can be a layout for designing a custom home. Templates make powerful gated offers because the prospect can put the tool to immediate use.

Software

Software can work well as a gated offer. You might, for example, offer full access to a free software tool that you developed or a free trial (that lasts for 14 days, perhaps) of your software in exchange for an email address. Software companies often offer a free trial of their software as a gated offer. A software gated offer can turn a lead who is on the fence about purchasing the product with a risk-free means of acquiring it, while also providing the company a way to follow up with that lead.

Discount and coupon clubs

Discount and coupon clubs offer exclusive savings and early access to sales. This is an effective type of offer that acquires contact information and allows you to continue the conversation by reminding members of specials and rewards available to them.

Quizzes and surveys

Quizzes and surveys are fun and engaging for people to take and can be a great way to generate new leads. For instance, a beauty company might offer a "What's Your Skin Type" quiz. These types of content are intriguing to members of your market because they want to know the results of the quiz or survey. To obtain the results of the quiz or survey, the prospect must first opt in by entering an email address. If the quiz or survey results provide value to your market, this type of gated offer can be powerful.

Assessment

You can develop a gated offer that assesses or tests prospects on a particular subject. At the end of the assessment, offer prospects a grade and information on actions they can take to improve their grade, which would likely be a tool or service that you provide. For example, this assessment can serve as a rubric for grading a blog post. Figure 3-5 shows an assessment offer that has been generating leads for HubSpot, a company that sells marketing software, for years. Leads can use the assessment from HubSpot to grade their marketing and make it better.

Filling out the gated offer checklist

At our company, we've tested gated offers in a lot of different niches and developed an eight-point checklist of factors that can improve your overall level of success by making more effective gated offers. You don't have to be able to check off every one of the factors in the checklist, but if you find that your gated offer meets very few of these criteria, you have reason to be concerned.

We tell you about each of the factors on the checklist in the following sections.

FIGURE 3-5:
HubSpot
generates leads
with its gated
offer of its
"Website Grader"
assessment.

Source: https://website.grader.com/

Point 1: Is your offer ultraspecific?

The more specific the promise of your gated offer is, the better it will perform after you provide that promise. By delivering on your promise, you have given value. This, of course, assumes that the promise you are making is compelling to the market you're approaching. Make sure that your gated offer isn't vague and that it offers an ultraspecific solution to an ultraspecific market.

Point 2: Are you offering too much?

Believe it or not, your gated offer will perform better if it delivers on "one big thing" rather than a number of things. We live in a multitasking world, so you want to be sure that your gated offer focuses on one topic or theme and provides one path for your lead to take. If you include too many paths or offers, your leads can get distracted and go off course as they try to follow all the ideas presented in your gated offer, thereby causing them to not opt in. If possible, offer a single solution to a single problem rather than numerous solutions to numerous problems.

Point 3: Does the offer speak to a desired end result?

The members of your market are searching for solutions. What does your market *really* want? If you can craft a gated offer that promises that solution, prospects will gladly give you their contact information (and their attention) in return.

Point 4: Does the offer deliver immediate gratification?

Your market wants a solution and wants it *now*. Establish and communicate how long it will take your leads to consume and derive value from your gated offer so that they know what to expect. If it takes days or weeks, your gated offer is not delivering immediate gratification — not by a long shot.

Point 5: Does the offer shift the relationship?

The best gated offers do more than inform; they actually change the state and mind-set of your prospects so that they're primed to engage in business with your company. After your leads have taken advantage of your offer, determine whether the value it provides will actually teach the leads how and why they should trust and buy from you. For example, if you sell gardening tools and supplies, a check-list entitled "15 Tools You Need to Create a Successful Container Garden" educates prospects on the tools they need while simultaneously moving them closer to purchasing the products you sell.

Point 6: Does the offer have a high perceived value?

Just because your gated offer is free doesn't mean that it should *look* free. Use good design through the use of professional graphics and imagery to create a gated offer of high perceived value in the mind of your lead.

Point 7: Does the offer have a high actual value?

The right information at the right time can be priceless. The gated offer that delivers something priceless will enjoy very high conversion rates, but if you're promising value, you *have* to deliver on it. A gated offer has high actual value when it lives up to its promise and delivers the goods.

Point 8: Does the offer allow for rapid consumption?

You don't want your gated offer to be a roadblock in the customer's journey toward becoming a customer. Before customers buy from you, they want to receive value from your gated offer. You want the gated offer to help move the lead to the next step, so ideally the gated offer should deliver value immediately. In other words, avoid long e-books or courses that take days or months to deliver their value.

TIP

Why do we keep insisting that your gated offer be quickly and easily consumable? Because after your gated offer has been consumed, you want to make the next offer whenever possible. There is (usually) no better time to make an offer than directly after someone has taken a prior offer. However, few will buy from you if they have not received the value from the last offer you made — your gated offer. So be sure that your gated offer quickly delivers value, allowing you to then make an offer to purchase something, which we discuss in the next section.

Designing Deep-Discount Offers

Acquiring leads is the goal of the gated offer discussed in the previous section, but how do you acquire buyers? Remember that the key to success online is the sequence of the offers you make to new leads and customers. The best way to acquire buyers is by making an offer at such a deep discount that it is difficult to refuse. A *deep-discount offer* is an irresistible, low-ticket offer made to convert leads and cold prospects into buyers.

REMEMBER

The goal of a deep-discount offer is not profit. In fact, selling deep-discount offers may come at a net loss to your company. Offering deep discounts may therefore seem counterintuitive, but the goal of this type of offer is to acquire buyers. Deep-discount offers change relationships; they turn a prospect into a customer, and that's a big deal. After a prospect makes a successful purchase with your company, she is far more likely to buy from you again. Deep-discount offers bring you one step closer to achieving your goal of converting a prospect to a repeat buyer and possibly even a raving fan.

In the following sections, we discuss the six different types of deep-discount offers you can employ.

Using physical premiums

As the name suggests, physical premiums are physical products. Offer something that your market desires and discount it deeply. DIY Ready, a company in the DIY and home décor space, offers a $19 bracelet kit for free. The new customer need only enter his or her credit card to pay for shipping and handling to receive the bracelet kit. This is a physical product that do-it-yourselfers find highly desirable. Figure 3-6 demonstrates what this physical premium offer from DIY Ready looks like.

FIGURE 3-6:
A "Free +
Shipping" offer is
a typical deep-
discount offer.

Employing a book

A physical book can make an excellent deep-discount offer. Books have an extremely high perceived and actual value. If you need to establish authority and trust with your market before making more complex or higher-ticket offers, the book is a great deep-discount offer to employ. Consider offering the book at a steep discount, or free plus shipping and handling. Although we don't recommend a physical or digital book for generating leads, it's a highly effective way to convert prospects and leads into customers. Remember, the objective of a deep-discount offer is to change the relationship with a lead or prospect and turn the person into a customer.

Leveraging the webinar

Webinars are one of the most versatile offers available to digital marketers. You can conduct free webinars to generate leads, plus you can offer a webinar as a product. Remember that when you're charging for anything and particularly a webinar, you should deliver value beyond what you've charged to attend.

TIP

When employing a webinar to serve as a deep-discount offer, you may not want to use the term *webinar* in your offer. People generally associate that term with something free. Consider calling your deep-discount-offer webinar a teleclass, online training, or boot camp instead, and it can be prerecorded or held live.

Selling software

Software and application plug-ins are effective deep-discount offers because software saves people time and energy, so these are highly sought-after commodities. When you use software as a deep-discount offer, the deep discount price is likely to cause a "buying frenzy," resulting in a highly successful acquisition campaign.

Splintering a service

If your business has a high-dollar product or service, you can take a small piece of that product, also known as a *splinter,* and sell it *à la carte.* The key is to offer a piece of your service that can stand alone at an incredibly low price.

An example of a company that uses this approach is Fiverr, an online marketplace that offers tasks and services starting at $5. Figure 3-7 shows one of these Fiverr services, which include creating business logos. This is an excellent example of offering *part* of a highly sought-after service at a deep discount that will help turn a lead into a customer and can ultimately lead to more sales. After a person has bought from you, he's likely to buy from you again.

Because you're breaking out a part or splinter of your service, you don't have to create a new service. Instead, you're offering a portion of an existing product or service.

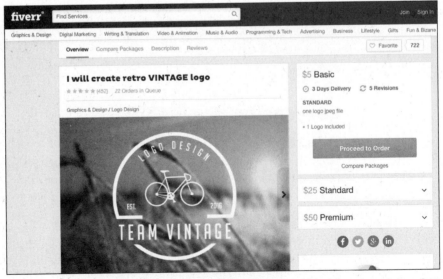

FIGURE 3-7:
Through Fiverr, larger services can be splintered into smaller, single projects.

Source: https://www.fiverr.com/gfx_expert2/create-retro-vintage-logo

Brainstorming "little victories" to offer your leads

Because deep-discount offers are low priced, low risk, and highly desirable, they help your leads overcome doubt about your business or product. Less monetary risk is involved for the leads, so they're willing to take a chance and become customers. However, it can be harder for a marketer or a business owner to overcome the self-doubt that leads may have about themselves or their ability to reach the "After" state that your product or service promises to take them to. That's why the best deep-discount offers lead the customer to a "little victory."

A "little victory" is something that helps inspire your leads and gives them confidence that they can accomplish whatever solution or goal you're offering, as well as the confidence that your product or service will help to get them there. A little victory gives your prospects hope and a taste of achieving the whole thing — of making it to the other side of the tunnel, so to speak. Keep in mind that little victories are usually quick to achieve and help deliver value to your customer.

For instance, if you're in the fitness world, you can offer your seven-day juice cleanse at a deep discount as a deep-discount offer. When describing the offer to potential buyers, you state that completing this juice cleanse is the hardest part of your program — because getting started is often the hardest part. If they can get through your seven-day cleanse, they'll know that the toughest part is behind them.

As you go through your products and services to determine which will make the best deep-discount offer, ask yourself what little victory this product or service can provide your customers. Brainstorm how it will give them hope, how it will help to get them over the hump of self-doubt. Helping your customers see that success is possible not only for the smiling customers in your testimonials but also for *them*, personally, will help make your offer more potent and enable you to build positive relationships with your newly acquired customers.

Filling out the deep-discount offer checklist

Previous sections talk about the various forms your deep-discount offers could take and the importance of little victories. Next, look over the five-point deep-discount offer checklist, presented in the following sections, so that you can ensure that your offer can convert leads and prospects into buyers.

Point 1: Does it lower the barrier to entry?

To start, your deep-discount offer should be low risk. The offer shouldn't be expensive, time consuming, or difficult to understand. The best offers at this stage are often impulse buys, like the pack of gum you grab while you wait in line at the supermarket. The price of your offer depends on your market. Leads shouldn't have to pause to consider whether they can afford your deep-discount offer; the price should remove that barrier. Again, the purpose of this offer is not profit. A good rule of thumb is to make these offers at $20 or below.

Point 2: Is the value clear?

Make your deep-discount offer easy to understand. You want to be able to quickly explain the value and entice the lead into buying. Therefore, your deep-discount offer should not be complex. Impulse buys are not complicated offers.

Point 3: Is it useful but incomplete?

WARNING

The keyword here is *useful*. Your deep-discount offer should not be a bait-and-switch offer. If the deep-discount offer doesn't deliver on its promise, you'll tarnish your relationship with that customer. You may have gained a quick sale with the deep-discount offer but lost a potential lifelong customer. This offer must be useful in its own right, but it is not the whole package.

Point 4: Does it have a high perceived value?

As with the gated offer before it, use good design to create a deep-discount offer with a high-quality look and feel. You don't want your new customers to feel ripped off; instead, you want them to feel as though the deep-discount offer they just bought from you was a steal.

REMEMBER

People don't buy products and services online, but rather buy pictures and descriptions of products and services online. If you want to sell online, you need to employ design and copywriting that communicate the value of the products and services you're offering.

Point 5: Does it have a high actual value?

Be sure that your deep-discount offer makes good on its promise and delivers value. This situation builds trust with your new customers, and when they're ready to buy again, they will remember the positive experience they had with you.

Discovering your deep-discount offer

The offer you use to acquire customers likely exists inside your *core offer*, which is a higher-priced or more complex product or service. Your core offer is often your flagship product or service. Look at your core offer and see what piece or pieces can stand on their own. What can you splinter off and still deliver value with that piece?

Here are some questions to ask to help you discover your deep-discount offer(s):

>> **What's the cool gadget that your market wants, but doesn't necessarily need?** What's your impulse buy? What's your stick of gum?

>> **What's the one thing everyone needs, but doesn't necessarily want?** This can be a product or service that people know they need but aren't exactly excited about. The product may not be "sexy," but it's critical to a process that people engage in. For instance, if someone has a candle-making hobby, the wick may not be as fun or interesting as the colored waxes or scented oils, but it's an essential ingredient.

>> **What's a valuable service that you can perform quickly and inexpensively, one that will deliver results in advance and get your foot in the door?** This idea goes beyond giving someone a free quote or estimate; it gives customers a taste of how you can positively affect their lives. For example, a roofer could offer a deep discount on gutter cleaning as a deep-discount offer. After completing the job, the roofer could point out any necessary improvements that the roof or gutters need. That's a deep-discount offer that provides value first and then gets your foot in the door.

>> **What little victory or victories does your deep-discount offer provide?** How do you help the customer overcome self-doubt?

Maximizing Profit

As this chapter explains, you use ungated, gated, and deep-discount offers to acquire new customers and buyers. But when do you actually make a profit? The cost of acquiring new customers is often the most expensive one that businesses incur. After you have a buyer, asking that buyer to buy from you again makes sense. You want to turn that customer you spent so much time and money acquiring into a *repeat customer*.

The marketing campaigns you employ to sell more, or more often, to the leads and customers you've acquired are called Monetization campaigns, and these campaigns have a number of different types of offers to employ. In the following sections, we tell you how to implement and improve your monetization offers.

REMEMBER

Most companies are running Monetization campaigns (making high-dollar and complex offers, which we discuss in Chapter 2) directed at ice-cold prospects and brand new leads. Although it would be fantastic to be profitable without needing to warm up a prospect with ungated, gated, and deep-discount offers, making that work is very difficult. The sequence of the offers you make to people is extremely critical to avoid being the business that is asking its prospects for too much, too soon.

Making an upsell or cross-sell offer

The first type of monetization offer we discuss is the immediate upsell, and it's one you're probably already familiar with even if you've never heard the term. An example of the immediate upsell is the famous "Do you want fries with that?" offer made at McDonald's. Upsells offer customers more of what they already bought. The purchase they are currently making and the upsell should lead the customer to the same desired end result. In the McDonald's example, adding fries to your order gets you a bigger meal. The cross-sell offer, on the other hand, makes an offer related to the first purchase. For example, a clothing retailer might offer dress shoes to a man who just purchased a suit.

Amazon.com (and virtually every other successful online retailer) uses upsell and cross-sell offers to increase the number of items people purchase. Amazon's "Frequently Bought Together" and "Customers Who Bought This Item Also Bought" sections contain immediate upsell and cross-sell offers to help ensure the sale and possibly increase the basket size. For example, after we select a book for $17.98, Amazon suggests other products that we may want to make with this purchase, as shown in Figure 3-8. If we accepted all the suggested upsells, the amount of our purchase would increase from $17.98 to $44.96.

In Figure 3-8, the item being searched for is *Harry Potter and the Cursed Child,* and Amazon offers some related Harry Potter books that would serve as an upsell and increase the basket size. But Amazon also offers cross-sells in the form of other fantasy books that may appeal to a fan of Harry Potter because they are of the same genre.

FIGURE 3-8: Amazon expertly uses upsells and cross-sells to increase the basket size of its customer and get the sale.

Because the cross-sell may not be as relevant to the first purchase, a cross-sell can feel like it's coming out of left field, which can be jarring to and unwanted by the customer. That's why you have to be careful with cross-sells, or you risk annoying your customers. Imagine buying a Mac computer and having Apple ask before you've even left the store whether you want to buy an iPhone or an iPad. That said, if the cross-sell truly complements the initial purchase, your customers will welcome the offer, and you'll welcome the additional revenue.

Building bundles and kits

Bundles and kits are other forms that your monetization offer can take. A bundle or a kit is taking one of your stand-alone products and combining it with other like items that you or one of your business partners sell. For example, if you sell men's razors, you might bundle the razor with a shaving kit that includes all the essential items a man needs to shave with, from the brush to the after-shave. This "essential shaving kit" will cost more than an individual razor, which increases your revenue per sale. Do you have products or services that you can combine to create a new value proposition?

Tacking on a slack adjuster

Slack adjusters can have a dramatic impact upon the bottom line. A *slack adjuster* is a product or service that you offer at a price point much higher than your typical offer. The price is generally 10 to 100 times higher than your usual offers. Although this product or service will appeal to only a very small portion of your market, those that do make this high-ticket purchase will have a dramatic impact on your revenue.

For example, Starbucks sells cups of tea and coffee, but the company also sells coffee makers. The coffee maker is far more expensive than the $6 cup of coffee. Most people stick to their usual beverage and ignore the coffee maker, but a few buy the coffee maker. When a product is that much more expensive than the core offer, only a small number of slack adjuster sales is needed to make an impact.

Recurring billing

Sometimes called a continuity offer in digital marketing circles, a recurring billing offer charges the customer periodically — usually each month or year. This may take the form of a club or some other type of membership, or a subscription such as a monthly gym membership. In the latter case, the gym charges a membership fee 12 times a year. You also find recurring billing in content and publishing with subscriptions to Netflix or *Cosmopolitan* magazine, and in e-commerce with products like Dollar Shave Club and Birchbox. Look to your products or services and consider how you can make a sale once and get paid over and over again.

Recurring billing can be a difficult sell because of the commitment that goes along with it. To overcome this issue, clearly communicate the advantage provided by the recurring billing offer and lower the perceived risk by clearly communicating the cancellation. For instance, the cooking delivery company Blue Apron often states in its offers that you can cancel anytime. In the dating analogy earlier in this chapter, a recurring billing offer is akin to a marriage proposal. Customers must decide whether they want to commit to you for an extended period.

2

Using Content to Generate Fans, Followers, and Customers

Use content to raise awareness, generate leads, segment your audience, move your audience through your marketing funnel, and ultimately generate sales.

Learn methods to brainstorm blog ideas, techniques to write headlines that capture your audience's attention, and strategies for working with outside blog contributors. Follow the ten steps to audit your blog and ensure its quality and effectiveness.

Defeat writer's block with 57 blog post ideas that inform, entertain, and engage your prospects while displaying your brand's personality and humanity. Quickly produce high-quality blog posts that build a rapport with your audience.

Chapter **4**

Pursuing Content Marketing Perfection

ontent is at the heart and soul of any digital marketing campaign — the foundation on which your search, social, email, and paid traffic campaigns are built. Without content, Google has nothing to discover on your website, Facebook Fans have nothing to share, newsletters have no news, and paid traffic campaigns become one-dimensional sales pitches.

Content goes beyond blogging; content includes YouTube videos, product and pricing pages on e-commerce sites, social media updates, and much more. Each piece of content acts as a stepping stone on the path from lead to customer, and from customer to engaged, frequent buyer.

Part 2 of this book is about generating fans, followers, and customers using content. This chapter begins that quest by outlining the often-misunderstood strategy behind content marketing. We examine the many different forms that content marketing takes and its uses throughout a prospect's journey toward becoming a loyal customer.

Knowing the Dynamics of Content Marketing

At its core, the Internet is a place where people gather to discover, interact with, and share content. Whether that content is a funny cat video that gives you a much-needed laugh, an inspiring podcast about a single mom surviving cancer, or an article teaching you how to fix a leaky faucet, content is what people crave.

Engaging with valuable content is a natural, or "native," experience on the Internet. People are drawn to content that teaches them something, inspires them, or makes them laugh or cry, and people share and talk about content that has provided them some form of value.

With the low-cost (or no cost) of publishing platforms such as WordPress, YouTube, and iTunes, even the smallest of brands can produce content for the web. This ease of publishing, however, is a double-edged sword because the constantly changing nature of the Internet requires the rapid production of content. Although your brand stands to reap the enormous rewards associated with content publishing, doing so without a plan can lead to frustration.

People have a nearly insatiable demand for content on the Internet. According to the most conservative estimates, every minute more than 1,000 blog posts are produced and 72 hours of new video are uploaded to YouTube. This glut of content underscores the importance of proceeding with content marketing only after you have made a plan, because you must create quality content to cut through the noise. And quality demands a plan. Without a plan, your content assets still have a chance to go viral, but that's more than likely to be the result of dumb luck. A plan helps to ensure the success of your digital marketing campaign.

TIP

Marketers often confuse the term *blogging* with *content marketing.* Although blogging is a powerful and versatile content marketing channel, it's only one part of a well-balanced content strategy. If you're among the many marketers who blog with no clear direction, you should commit a few hours to designing a content plan before writing another blog post. Well-executed content marketing includes planning what content you will produce, for what audience, and for what purpose. Many companies and personal brands that are frustrated with digital marketing can trace that frustration back to the time-consuming act of creating content with no clear audience or objective. You'll find the entire process much easier and much more lucrative when you have a good sense of your direction.

Finding Your Path to Perfect Content Marketing

Although "perfect" content marketing may sound like hype, it's actually obtainable. When you gain an understanding of the true principles of this critical discipline and content marketing's connection to all other facets of your digital marketing mix, you can quickly see the path to content marketing perfection.

Content marketing is about anticipating the needs of your customers and prospects, and building content assets that satisfy those needs. For example, the cloud-based software company Freshbooks anticipated a prospective customer's need for pricing information. The web page shown in Figure 4-1 represents perfect content marketing in this scenario: The content succinctly and clearly communicates the differences in its plans and the varying price levels, provides contact information for those who may have more questions and want to talk to a representative, and offers a free trial. The content on this page completely satisfies the need for pricing information.

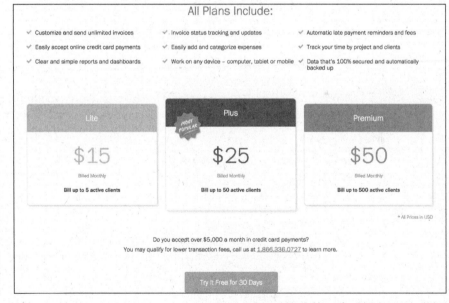

FIGURE 4-1:
This content on Freshbooks is designed to meet a prospective customer's needs when looking for pricing.

Source: https://www.freshbooks.com/pricing

For a prospective customer of Freshbooks to make an informed buying decision, the pricing page is necessary. Before they commit, people want to know what they're buying and how much it will cost. Failure to conveniently provide that information for the prospect will result in lost sales.

Understanding the marketing funnel

The path from stranger to buyer is often conveyed using the metaphor of a funnel. Ice-cold prospects enter the wide top of the funnel and some, you hope, exit through the much narrower bottom of the funnel as customers. Content can, and should, assist the prospect in graduating from one stage of the marketing funnel to the next.

A basic marketing funnel has three stages that take a prospect from stranger to buyer:

TIP

>> **Awareness:** The prospect must first become aware that he has a problem and that you or your organization can provide a solution.

Raising problem and solution awareness is where your blog will shine. Use your blog to educate, inspire, or entertain prospects and existing customers.

>> **Evaluation:** Those who move through the awareness stage must now evaluate the various choices available to them, including your competitor's solutions and, of course, taking no action to solve the problem at all. People can, after all, decide to live with the problem and not purchase the product or service that could solve that problem.

>> **Conversion:** Those who move through the evaluation stage are at the moment of truth — purchase. The goal at this stage is to convert leads into frequent and high-ticket buyers.

REMEMBER

These three stages of awareness, evaluation, and conversion form what is known as a *marketing funnel*. Figure 4-2 conceptualizes the marketing funnel.

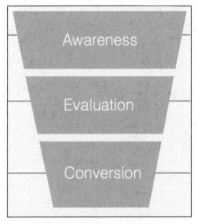

FIGURE 4-2:
The three-step marketing funnel.

Source: http://www.digitalmarketer.com/
content-marketing/

Cold prospects cannot evaluate your solution until they are first aware of the problem *and* of your solution. If prospects are unaware of the problem or the solution that you offer through your product or service, they obviously won't buy. Therefore, conversions are impossible until prospects have first evaluated the possible courses of action they can take, which include buying your product, buying a competitor's product rather than yours, or doing nothing and living with the problem. To move prospects through a marketing funnel, you need to provide content designed to satisfy their needs at each of the three stages:

>> Content at the top of the funnel (TOFU) that facilitates awareness.

>> Content at the middle of the funnel (MOFU) that facilitates evaluation.

>> Content at the bottom of the funnel (BOFU) that facilitates conversion.

TIP

Blogs are fantastic facilitators of awareness (top of funnel) — but they do a poor job of facilitating evaluation (middle of funnel) and conversion (bottom of funnel). Also, at the risk of pointing out the obvious, evaluation and conversion are super critical to your business. To move prospects through the middle and bottom of the funnel, you need other content types, as shown in Figure 4-3 and explained in detail in the following sections.

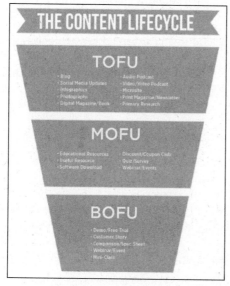

FIGURE 4-3:
You need different content types at each stage of the marketing funnel.

Source: http://www.digitalmarketer.com/
content-marketing/

Top of funnel (TOFU) content marketing

The prospects entering the top of your funnel are unaware of your solution and often unaware that they even have a problem that needs to be solved. As a result, you need content that people can freely access, as opposed to content that requires prospects to give you their contact information or make a purchase. After all, you have yet to prove your value to them.

At the top of the funnel, make free ungated content (which we cover in greater detail in Chapter 3) available that provides one of the following values

- » Entertains
- » Educates
- » Inspires

Choose two to three of the following content types to deliver TOFU content that will raise awareness about the solutions you provide through your products or services:

- » **Blog posts:** Arguably the most recognized form of online content, blogs are an excellent way of raising awareness. For example, the fashion company J. Crew raises awareness of the products it sells by creating blog posts about fashion styles and tips for accessorizing. The J. Crew blog reader (and potential customer) gets some inspiration and solutions to the problem of what to wear and how to look fashionable ; the post also alludes to the fact that J. Crew carries the clothing needed to pull off the look.

- » **Social media updates:** As with blogs, social media platforms (such as Facebook) are fantastic at creating awareness. Whether it's a Pinterest board by Dreyer's Ice Cream that lists every flavor of ice cream the company sells, or a tweet by Airbnb about the ten perfect Paris food experiences, these social media updates give their followers free, valuable information while also bringing the solutions their company provides to the forefront.

- » **Infographics:** Infographics are an interesting and engaging way to display content. Typically, infographics contain fun images with contrasting, eye-catching colors, and the way infographics break up text makes this form of content easily consumable by the viewer. Infographics are highly effective at delivering content that is both entertaining and educational, quickly. Whether it's an infographic by IMDb about the best of the year in movie entertainment, or an infographic by Casper Mattress providing tips on better sleeping habits, this type of content delivers value that a consumer wants, and it raises brand awareness effectively as well.

- » **Photographs:** Pictures are powerful because they can explain a lot in a single image. Photographs also help to break up blocks of text in a piece of content, which keeps that content from becoming boring or intimidating to read. With a photograph, a kitchen design company can show completed projects that effectively demonstrate what the company does while raising awareness of what the company can do for another customer's kitchen.

- **Digital magazines and books:** Digital magazines and books are popular, and are another way to distribute content and raise brand awareness. E-books and e-magazines are similar to the blog strategies discussed in Chapters 5 and 6. Therefore, you can look to your blog to inspire your content for your e-book or e-magazine.

- **Audio and video podcasts:** Another form of content that you can use at the top of the funnel is a podcast. With a podcast, you package and distribute your content differently from textual content. A podcast delivers consumable content on the go. Subscribers can listen to the podcast on their commute to work or during their workout, or any other time they choose. They have a more flexible way to consume the content, in contrast to a blog post or a social media update that is less conducive to multitasking. Also, you can use podcasts to effectively promote your product or service while providing value to your prospects. If you sell outdoor equipment, for example, each episode of your podcast can give tips and tricks about hunting, fishing, camping, and other outdoor activities while also subtly reminding your listener of the outdoor equipment available at your store.

- **Microsites:** A microsite is essentially an auxiliary blog about a specific topic that is put on a different site with its own links and address; a microsite is accessed mainly from a larger site. For instance, DadsDivorce.com is a separate domain of the men's family law firm Cordell & Cordell. DadsDivorce. com provides free content for divorcing fathers and is designed to raise awareness about the services and solutions Cordell & Cordell can provide.

- **Print magazines and newsletters:** This type of content can require a bigger budget than digital content, but if going this route falls within your budget, print magazines and newsletters are still a great way to raise awareness. For example, the *Lego Club Magazine* contains plenty of entertaining comic book style content for Lego's target customer. Magazines and newsletters help sales by inspiring shoppers based on what they see in print.

- **Primary research:** This is research you go out and collect yourself, such as surveys, interviews, and observations. Although this data can be difficult and time consuming to gather, primary research is powerful because only a finite amount of primary research exists. Specifically, when you take the time to create research, you're providing a service and saving people from having to do their own primary research. For this reason, primary research can stir a good deal of awareness among your prospects.

TIP

Do you need all these content types at the top of the funnel? Heck, no. Most businesses focus on posting content to a blog and to social media channels such as Facebook, Twitter, LinkedIn, and Pinterest. After you've mastered blogging and social media updates, you might want to add more top-of-funnel content to the mix, such as a podcast or a print newsletter.

REMEMBER

The big goal at the top of the funnel is to make prospects "problem aware" and "solution aware." In Figure 4-4, notice how Whole Foods uses its Whole Story blog to raise awareness for the seafood the grocery store sells. In this way, Whole Foods is reminding its audience of the products it sells, making its audience "solution aware" while providing people with recipes they find valuable.

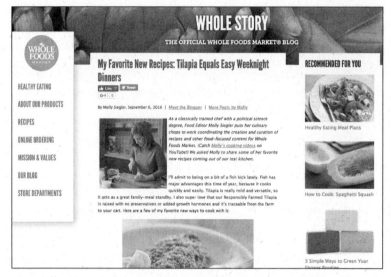

FIGURE 4-4:
Whole Foods raises awareness of products it sells while providing value to its blog audience.

Source: http://www.wholefoodsmarket.com/blog/my-favorite-new-recipes-tilapia-equals-easy-weeknight-dinners-0

Unfortunately, the top of the funnel is where most organizations begin and end their content marketing efforts. Smart content marketers know that, with a bit more effort, they can move prospects from awareness to evaluation at the middle of the funnel.

Middle of funnel (MOFU) content marketing

The big goal for content you use at the middle of the funnel is to convert "problem aware" and "solution aware" prospects into leads. You're looking to grow your email lists and gain more leads at this point of the funnel. At DigitalMarketer, we use free content to incentivize prospects to submit their contact information (such as their email address) and opt in to receive future marketing in exchange for valuable content. We call this type of content *gated offers*, which we discuss in Chapter 3.

REMEMBER

A *gated offer* is a small "chunk" of value that solves a *specific* problem for a *specific* market and is offered in exchange for prospects' contact information.

Gated offers often take the form of content such as the following:

>> **Educational resources:** As discussed in Chapter 3, educational resources for gated offers often exist in the form of free reports, white papers, primary research, webinar training, and sales material. These types of content resources educate the consumer on a particular topic related to your brand while highlighting features of a solution, product, or service you provide. An educational resource can include a case study packed with professional tips and a detailed breakdown of some of your strategies.

REMEMBER

Educational resources (and all forms of MOFU content, for that matter) must be of high quality or the consumer is likely to feel cheated. Also, if prospects feel that the content you gave them in exchange for their contact information is subpar, your brand awareness suffers. Keep in mind that the point of the MOFU is to help people evaluate your company and entice them to make a purchase. You entice with quality, not garbage.

>> **Useful resources:** Useful resources are tools such as

- Handouts or cheat sheets
- Resource lists
- Templates
- Software
- Surveys
- Assessments
- Discount and coupon clubs
- Quizzes and surveys

We explain these useful tools, which serve as powerful content for MOFU, in Chapter 3. Instead of using a consumer's time (such as an e-book that may take an hour or more to read), useful resources promise that they will not only educate your prospects but also save them time. These resources save them time because the content is easy to consume and the resource is complete; it doesn't depend on another resource to deliver its value but can stand alone. For example, a company that sells vegetable gardening tools can create a resource called the "Seed Starting Cheat Sheet" that allows people with an interest in gardening to quickly determine the best time to plant popular vegetables in the garden.

WARNING

Don't pin all your lead-generation hopes to a passive gated offer on your home page or the sidebar of your blog, because the gated offer can get lost among the many elements of your site. A missed gated offer won't capture leads. Be sure to also create a dedicated landing page for every gated offer (some call this a *squeeze page*) and drive traffic directly to that page using social media, email marketing, search engine optimization (SEO), and paid traffic. A dedicated landing page, which we go over in more detail in Chapter 7, increases opt-ins. See Figure 4-5 for an example of a landing page.

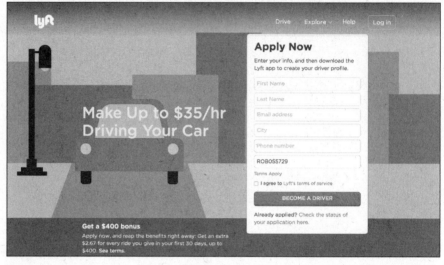

Source: https://www.lyft.com/drive-with-lyft?ref=ROB055729.

The goal at the middle of the funnel is to convert prospects who were unaware of your product or service into people with whom you can now follow up. As they say, however, you can't deposit leads in the bank. To generate revenue, you need content that assists your prospects in making decisions at the point of sale.

Bottom of funnel (BOFU) content marketing

At the BOFU, you're looking to convert leads into customers and customers into higher-ticket customers. What types of content will your new lead need to make an informed purchase decision? Your leads may be reading your blog and downloading your gated offers (all of which helps to convert them), but to move them on through to the point of making a purchase, you also need to offer content that helps them decide whether to buy.

Here are examples of content types that work well at the bottom of the funnel:

>> **Demos:** The downside of buying a product online is that customers can't hold the product in their hands — they have only an image (or two) and a

description to base their purchasing decisions on, which can make people hesitate to buy. Offering a demo can help with this problem. A demo shows the product or service you offer in action, so that consumers can see how it works. It's as close to touching the product as they can get from their screen. So find a way to demonstrate your product or service through content such as video, screen shots, webinars, or schematic drawings.

>> **Customer stories:** Customer stories are customer testimonials and reviews. Customer stories are fantastic at the bottom of the funnel because they allow a prospect to see how someone else experienced success with your product or service. You provide your prospects with peer reviews, which have a powerful effect on decision making. As shown in Figure 4-6, Salesforce.com supplies leads who are at the BOFU with plenty of customer success stories to prove that its product can take care of their needs.

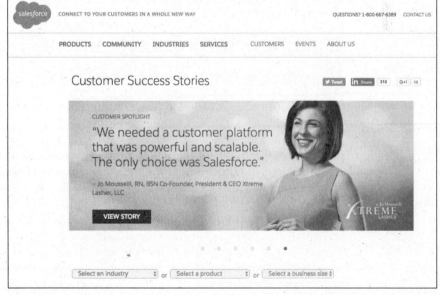

FIGURE 4-6: Salesforce creates content that converts at the BOFU by telling customer success stories.

Source: http://www.salesforce.com/customers/

>> **Comparison/spec sheets:** When someone at the BOFU is debating over different products, comparisons and spec sheets are handy resources that people use to compare products side by side (whether the comparison is between similar products that you offer or between your product and your competitor's product). For example, the tax preparation software company TurboTax might show a side-by-side comparison to the features and pricing of its competitor, TaxAct.

>> **Webinars/events:** As previously stated in this chapter and Chapter 3, you can use webinars and events at the middle of the funnel to gather leads, but you can also use them at the bottom of the funnel to convert those leads. At the bottom of the funnel, a webinar can be used to gather prospective customers in one place to ask questions about a complex, risky, or high-ticket product or service.

>> **Mini-classes:** A mini-class is a type of event that you set up to teach a relevant topic to your target audience. At the end of the short class, you make your pitch for your product or service. You need to provide quality educational resources with the mini-class, but in the end, the purpose of the class is to pitch a higher-dollar product related to the class you just held.

TIP

Is creating content that drives awareness at the top of the funnel important? Absolutely. That said, particularly for existing brands, the place to start building content is usually at the bottom of the funnel. Your prospects need information such as pricing or how you compare to a competitor, so build content that satisfies those basic questions before you start writing blog posts or uploading podcasts.

Exploring the prospect's intent

The key to perfect content marketing is to understand your prospects' existing intent so that you can anticipate their future intent and predict which path or paths they will take. In foreseeing this, you can create the content assets needed to address that intent 24 hours a day, seven days a week.

Returning to the Freshbooks example, the software company that we refer to earlier in the chapter, a customer in the evaluation or conversion stage of the funnel might intend to compare Freshbooks to QuickBooks. The web page shown in Figure 4-7 satisfies that intent at both the middle and the bottom of the funnel. Freshbooks gives the prospect a comparison sheet that allows the customer to see the differences between Freshbooks and its competition, QuickBooks. The company knows that prospective customers want to see how it stacks up against QuickBooks. Satisfying that intent in the evaluation stage helps prospects move into the conversion stage.

TIP

If you're having difficulty brainstorming ideas for content that will satisfy your prospects' intent, gather a group of people in your organization who have contact with your customers and prospects. Salespeople, customer service representatives, trade-show workers, and others who hear the voice of the customer and prospect should be present. These members of your team can help you discover holes in your content that would satisfy a prospect's intent.

Brainstorm lists of intent at the top, middle, and bottom of the funnel. Then decide what content assets need to be built to satisfy that intent from awareness through conversion.

Accounting Purpose-Built for Small Business Owners

Frustrated by slow, bloated accounting software? FreshBooks is easy to use, backed by award-winning support and loved by millions.

	FreshBooks cloud accounting	QuickBooks
Invoices, expenses, and reports	✓	✓
Web and mobile access	✓	✓
Free online and phone support	✓	✓
Designed for service-based small business owners	✓	✗
Built-in time tracking features	✓	✗
Project tracking	✓	✗
Multi-currency billing	✓	✗
Late payment reminders	✓	✗
Award-winning customer support	✓	✗
Industry leading customer happiness score	✓	✗
Free trial period	30 Days	30 Days
Paid plans start at	$12.95/month	$12.95/month

* All prices in USD

FIGURE 4-7: Freshbooks uses a comparison sheet to move a prospect closer to conversion.

Source: `https://www.freshbooks.com/compare/quickbooks-alternative`

Providing a path to the next step

As a marketer, you need to provide a path from one piece of content to the next. People are busy and don't have the time or the patience to go digging through your site for the proper piece of content. They need to be able to find what they're looking for fast.

Failing to provide an easy-to-follow path to the next step isn't just bad marketing, it's a bad user experience, one that will cause people to hit the Back button on your site and leave it altogether. Smart content marketers anticipate the next logical intent and remove as much "friction" as possible to create a clear path to conversion.

The goal of every piece of content is to get the prospect to ascend to the next logical step in the customer journey. In the Freshbooks pricing page example shown in Figure 4-8, notice that Freshbooks has created a clear ascension path to a "Risk-Free Trial" of the software. Creating an ascension path is good marketing and results in a good user experience.

TIP

How well an ascension offer performs depends on the relevance of the offer. Take time to anticipate the next logical step in the customer journey and create offers that are applicable to the piece of content they are currently consuming. For example, asking a visitor to listen to a podcast episode (a top-of-funnel content type) would be neither logical nor relevant from the Freshbooks pricing page in

Figure 4-8. This person is visiting the pricing page because she is interested in buying, and the smart marketer anticipates that intent and makes the next logical offer — a free trial.

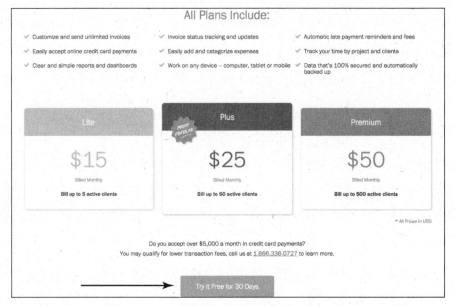

FIGURE 4-8:
Freshbooks anticipates the next logical intent of a visitor who needs to obtain pricing information.

Segmenting your marketing with content

You won't truly understand your audience and what people really want until they have given you one of two things: their time or their money. They may answer survey questions and make comments that they are interested in this or that, but until they have committed a precious resource — time or money — you don't know for sure what interests them. This is good news for anyone creating content online, because when people spend time with content, they are showing interest.

For example, imagine that you own a company that sells healthy and nutritious meals to busy professionals, and you've been creating blog content about nourishing recipes. Your content falls into three main categories of recipes: vegan, vegetarian, and gluten free. What do you know about someone who visits a blog post about vegan recipes? Likewise for someone visiting a blog post about vegetarian recipes? It's pretty clear, right? These people have "raised their hands" and told you that they are (or are interested in becoming) vegan or vegetarian.

When people spend their valuable time consuming content, they are segmenting themselves. They are telling you what interests them. And thanks to the magic of ad retargeting, you can follow up with these prospects by using a relevant ascension offer without having to acquire their contact information.

Retargeting is the process of advertising to people based on their prior behavior. For example, you can configure retargeting ads so that they appear only to customers who bought a particular product or visited (showed interest) a particular product page or blog post. This approach allows you to show a very specific piece of content that is more likely to resonate with the segmented audience. Turn to Chapter 10 for more information on ad retargeting strategies.

Appearing everywhere your customer expects

Marketers who want to create perfect content need to publish where their customers are. That means publishing content that meets prospects' intent in any channel, and at every stage of the funnel where groups of prospects are searching for and sharing content. These channels include but are certainly not limited to the following:

>> A website or blog

>> Facebook

>> Twitter

>> LinkedIn

>> Pinterest

>> Instagram

>> YouTube

You can publish a single content asset across numerous channels to maximize exposure. For instance, at DigitalMarketer, we turned a presentation about how to launch a podcast into a webinar, and then into a podcast episode, and finally into a blog post. Because our audience responded so enthusiastically to this content, we saw the value and the need to repurpose it and distribute it throughout our channels.

Consider what content from your company has resonated with your audience. For example, can that video demo of your product be republished on your YouTube channel? Can you repurpose an article from your blog into a webinar, or a podcast episode into an article for LinkedIn Pulse? The opportunities to repurpose content are virtually limitless.

Customizing your content

You produce perfect content marketing materials to satisfy the intent of your *customer avatars* (also known as target audience or customer persona). But not all avatars are the same; they, like their real-life counterparts, don't all want or need the same solution. That's why customizing and then segmenting your content is essential. A particular piece of content can satisfy the intent of multiple avatars, or you can use it to target a single avatar.

For example, we produced a blog article called "6 Trending Digital Marketing Skills to Put on a Resume" to raise awareness (top of the funnel) for our marketing certification programs. This post probably wouldn't interest small business owners, but that was fine — we weren't targeting them. This article was specifically targeted to our "employee" avatar whose intent is to acquire skills that will land her a better job. Included in the post are two calls to action, which, as mentioned in Chapter 2, is an instruction to your audience designed to convey urgency and provoke an immediate response. In the case of the trending skills blog post, the calls to action are customized to appeal to the "employee" avatar.

Executing Perfect Content Marketing

As we say earlier in this chapter, to execute perfect content marketing, you need a plan. Each offer you make often requires the creation of different pieces of content. As a result, the ideal is to make a content plan for each of your major offers using a resource we call the Content Campaign Plan. The Content Campaign Plan aligns your content marketing with business objectives such as generating leads and sales. You can see the Content Campaign Plan template in Figure 4-9 and can fill out your own by visiting www.digitalmarketer.com/content-campaign.

Following are the steps for creating your first Content Campaign Plan:

1. Choose avatars.

2. Brainstorm content assets.

3. Choose the vehicle and channel.

4. Plan for ascension.

Read on to find out more about each of these steps.

OFFER	AVATAR 1	AVATAR 2	AVATAR 3	AVATAR 4	AVATAR 5	
AWARENESS						
EVALUATION						
CONVERSION						

ASSET	DESCRIPTION	AVATAR(S)	VEHICLE(S)	CHANNEL(S)	OWNER	ASCENSION
ASSET A						
ASSET B						
ASSET C						
ASSET D						
ASSET E						
ASSET F						
ASSET G						

FIGURE 4-9: The Content Campaign Plan organizes your content strategy for each individual product or service offer.

Source: https://docs.google.com/spreadsheets/d/1Z29wImP17PgJwQMv2TFr-RyOu_THBu1pX1OxJgjUtEw/edit#gid=0

Step 1: Choosing avatars

Decide which avatars (also known as a buyer persona) this content targets. Because each avatar has different intents, motivations, and problems he responds to, each avatar requires different content to move him through the awareness, evaluation, and conversion stages. You therefore need to determine which existing content to use or what new content to create to move the avatar through the top, middle, and bottom of the funnel.

For example, a wealth management firm attempting to sell financial planning should approach a young professional much differently than a near retiree. Some content will appeal to both, but the most effective content will speak directly to a specific avatar.

Step 2: Brainstorming content assets

Use what you know about your customer avatar to create descriptions for content that you can create to reach that persona.

REMEMBER

Plan to create content at all three stages of the marketing funnel: awareness, evaluation, and conversion. In the wealth management firm example, what content could the firm produce at the top of the funnel to increase awareness for the young professional avatar? What could it produce to move the retiree avatar through the conversion stage?

Step 3: Choosing the vehicle and channel

The *vehicle* of the content refers to the form the content will take. Will it be text, an image, a video, or an audio asset? The *channel* refers to where the asset will be published — such as your blog, a Facebook page, or a YouTube channel.

The vehicle can sometimes determine the channel, and vice versa. For example, a video asset often gets published on YouTube, Facebook, and your blog, whereas an image asset is more likely to be on Pinterest.

Step 4: Planning for ascension

In the final step of the Content Campaign Plan, you connect your content to your business goals. Build offers into each piece of content that allow prospects to get more value, either by consuming more content, giving you their contact information for follow-up, or buying a product or service.

TIP

Any call to action is better than none at all, but the highest-converting ascension offers are relevant to the content the prospect is consuming. For example, a blog post entitled "10 Ways to Grow More Nutritious Organic Tomatoes" would do well to make an offer like "50% Off and Free Shipping on Organic Tomato Seeds" rather than an offer for carrot seeds.

If you want to create content that converts prospects at all stages of the funnel, create a Content Campaign Plan and execute it. It works.

Distributing Content to Attract an Audience

Today, content plays an important role in all major forms of traffic generation. Convincing cold (and even warm) prospects to visit your website is difficult without first leading with valuable content.

The processes you develop to distribute content, and thus generate traffic to it, are as important as the processes surrounding the creation of that content. Entire chapters of this book are devoted to the nuances of traffic generation using the methods of email marketing, search, social media, and paid traffic. However, it's worth mentioning how each of these major traffic generation methods interact with the content you produce.

Marketing through email

Email is still the best method for making offers and sending more content, so growing and maintaining your email lists are critical tasks, which is why growing your email list is built into your content strategy. After you've produced a content asset, such as a blog post or a podcast episode, use your email list(s) to drive traffic to that piece.

To write the email for your new piece of content, first create the subject line of the email message. Often the subject is the same as the title of the content, but there are other strategies to naming your email subject line, such as scarcity headings like "FINAL notice (Just hours left . . .)" or by piquing curiosity with subject lines like "THIS is why I do what I do . . . ." We describe these strategies in more detail in Chapter 11.

Next, open your email with a short, punchy introduction that pulls people into the main body of your email, where you pique the email subscriber's interest and describe what he can expect from the content. Explain this email's relevance to the reader and what he has to gain from it (also known as the *benefit*). Also, be sure to include a call to action that instructs the subscriber to click the hyperlink to your content. Use two to three hyperlinked calls to action to make clicking them as convenient as possible.

Capturing leads through search marketing

Search engines, such as Google and Bing, are important content distribution channels to leverage. When prospects reach your site by querying a search engine (they might be searching for "dslr camera reviews" or "crepe recipes" in Google or Bing) but haven't selected an ad, they are using search marketing. The traffic driven to that content wasn't paid for but was found naturally by the users.

TIP

Today, search marketing is simple. The search engines, particularly Google, have become adept at sending traffic to the content that is most likely to satisfy the intent of the searcher. If you are committed to creating content assets that satisfy the intent of your various customer avatars, you'll get plenty of love from Google and other search engines. You can learn more about search marketing in Chapter 8.

Using social media to drive traffic to your site

After you have created a piece of content, use the social media platform(s) that your business participates in to drive traffic to that content. We describe how to use social media in greater detail in Chapter 9, but for now, be aware that driving traffic on social media may take several forms, such as a tweet on Twitter or an update on Facebook or LinkedIn. This update announces the new content and provides a hyperlink to it.

When you write text for a social media update, your brand's personality should determine how you announce this new content. For instance, if your brand is a refined jewelry store, you may want to use a formal tone in your copy.

The length of the copy depends on restrictions (such as on Twitter) and the complexity of the offer. Simple offers don't require the same amount of description as complex offers do. Regardless of the length of the copy, be sure that the social media update piques the viewer's curiosity, describes the benefit of the content, and has a clear call to action, such as the home improvement store Lowe's Facebook post shown in Figure 4-10. This social media update meets all three of these requirements effectively.

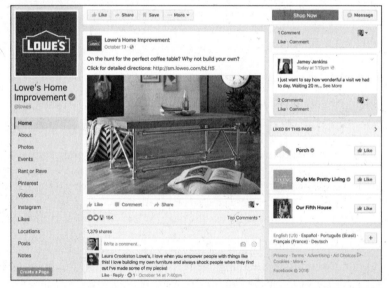

FIGURE 4-10:
On Facebook,
Lowe's
establishes the
benefit of the
content and gives
a clear call to
action for the
viewer to click.

Source: https://www.facebook.com/lowes/posts/10153827254486231:0

Paying for traffic

As the name suggests, paid traffic takes the form of ads that promote your content and helps your content gain reach, or exposure. You can display ads on many different platforms, including search engines and social media. Paid traffic can be highly effective at generating leads because it helps you to segment your visitors and make use of retargeting.

When a prospect visits a piece of content, she places herself into a particular segment of your potential buyers. She's indicating an interest in the offer, topic, problem, or solution found on that page, and you can take advantage of ad retargeting networks such as Google and Facebook to show ads to this prospect based on the content she has visited.

Although many marketers may be reluctant to pay to send traffic to content, such as blog posts and podcasts, paid traffic has a major advantage: It's predictable. When you cut a check to Facebook, for example, to promote a piece of content, you will get traffic. This is why, at all times but especially when buying ads for your content, you must ensure the exceptional quality of your content. The last thing you want to do is spend money to send traffic to poor-quality content.

Use paid traffic to promote quality content that gives value to the consumer and aligns with your business goals. This will help you move people from one part of the funnel to the next, progressing from ice-cold prospect to a lead to customer to repeat customer and, ideally, to raving fan.

Chapter **5**

Blogging for Business

The topic of blogging deserves in-depth discussion. Blogging is one of the most powerful and versatile digital marketing tools at your disposal. You can think of your blog as a home for content of every type, including text, graphics, audio, and video. Functionally, though, a blog is just a tool that helps you manage certain pages of your website.

The power of a well-executed business blog lies in its capability to generate awareness for your company, brands, customer-facing employees, products, and services. When done right, the business blog becomes a critical part of your marketing mix. If done improperly, however, a business blog can become a frustrating, time-consuming chore that gives you zero return for your effort.

Although you should always keep the customer journey in mind, the main purpose of your business blog is to create aware and engaged prospects who eventually convert into leads and sales. Although in other content areas, building ungated, gated, and deep discount offers (discussed in Chapter 3) into your content is critical, the goal of your blog is not the immediate conversion of a prospect into a lead or customer.

REMEMBER

Marketing is about the sequence of the offers you make to prospects, leads, and customers. Your blog content is one of the entry point offers (EPOs) that you make to cold prospects who know nothing about you or your company. But content is also something you can distribute via email, social media, and paid traffic to even your best customers to keep your business at the forefront of people's minds and provide additional value.

In this chapter, we give you strategies for successful business blogging. We point you toward effective tools to use for blogging ideas, tell you how to find and work with content creators to keep your blog diverse and interesting, and help you brainstorm effective headlines for your blog articles. The final part of this chapter provides a list of the elements by which you can "audit" your blog to make sure it's as effective as you can make it.

Establishing a Blog Publishing Process

To produce a blog that has an impact on the bottom line, you need a process. The unsuccessful business blog fails to plan. Putting together a blog-publishing process helps you do the following:

>> Fine-tune aspects of your blog such as style, tone, topics, offers, mediums

>> Plan your content and identify content gaps while considering what your audience *wants* you to write about

>> Maximize your content's immediate impact as well as its long-term impact as a resource

Your blog-publishing process should include a way to generate blog post ideas, utilize content segments for consistent planning, find and work with content creators, edit content, and broadcast new content. The following sections break down the details of each part of this process.

Brainstorming blog post ideas

In Chapter 6, we offer you 57 content and blog post types you can use in multiple ways, which will ensure that you never run out of post ideas or ways to frame your content again. In this section, you learn which tools are available to you while you're brainstorming.

Get inspiration from your customer avatar

The customer avatar process outlined in Chapter 1 gives you an abundant source of information for brainstorming blog post ideas for your blog. What blog posts, videos, podcasts, and so on should you create to attract and convert your avatar?

Start by looking at the five components of your avatar:

>> **Goals and values:** What is the avatar trying to achieve? What values does he hold dear?

>> **Sources of information:** What books, magazines, blogs, and other publications does the avatar reference for information?

>> **Demographics:** What is the age, gender, and marital status of the avatar?

>> **Challenges and pain points:** What holds the avatar back from achieving her goals?

>> **Objections:** Why might the avatar choose not to buy your product or service?

Answer each of those questions about your avatar and use those answers to brainstorm ideas for content. Use the information you know about your target market to create content that solves your avatar's problem, enters the conversations she's having, speaks to her goals, and meets her objections head-on.

Do some research on BuzzSumo

BuzzSumo is an online tool that allows you to analyze what content is performing well on social media for a topic. The number of social media shares that a blog post receives is a good indication of content that the audience likes. The topics receiving the most attention from social media are the ones you should consider for your blog.

Start by searching keywords and phrases that your audience is likely to be searching for. With the BuzzSumo tool, you can also adjust the content type that you search for. You can choose from these categories: Articles, Infographics, Guest Posts, Giveaways, Interviews, and Videos. BuzzSumo allows you to adjust the date range for the content it searches, so if you're searching for content that's been making a *buzz* lately, or content that was published in the last year, your options are open.

Want to see how your competition's content is performing? Type in its domain to see all its content in order of social popularity. Figure 5-1 shows the BuzzSumo ranking of content on Typepad's blog by social popularity. Want to see what is performing well with people you admire in your industry? Search their names and BuzzSumo generates their most popular content.

Monitor your own data

The savvy blogger watches how the audience responds to content by monitoring data points. These data points help you determine what you should produce more of in the future.

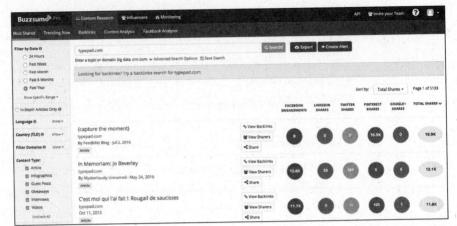

Source: https://app.buzzsumo.com

FIGURE 5-1:
Use BuzzSumo
to identify
content that is
working well.

Google Analytics is a free tool that allows you to view data about how your visitors are using your website. You can use Google Analytics to determine which blog posts on your website receive the most traffic, which posts people spend the most time on, and where the traffic comes from (for example, Twitter, Google, and email).

You should also keep an eye on the number of social shares on each blog post. If you use a content management system like WordPress or Squarespace, you can install social sharing buttons that allow blog visitors to easily share your content with their network on sites like Twitter, Facebook, or Pinterest. Figure 5-2 shows a blog post with high social engagement and shares. The data-driven blogger can find inspiration and create content that mimics posts with high social share count.

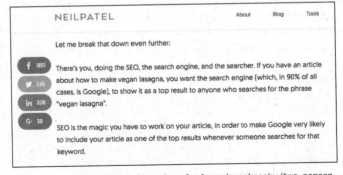

FIGURE 5-2:
A recent
post from
DigitalMarketer
with high social
engagement.

Source: https://www.buzzfeed.com/annakopsky/two-person-halloween-costume-ideas-you-have-permission-to?utm_term=.cm7xOkVyM#.naZgR4NkG

And finally, when distributing your content through an email newsletter, keep an eye on the open and click-through rates on each email. Content that interests your audience gets a relatively higher percentage of opens and clicks than content your audience finds less interesting.

Use information pulled from your internal data sources to shape your content calendar, prioritizing what the data tells you concerning your audience's interests.

Establishing content segments

Your blog should not be reinventing itself from week to week and month to month. You and your audience can derive more value from your blog if you create a predictable structure to the types of content you publish. To offer a predictable structure, you create content segments. A *content segment* is a blog post format that repeats on a set schedule and follows a similar style and template.

You're likely already familiar with content segments whether you're aware of it or not. The radio, television, and print mediums have used segments for decades. For example, the Letters to the Editor segment is a staple of the newspaper industry that appears day after day. Buzzfeed, an online social news and entertainment website, runs a daily post called "Here's What People Are Buying on Amazon Right Now." Figure 5-3 shows Moz, a company that creates SEO software and resources for digital marketers, featuring a weekly video blog post called "Whiteboard Friday."

FIGURE 5-3: An excerpt of a segmented post from Moz.

Source: https://moz.com/blog/how-to-appear-in-googles-answer-boxes-whiteboard-friday

Many of the post types that we introduce you to in Chapter 6 are adaptable as segments. For example, you can run the link roundup post (covered in Chapter 6) every week or month on your blog. Simply curate and compile a list of links that your audience would find interesting and publish it along with a description of what people can expect if they visit that link.

Segments are great pieces to have on your calendar for a variety of reasons. One is that you can offer outside writers consistent exposure on your blog. Another reason is that they're easily repeatable and quickly consumable because the format is always the same. Your audience will recognize them and grow to expect them as you continue to publish them, providing people with consistent value.

Working with content creators

To produce the content necessary to grow your blog, you're likely to need a team of writers. An outside writer is someone not associated with your brand who creates content assets for your blog. Those content assets are typically written articles, but the content can also take the form of audio, video, and images for your blog. Acquiring quality outside content creators gives your blog a broad range of perspectives and can help give authority and reach to your blog. This is especially true if the content creator is an *influencer,* that is, someone who has an above-average impact in his or her niche. Influencers often have a following of their own and are connected to key players in media outlets, consumer groups, or industry associations.

Finding content creators

One place to start when you're hunting for content creators is to search for blogs that are similar to yours in topic. Use a search engine, such as Google, and enter one of the following search queries:

> [your blog topic] blogs
>
> [your blog topic] blogger
>
> [your blog topic] author
>
> [your blog topic] speaker

For instance, if your blog is on the vegan lifestyle, you can search for "vegan blogs" and find links to top vegan blogs and authors who have contributed to those blogs.

TIP

Don't just search the first page of the search engine results page. Search deep into the results pages, many pages in — this is where you might stumble upon a good writer who may not be receiving very much traffic. These bloggers are very receptive to contributing content to other blogs to receive more exposure for their own blog.

You can also search for content creators on Twitter. Most content creators use Twitter to distribute links to their content. Use an app such as Followerwonk to search Twitter Bio's for terms like the following:

[your blog topic] blogger

[your blog topic] writer

[your blog topic] author

[your blog topic] speaker

Another way you can find content creators is to visit blogs that are writing about topics that are the same as, or related to, your own and contact their guest bloggers. Often, these are freelance writers and bloggers who would be willing to write for your blog for money and exposure to your audience.

Next, you may be able to find content creators from your best commenters. These are people who leave the most in-depth and thoughtful comments on your articles. Not only are these commenters engaged with you, they know your style, and they may be writers and speakers looking for exposure.

Finally, you can create a Write for Us page on your site or blog so that interested writers can contact you. But be careful: You can get many low-quality content creators sending requests from your "Write for Us" page, which is why you want to include guidelines. Listing what you expect from content creators helps to detract the ones who aren't fit for your blog as well as draw the kind of authors you're looking for. Here are the elements to include on your Write for Us page to attract high-quality writers:

>> **Acceptance of bylined articles:** Most writers want to know that you will include a byline with a link to their website; let them know you do.

>> **Statement that you pay for articles:** If you pay for articles, you increase the response rate by letting writers know on the Write for Us page. You don't have to include how much you pay.

>> **Content categories:** Outline the topics you want guest writers to write about.

>> **Examples:** Link to sample articles that model the posts you want from guest writers.

>> **A form:** Include a form that the interested writer can fill out to contact you. Ask for the writer's name and email, at a minimum. To filter out low-quality submissions, ask interested writers to submit writing samples; at our company, we ask for three writing samples.

MarketingProfs does an excellent job of creating a very detailed Write for Us page to help find quality content creators; see Figure 5-4 for an excerpt.

Write for MarketingProfs

Yes! We accept **bylined "how to" articles** and **opinion pieces** for our website and daily newsletter, MarketingProfs Today.

We also publish daily **summaries of research findings** based on polls, surveys, and research studies conducted by marketers, academia, PR firms, and other researchers.

1. Contribute bylined "how to" articles for MarketingProfs.com

Bylined articles of **800-1,000 words or so of body text**, written from an objective viewpoint and conveying valuable **how-to** content (**practical** advice, **actionable** tips, and **useful** know-how) in a fresh, approachable voice are more likely to meet MarketingProfs standards—and therefore more likely to be accepted for publication. See, as examples, the following three articles:

1. 13 'Old-School' Marketing Techniques That Take Your Facebook Fan Page From Wimpy to Wow

2. Run Your Website Like a Magazine

3. 10 Ways to Entice Your Whole Company (Not Just Marketing) to Blog

We will inform you if your article has been accepted for publication; expect to hear from us within a week or so of our having received your email. If we choose not to accept your article, you may or may not hear from us, depending on how crowded our inbox is.

Articles accepted for publication will be edited for clarity and brevity and to conform to the MarketingProfs house style. We will likely change your title, too, so you might want to suggest some alternatives.

So, if you are interested in joining the hundreds of MarketingProfs contributors of how-to marketing articles—on a one-time or a regular basis—here are some guidelines:

1. Articles should be original to the author and **unpublished elsewhere**.

2. Articles should offer readers **clear advice, takeaways, and practical how-to tips** about a specific marketing topic or approach to marketing. Bullet points are good. Meandering text is not—but keep in mind that **800-word minimum**.

3. At the beginning of your article, **list two or three bullet points summarizing its key takeaways**—the lessons learned and the how-tos contained in the article. They will be published along with the article.

4. Include a **brief bio** of 25 words, including LinkedIn and Twitter contact info, if available, and a recent **headshot** (make sure your entire head is in the picture).

FIGURE 5-4: An excerpt from MarketingProfs' "Write for Us" page.

Source: http://www.marketingprofs.com/write-for-us

Acquiring content creators

After you find content contributors who interest you, it's time to reach out to them. Understand that outside content creators will produce content for your blog for one of two reasons: money or exposure (or both).

For writers doing it for the first reason, the process is simple: You cut them a check, and they create a piece of content for you. As a rule, the more specialized the knowledge your writer needs, the more the content will cost you. It's a supply and demand thing. If you're unsure how much the going rate for a writer is, you can visit sites such as Craigslist and ProBlogger Job Board to browse through the open jobs.

Aside from money, what you can offer writers is exposure to your audience. If your blog has impressive amounts of traffic, social shares, or comments from readers, share that information with the outside writers you are courting. You will find that the more exposure you have to offer writers, the less you will have to pay for their content. In fact, after your blog reaches a critical mass, you won't need to pay a dime for content — writers will come to you for the exposure.

Keep in mind that the reach the writer brings to the table will affect how much you have to pay him or her. The more influence and followers your guest writer has, the more money and exposure that author will require from you.

Ensuring success with content creators

The best way to ensure success from an outside writer is to be prepared with guidelines for your blog. These guidelines, like those on the Write for Us page, communicate what types of content perform best on your blog, what audience you gear your articles toward, and other standards for an outside writer's work to meet. For instance, if your blog doesn't accept certain kinds of images (stock or personal photography, for example) indicate those restrictions in your guidelines. If you require your images to be a certain size, with a certain resolution and with a specific border, list those requirements. Your guidelines are the information your writers need to shape the content you want them to provide you, and having guidelines will save you a mess of editing, formatting, and image polishing when you receive their final work. After connecting with outside writers who have indicated interest in writing for you, send them your guidelines so that they know what to expect. You can send the guidelines in a separate document or paste them directly into your correspondence.

Next, lead with examples by showing writers articles on your own blog that you want their article to model. Also, provide links to content that has done well in the past to help the writers get a sense of what direction to take the article.

After writers know what you expect based on your guidelines and the examples you've provided, ask the writers for information about the post they intend to write for you. Have them give you the following information:

>> **The working title:** The title of a blog post, also called a headline, is a promise to the reader. The working title isn't necessarily the headline that will be published on your blog, but it is a guiding statement for the writer as he produces the post.

>> **The outline:** You want to know how the post will lay out, details for each section, and what images the writer expects to use. The more detail you receive from the writer upfront, the greater the chance for the article's success.

When writers send back the working title and outline, approve or make suggestions and ask questions until you're satisfied that their efforts will generate a post that is publishable on your blog.

Last, discuss timeframes and deadlines. Depending on the type of post, expect the writer to take between one and three weeks to develop the first draft. If you've never worked with someone before, ask her to write the first 25 percent and send it to you or your editor for review. This preview will allow you to make adjustments and work with the writer before she completes the post.

Be sure to respect the writers' time as they've respected yours and set expectations on turnaround time. How long will they have to wait until you send back edits or questions? How long before they know their post is approved? When will you communicate their publish date to them? With guidelines, timing, and expectations set, you ensure that your content creating process can go off without a hitch.

Editing the first draft

After a contributor has submitted a first draft (on time, you hope!), you approach the draft for a technical edit. This is the edit you perform to ensure that this piece of content is publishable in its current state, or can be brought up to standard without an overhaul of the content.

First, compare the final post to the headline and outline the writer submitted earlier in the process. Does it deliver on the promise in the working title? Does it stay true to the outline? Point out any areas of concern you have. Pay particular attention to areas that deviate from the stated promise in the working title or that the writer omitted from the expected outline.

Next, run down your guidelines to verify that the post meets your publishing criteria. Is the tone right for your blog? Does it deliver the types of content your audience expects from your blog? Do images meet the standard and specifications set by your guidelines? Does your writer have the necessary permissions secured to use images in the content?

After you established that the post does or does not meet your guidelines, go through the meat of the post to see what edits you need to make. What does the writer need to expand on? What should he remove? What can he clarify for the audience?

Decide whether the post needs to go back to the writer for further revisions and edits, or if you will publish as is or with minor edits from you or your editorial team. If you return the post to the writer, communicate a follow-up deadline in order to reach your publishing date. Your notes should clarify exactly what you're hoping for in the revisions, and what edits need to be made.

Copyediting the post

After you have a publishable post (one that fulfills the promise and meets your standards), you should perform a thorough copy edit. Edit the post to meet your language style (do you capitalize certain words by company standards? Hyphenate words that others don't?), or add clarifying sentences that you believe your audience needs to connect the dots.

Next, go through the post line by line, checking for misspellings and grammar errors, among other things. You should edit for formatting, flow, tone, and to ensure that links, images, and video work as expected. The goal of the copy edit is to ensure that the content is free of errors, including misspellings, grammar errors, and broken links.

Applying Blog Headline Formulas

Everything we discussed in this chapter is a moot point if you don't create blog post titles, also called headlines, that entice and engage your audience. The headline is the most important part of your post because it cuts through the noise to grab your readers' attention and convince them to give you their precious time by reading your article.

But how do you come up with these stellar blog headlines that increase clicks? You follow a formula. There are six different categories that great blog headlines fall into, and we're going to detail each.

Tapping into self-interest

The first headline formula is the self-interest headline. These are your bread-and-butter blog post titles and should be used frequently. Self-interest headlines are usually direct and speak to a specific benefit that your audience will gain by reading your blog post. These headlines start to answer the "What's in it for me?" question, as well as help prequalify readers by giving them a clue about what the article entails.

Here are some sample self-interest headlines:

Grow Your Website Traffic with the 3-Step Content Marketing Plan

How to Retire in Style Even if You Haven't Started Saving

Top 10 Organic Food Markets in Austin, Texas

Piquing curiosity

If self-interest headlines work because they communicate a direct benefit of reading a blog post, curiosity-based ones succeed for the exact opposite reason. These headlines pique the interest of readers without giving away too much information, which leads to a higher number of clicks. Curiosity headlines create an itch that needs to be scratched, and readers have a hard time resisting reading the blog post. Be careful, though, because curiosity-based headlines can fall flat if you miss the mark. Because curiosity headlines are more ambiguous, you might annoy your reader when the content fails to live up to the expectations set by the headline. So make sure that your curiosity headline doesn't mislead your reader.

Here are some examples of curiosity headlines:

25 Things You Didn't Know Your iPhone Could Do

Grill the Perfect Beef Filet with the "Butterfly Process"

This is Why You Should Never Drink Raw Milk

TIP

It's rarely a good idea to use pure curiosity in a blog post title. Instead, as with the example preceding headlines, combine curiosity with benefit to craft a powerful blog post headline. For example, you might be interested in reading a blog post about grilling the perfect beef filet, but the added curiosity created by the "Butterfly Process" makes the headline even more compelling.

Employing urgency and scarcity

The most powerful way to get someone to read your blog post is to impart urgency or scarcity with your headline. Headlines that communicate urgency and scarcity tell readers they must act *now*, or they'll miss something. Don't overuse this technique, or you'll likely aggravate your audience. Use urgency and scarcity headlines only when you truly have a deadline, limited quantity, or limited availability.

Here are some urgency and scarcity headlines:

Get Tickets Now! Woody Allen Speaking at Lincoln Center on October 15th

Free Photography Classes: Last Chance for Open Enrollment

New Book Reveals Ancient Weight Loss Secret; Supplies are Limited

Issuing a warning

Often, people will be more motivated to take action to avoid pain than gain a benefit. Well-crafted warning headlines, like the following, incorporate the promise that you can protect yourself from a threat if you take action:

The Big Lie Hiding in Your Apartment Rental Contract

Warning: Don't Buy Another Ounce of Dog Food Until You Read This

Is Your Child's Mattress Harmful to His or Her Health?

Borrowing authority

A fundamental characteristic of humans is that we look to the behavior of others when making decisions. You can leverage this trait in your headlines by mentioning a person's success story, citing familiar and influential names, or highlighting how many people are already using a product or service.

Smart marketers use this "social proof" — the propensity for people to make choices based on the choices other people have made — wherever they can. The more people making that choice and the more influential those people are, the more influential the social proof.

Consider these "social proof" headlines:

> Why 1000's of Bostonians Will Gather in Boston Common on December 8th
>
> What Dr. Oz Eats for a Midnight Snack
>
> The New Justin Timberlake Video Everyone is Talking About

Revealing the new

Keeping your audience informed about new developments in your field builds authority and keeps your audience tuned in. Blog posts that center on the cutting edge need a headline that stands out and conveys the newness or urgency of the latest information. These headlines often work well when combined with a curiosity element and are known as news headlines.

Take, for example, these news headlines:

> Ancient Human Cancer Discovered in 1.7 Million-Year-Old Bone
>
> Vibrant New Species Discovered Deep in the Caribbean
>
> New Tool Changes Webinars Forever

Auditing a Blog Post

When you're reading or editing a blog post, putting your finger on the *specific* reasons a post is falling short of fabulous can be difficult. Communicating what needs to be improved to a writer or content team can be even more difficult — that is, these things are difficult if you don't have a process or don't know what to look for. To audit your blog post, you should examine ten elements. The following sections discuss each element to help you learn to evaluate and improve each one.

Presents an exceptional headline

In the section "Applying Blog Headline Formulas," earlier in this chapter, we list the six categories that headlines often fall into. No matter which headline formula, or combination of formulas, you're using, exceptional headlines have three aspects in common.

>> The headline contains a promise of what people will gain from reading the post.

>> Although the headline uses as many words as needed to convey the promise, it's concise and avoids fluff words, which are redundant, unnecessary words or phrases that add little to the headline and slow the reader down, such as *really, just, very,* and *rather.* Here's an example of a headline with fluff words:

Why It Is Very Important to Basically Avoid Fluff Words That Are Rather Empty and Sometimes a Little Distracting in Your Headlines and in Your Writing

Here's a better, more compelling headline:

How Fluff Words Are Driving Your Readers Away and How You Can Avoid Them in Your Writing

>> The headline is compelling without being misleading or full of hype.

Headlines that don't work well are often merely statements or incomplete phrases. For example, consider three blog headlines found on a fitness and nutrition website:

Chocolate for Breakfast

Benefits of Meditation

Win the War Against Childhood Obesity

Notice how all three headlines are simply statements of (presumably) fact. They can be dramatically improved, and often by a simple alteration such as

Chocolate for Breakfast?

7 Benefits of Meditation

How to Win the War Against Childhood Obesity

Although these modified headlines aren't perfect, they're considerably more effective than their originals. Adding a question mark to the first headline is a better way to pique a reader's interest. Putting a number in the middle headline eliminates vagueness and adds specificity. Finally, the addition of "How to" in the last headline turns a statement into a promise.

If you're struggling to come up with a headline for your piece, you can often find one hiding in the opening or closing of the article. Look for the promise statement that conveys the benefit of the article in your introduction or conclusion. You'll likely find the beginnings of a headline there.

Includes a strong introduction

The weakest part of an article is often the introduction. Sometimes a blog post can go from being good to great if you just chop off the first five paragraphs to get the reader to the point quicker. Exceptional introductions contain the following elements:

>> Intro copy is extremely easy to consume and develops a rhythm for the post.

>> Intro copy draws readers in and compels them to read the entire article.

When writing your introduction, here's a trick you can use: Open the post with a punchy, curiosity-building sentence. Keep it short (rarely longer than eight words). The first sentence is intended to create a "greased chute" (a term coined by copywriter Joe Sugarman) that starts the reader "sliding" down the page.

Here are a few examples of this type of opening line:

You've finally found it.

Here's the big misconception . . .

Stop me if you've heard this before.

After you get readers started down the "chute," keeping them moving is much easier; getting them started is the difficult part.

Offers easy-to-consume content

One of the goals of a blogger is for people to read the entire article, from start to finish, and not bounce to somewhere in between. Blog content isn't doing its job if it isn't easy to consume. To ensure that your content is easy to read, be sure that

>> Copy is formatted in a way that makes the article easy to consume.

>> Transitions between ideas and subheadlines are smooth.

Blog articles aren't like books. An exceptional blog should not consist of dense, long paragraphs with few to no images or video. Long, uninterrupted blocks of text are intimidating to a reader, not to mention visually unappealing. Help move the reader through the content by breaking up text with the following:

- » Bulleted lists
- » Numbered lists
- » Block quotes
- » Subheadings
- » Artwork and images (such as pictures, GIFs, infographics, and embedded videos)
- » Bold font
- » Italics

Next, look for changes between ideas and other areas where readers might slow down or stop reading. At the points that may block readers, make sure to include transitions. Transitions help to tie the article together, enhance reader comprehension, and help keep readers engaged and moving down the page to the final sentence. Figure 5-5 shows an excerpt of a blog post that uses figures, headings, bulleted lists, a bold font, and short paragraphs to break up text and make the content easy to read.

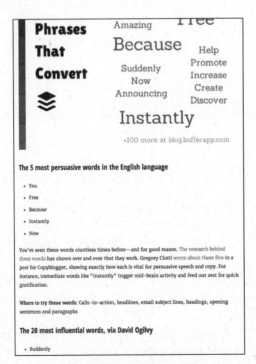

FIGURE 5-5:
A blog post uses formatting in a way that makes the content easy to consume.

Source: https://blog.bufferapp.com/words-and-phrases-that-convert-ultimate-list

A final point: Break up paragraphs. Long paragraphs in blog posts are like speed bumps, slowing readers down and deterring them from fully consuming the article. When you're laying out your blog post, break up paragraphs that are longer than three lines to improve consumption.

Satisfies your goal

Although a blog has many goals, such as branding, providing your audience value, and establishing yourself as an authority, the main goal of a blog is to generate quality leads that ultimately lead to sales. The keys to higher conversion rates from blog content are as follows:

>> **Relevance:** The offer you make in the post needs to relate to that article's topic. The more congruent the offer, the more likely you'll secure a conversion.

>> **Consumption:** If the copy is difficult to get through, readers will leave your page in frustration.

To help meet the goal, be sure to include the following in each article that you publish:

>> A clear call to action (CTA) that is relevant to the subject matter of the article.

>> Effective copy and design for the call to action so that it compels readers to take the desired action.

>> A call to action that is located in one or more prominent positions within the post, giving it a better chance of being seen.

Figure 5-6 shows a call to action from *The New York Times* that pops up over the blog post, catching visitors' attention before visitors leave the site. This CTA has a simple message and design that helps to grab attention and generate clicks.

Includes quality media

The images, videos, and audio files that you include in an article make up the media of your post. Quality media that loads quickly is extremely important to the success of an article. Media that takes longer than three seconds to load, or is of poor quality, causes readers to become frustrated and seek out blog content that doesn't make them wait or that looks fuzzy. Committing to the production of high-quality media is one way to stand out in an industry saturated with content. Therefore, be sure to include high-quality images, videos, and audio that are clean and crisp. Also, look for instances where media can further explain or enrich a point made in an article.

FIGURE 5-6:
An article from
the NYT with a
strong CTA.

Source: http://www.nytimes.com/2016/11/15/world/europe/
putin-calls-trump.html?_r=0

Hiring a full-time photographer or graphic designer may not be necessary, but try to avoid using stock images and video. Often, stock forms of media look too staged or forced, plus they don't always match well with the topic of your piece.

Provides a compelling close

Your article's closing paragraph can take your post from good to great. Effective conclusions tie the piece together. Therefore, by the close, any curiosity loops that your heading may have opened need to be answered, and you must have delivered on the promise of the article; otherwise, readers feel cheated and might form a negative impression of your brand. You can finish a post by using humor, wit, or insight, or otherwise incite emotions that compel readers to comment, share, or visit more pages on your blog.

REMEMBER

The conclusion is the make-or-break portion of your article that makes readers decide to share the post, comment, click your call to action, or dive deeper into your site. Your closing doesn't have to be epic, but be sure that the article doesn't end abruptly. The simplest way to close a piece is to restate the intro and ask the reader to comment and share.

Uses search engine optimization

Done right, effective search engine optimization (SEO) helps your blog posts rank higher in search engines, such as Google, which will improve your chances of having your blog posts found by your audience. (We go into greater detail about SEO tactics in Chapter 8.) To optimize your blog post, choose a relevant keyword or keyword phrase that is unique to your post and include that keyword in the

>> Title tag

>> Body text

>> Image alt attribute

>> Universal resource locator (URL)

>> Meta description

Another important way to optimize your blog is to cross-link related and relevant sites to your blog article. You can link to other sites that aren't associated with your brand but are relevant to the topic of the article. You can also cross-link to other blog posts you've written that elaborate on or enrich a point that you make in your latest post.

Categorizes your topics

As your blog expands, you may find yourself covering a larger base of topics. This is where categorizing and organizing your blogs posts comes into play. For instance, an economics blog may cover a wide variety of topics, such as tax tips, financial planning, budget and saving, and others. To help readers find what they are looking for, include categories, also called tags, on each post you publish.

Including categories helps to improve user experience, which in turn increases the value that you bring to your audience. Although it's often as simple as selecting a box by using your mouse, selecting the right category for your blog posts is an important checkpoint of any blog post audit.

Completely delivers on the promise

If the goal of the headline and introduction is to make a compelling promise, the job of the body of the blog post is to ensure that the article delivers completely on that promise. If the post doesn't fulfill the promise made, amend your headline or get back to work on the blog post. Nothing destroys the reputation of your blog quicker than writing a great headline and failing to deliver in the article.

That said, this element of the audit is about more than simply delivering on the promise. You're also making sure that every idea presented in the post is appropriately "fleshed out" and doesn't leave your audience confused or needing more information to understand the point. Look for areas in the post that you can strengthen by adding

>> Media (images, video, audio)

>> Examples

>> Data

>> Internal or external links to more information

Go the extra mile with each and every article, and you'll see results. Consider producing fewer posts that are exceptionally complete, as opposed to a high volume of content that leaves the audience wanting.

Keeps professional consistency

What's the voice or personality of your brand? Is it professional? Snarky? Academic? Whatever it may be, produce content that reinforces your brand. For instance, a law firm blog probably shouldn't use curse words in its articles. But an edgy motorcycle blog has a better chance of getting away with using certain four-letter words because doing so might be more consistent with its brand. Therefore, whatever the topic of your article, be sure that it remains in line with your brand's personality.

Also, and perhaps more important for some organizations, ensure that the newest blog post doesn't contradict something else that you've published on the blog or anywhere else. For example, if you have a fashion blog with a post last year about the sins of wearing undershirts, but your newest blog post centers on the importance of undershirts and doesn't address what has changed since your past article on the topic, you're going to confuse and lose readers because of your inconsistency.

» **Producing high quality blog content with speed**

» **Creating blog posts that build trust with your audience**

» **Using your blog to network with influencers**

Chapter **6**

Taking Stock of 57 Blog Post Ideas

very blogger knows how crippling the dreaded blank screen can be, and how hard it can be to come up with new ideas. This is why this chapter is so important. These blog post types can be applied to both business-to-business (B2B) and business-to-consumer (B2C) blogs.

In the following pages, we reveal a list of 57 blog post ideas that should keep you from ever running out of blog post ideas again. We also cover, in detail, three blog post types that are quick and easy to create while still providing you with stellar content your company can be proud to promote.

Defeating Writer's Block

The key to defeating the blank page is understanding that there are actually many different types of blog posts. After you understand the formats through which you can deliver blog content, you'll never have writer's block again.

In Chapter 4, we discuss the concept of creating content segments. In the context of blogging, a *segment* is any content type that you repeat periodically, usually weekly or monthly. An example is a link roundup post, which displays a list of interesting links from outside sources. Many blogs publish a link roundup post once per week or once per month. By creating blog content segments that recur every week or month, you make planning your blog content much easier.

The various blog post types fall into categories that we cover in the following sections. If you create a lot of blog content, make sure to dog-ear this chapter and keep this book close to your work station. Try a few of the 57 blog post types described in this chapter and make one or two of them consistent segments in your editorial calendar.

Writing useful content

When people do research, they search for useful content on the Internet. They look for how-to guides, case studies, and resources that can help solve their problems, inspire them, or point them in the right direction. Writing content that is both free and useful endears you to your market and establishes you and your business as the authority in your niche. The following sections offer 13 types of useful blog post ideas that any brand can use.

List post

The list post is simply that, a list. Some may affectionately refer to it as a "listicle." A list post is one of the easiest to put together and can be very versatile. Not to mention that people just love lists — they're helpful and quick to read. For your blog, create a list of books, tools, resources, or any other topic that your market finds useful and is also relevant to your call to action.

Typically, list posts have quick introductions and then get right to the body of the post. By their nature, list posts are text heavy, which can be intimidating to readers. Be sure to use images wherever you can, which helps to break up the text, making your post easier to read and more likely to be shared.

Case study post

The term *case study* carries more perceived value than the term *article, blog post,* or *video.* Case studies provide great detail and go beyond simple testimonials by showing real-life examples. Using case studies, you can highlight your successes in a way that helps you turn a prospective customer into a customer.

In the case study post, get specific and talk strategy. Outline and unpack the details of something, such as a project, event, or process. Tell your story from start to finish, including the failures and "speed bumps" that you face; doing so offers authenticity to your case study post and makes your brand more relatable because it proves that your brand is composed of humans with faults, just like the rest of us. Finally, be sure to include real numbers, graphs, and figures that back up your examples. Figure 6-1 shows a case study post from ConversionXL.

FIGURE 6-1: An excerpt of a case study post from ConversionXL.

Source: *http://conversionxl.com/improve-mobile-ux/*

How-to post

The how-to post is another staple blog post type. In the article, you describe how to execute a process and use images, video, or audio to enrich the post and make it as easy as possible for your reader to take action.

This type of post contains a quick introduction and then gets into the process you're presenting; you might outline your process in the intro in the form of a bulleted list before going into more detail in the body of the post. It can help to break the how-to information in the body of the piece into steps, phases, or categories so that your readers can digest the information more easily.

Frequently asked question (FAQ) post

The FAQ post is a great way to bring traffic to your website from search engines. If you continually get repeat questions from customers or prospects, there is a good chance that people are using search engines to find the answers to these same questions. Create articles with detailed explanations around these FAQ topics.

The should-have-asked-the-question (SAQ) post

The SAQ post is a variation of the FAQ post. This is a question that customers or prospects don't ask — but they should. For example, a real estate company could create a post called "Questions You Should Ask Before Hiring Any Realtor." Your SAQ post should center around questions that customers should ask before they buy your product, or questions they should ask to learn more about your industry.

Checklist post

As the name suggests, a checklist post lists the steps a person should take to complete a specific task. For example, an airline blog might post a checklist containing the items people should bring when traveling abroad, or what parents should bring to keep young children entertained on long trips.

If you can break your content down into a checklist, it often performs better. People like the checklist format because it's easy to digest, and people find taking action easier when you itemize the content in this way.

Problem/solution post

This type of blog post has an easy format: First, define a problem; then present the solution. The solution to the problem might take the form of a product or service you sell, or it may be something that people can freely obtain. The problem/solution post is a valuable piece of content because people are always looking for ways to solve their problems. If you can provide a real solution for someone, that person will be grateful to you.

The problem/solution post can cross over into the territory of other blog post types such as the FAQ post, the how-to post, or the checklist post.

Research post

Conducting your own primary research around a topic in your niche is one of the best ways to build blog content that gets attention. That's because primary research is hard to gather and extremely time consuming. Collecting all the research for someone and providing it for free all in one place is a great way to endear your brand to prospects as well as establish your brand as an authority on the particular topic.

That said, you don't have to do all the research yourself. You can simply curate research from third parties and pull it together into an article, infographic, or other type of content that your market will find valuable and intriguing.

Stat roundup post

This post (like the research post) works best when you can use statistics that you have produced because it adds to your authority. That doesn't mean you can't use third-party information, but if you're looking to build awareness and clout around your brand, using your own statistics is the way to go. That said, don't ignore other resources altogether. Consider pulling together stats from multiple locations to create a very solid, well-rounded statistics post.

Ultimate guide post

The ultimate guide post is just what it sounds like: a detailed, comprehensive post on a topic in your niche. An ultimate guide post done right is an article that people will bookmark and continuously return to, so don't skimp here — take your time and deliver the definitive post on the topic. This type of post helps to bring people back to your site, establish you as an authority in your market, and prove that you know what you're talking about.

The idea behind the ultimate guide is that the reader shouldn't have to go anywhere else to gain more information on this topic. This post will be *long*, with thousands of words, and many figures and examples. If people can read and digest this post in ten minutes, it's probably not the ultimate guide.

Series post

Look for opportunities to break a topic into a series. An exceptionally lengthy or complex piece (such as the ultimate guide post) is a good candidate to be broken into parts and distributed as a series post.

Announce in the introduction of the post when readers can expect the next article in the sequence to be published. Also, you should have set days when you publish the series. For instance, make it each day over the course of a week, or every Monday over the next month. By announcing and having a set time frame, your readers know when to expect the next part, which helps to maintain engagement in the post. Be sure to link these articles together as you publish them. That way, if people miss the first or the second part of the series, they can easily find the post(s) needed to catch up. Figure 6-2 shows an example of a series post from the health club chain LA Fitness.

Definition post

In niches in which the market needs to be educated, the definition post is an absolute must. As the name suggests, it's an article that defines a topic, and it works well in industries and markets that have their own terms and lingo. For the definition post, you can create content around a particularly confusing or complex topic and then explain and inform your readers about that topic.

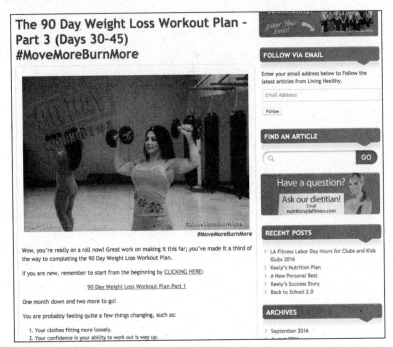

FIGURE 6-2:
An example of a series post from LA Fitness.

Source: http://blog.lafitness.com/2014/02/13/the-90-day-weight-loss-workout-plan-part-3-days-30-45-movemoreburnmore/

For the definition post, consider creating a series of posts that define aspects of your niche. You get bonus points if you can logically define something in your market that is unique, unusual, or controversial. Presenting one or more of these aspects helps you stand out while also creating engagement in your post.

YouTube cut-up post

This post leverages a popular YouTube video to create stellar content. It can be your video or, if you have permission, someone else's video. To create this article type, take screenshots at different stages during the video and add text explanations. Then embed the entire video into your post. This is a super-fast and easy way to create high-value and engaging content from video.

Being generous

One of the easiest ways to grow your blog is to be generous by promoting other people. When you promote others, they promote you; it's mutually beneficial. Call out and link to businesses and influential people in your market who are doing something worthwhile. You can use other businesses as an example for your readers to learn from. Following are eight ways for you to create generous pieces of content.

Profile post

Write a profile or bio of an influential person in your niche. You don't have to ask his or her permission first, but you can if you want. Be sure to notify this person via email, phone call, or social media that you have profiled him or her. This way, the influential person will have an opportunity to share the finished post with his or her audience and point people back to you.

Crowdsourced post

In this post, ask three or more experts in your industry the same question and aggregate the answers into a single article. For example, if you're in the fitness industry, you might reach out to top physical trainers and ask them to outline their favorite cardiovascular workout. Then aggregate the responses of the experts into a single post to create an article with multiple opinions.

The content from a crowdsourced post is top notch, easy to put together, and will be shared by many of these influential people. Not to mention, this type of post draws large numbers of the influencers' followers to both your blog and your site. In our experience, when you get ten influencers to give you about 100 words each on a single topic, you've got a powerful blog post.

Interview post

For the interview post, reach out to influencers in your market and create a post around the questions you ask them. You can write the post in a typical newspaper or magazine style, or simply list each question asked and give each answer verbatim.

Even the most influential people are surprisingly willing to give you an interview — even if you have a small audience for your blog.

TIP

The easiest way for an extremely busy influencer to give you an interview is through an audio recording. Text interviews are time consuming, and video interviews can be technically challenging, often requiring the influencer and the interviewer to be in the same location. With audio, you can record the interview over the phone or use a tool like Skype.

Link roundup post

For this type of post, you gather multiple pieces of content from outside sources that your audience will find relevant and interesting. Provide a description of the content and link to it. It's that simple. The articles you link to may not even have a common thread other than they'd be relevant or interesting to your readers. This content can take the form of what your company is reading and then link to different blogs, articles, and books you've gained value from. Another option is to use a tool like BuzzSumo to find the most socially viral content on a given topic and aggregate it into one post.

A post like this can work well as a series that publishes once a week or once a month. Remember to notify those that you link to via email or social media to give yourself the maximum opportunity to get the post shared by the people you've included in your link roundup.

Quote post

Quotes are inspirational and thought provoking, which is why they make for an excellent blog article. Pull together quotes from multiple influencers across a specific topic to create a quote post. Again, if applicable, be sure to notify those you quote that you have included them in your post. Figure 6-3 shows a post by Business.com that collects and links to its favorite quotes from Social Media Marketing World. In the blog post, Business.com doesn't put the quotes in a numbered list but rather takes the time to make the quotes visually appealing and uses images that make the post more engaging.

FIGURE 6-3:
An example of a quote post from Business.com.

Source: http://www.business.com/social-media-marketing/
the-11-most-inspiring-quotes-we-heard-at-social-
media-marketing-world/

Best-of-the-web post

Similar to the roundup post, the best of the web often includes content, tools, and other resources you are willing to put your name behind and call the *best*. In the post, curate, link to, and briefly describe what it is and why it's the best. This post might take the form of your favorite blogs or your top picks for website design. It's another great way to provide value for your readers while also promoting influencers whom you want to work with.

Pick-of-the-week post

Going off of the best-of-the-web post, the pick-of-the-week post is a series post that is fairly popular among bloggers. This blog article might be your favorite blog, podcast, tool, or other item of the week. The content is usually relatively short and describes a single article, tool, or other resource that you curate, link to, and describe.

People-to-follow post

In this post, you recommend which experts or businesses your audience should be following. Collect a list of influential people, describe them, and provide links through which your audience can connect with the influencers via their website, social media channels, events, and books.

Entertaining the masses

When people come across content that entertains them, they're likely to share it on social media channels such as Facebook and Twitter. Producing entertaining content can be difficult, but if you can make it work, it can be a very effective type of blog post. Following are five blog post types that entertain.

Story post

Stories are engaging, which is why they make effective blog posts. In this article, you tell a story that would entertain your market. Story posts don't have to be epic pieces of content; not all stories have to be complex. For example, commercials create entertaining stories all the time in fewer than 60 seconds.

Satire post

In the satire post, be humorous through the use of irony or extreme exaggeration. This kind of content works well with timely issues such as politics or sports. *The Onion*, which is a farcical newspaper featuring world, national, and community news, is a prime example of a digital media company creating satirical content.

Cartoon post

For the cartoon post, center your article around a cartoon that makes your audience laugh and think about issues and events in your niche. This type of post works well as a series, and you can run it daily, weekly, or monthly.

Meme post

Memes are humorous pieces of content that spread virally across the web. A meme post can be similar to the satire post or the cartoon post. In the post, you create your own meme or pull together a curated set of memes from across the web. Figure 6-4 shows an example of a meme post from Small Business Marketing Blog called "The Business Owner's Guide to Blogging."

FIGURE 6-4:
Small Business
Marketing Blog
centers its blog
article around
a meme.

Source: http://3bugmedia.com/business-owners-guide-blogging/

Parody post

In the parody post, you create content that imitates a well-known person, product, or media property in your niche. Be sure to exaggerate the person's or item's strengths and shortcomings in your content.

Capitalizing on the timely

Timely posts detail the latest information on a subject. You need commitment to stay timely in some niches, but if you can pull it off, timely news is among the most effective blog content you can create because you will be one of the first to have new information out there. If you find that keeping up with the latest news and trends is too daunting a task, consider creating a series of posts that publishes timely information once per week. Following are five blog post ideas that deal with timely content.

Review post

Center your content around the review of a product, event, or anything else you have access to while it is newsworthy and relevant to both your industry and target audience. For best results, rather than paint everything in a positive light, be as honest as possible in your review.

Survey post

To create a survey post, choose an interesting or trending topic and survey your audience about it using email, social media, or in-person events. Then pull the results together into a blog post.

News post

Same as a news outlet, you can create content on your blog about events as they happen. Although you don't need to "break" the story, for best results, be sure to add a perspective that your audience will find valuable or entertaining.

Trend post

Some content creators can predict trends as they happen. If you're a trendspotter, create posts on your blog that ride that trend as it becomes popular.

Issue post

Choose issues that affect your audience and create content about these issues while they are timely and relevant to your readers.

Showing your humanity

Be human in your posts. Show that your brand isn't some faceless, unfeeling corporate entity. Use blog content to help show off the people who work at your business, as well as your company's personality, with the six posts we tell you about in the following sections.

Inspirational post

Some of the most effective content on the web is neither informational nor entertaining — it simply inspires. The health and fitness industries often use this approach. Inspirational posts can work well as a story post, a profile post, or a quote post, among others.

Holiday post

Some blogs go dormant on popular holidays, but that doesn't have to be the case. Holidays are a great way to display your company's humanity. Use the opportunity to deliver well wishes and create anticipation with your audience, as *Country Living* magazine did with its Halloween cake recipe article, shown in Figure 6-5.

Source: http://www.countryliving.com/food-drinks/
g604/halloween-cake-recipes-1008/

FIGURE 6-5:
Country Living helps fans get ready for Halloween in this holiday post.

You can also get creative with the holiday post; you don't have to recognize only the major holidays. Some obscure holidays may apply to your niche, such as National Hat Day on January 15, International Talk Like a Pirate Day on September 19, or Write a Friend Month in December.

Guard-down post

In this post, the author opens up about a private moment in his or her past. Some of the best content on the web is created by a content creator who lets his or her guard down by delivering a deeply personal experience that the audience can relate to.

Behind-the-scenes post

People love to peek behind the curtain and see how something gets done. If you have a loyal following, many will want to see what goes on behind the scenes of your business. Create content around this idea. You might show a day in the life of one of your managers, or show your approach to putting a video together. In this post, provide images and videos that enhance your written examples.

Off-topic post

Throughout this section, we emphasize the importance of staying relevant to your niche. Going with the idea that any attention is good attention, you might create a post that is completely different from what you typically post on. This maneuver can be risky, but if you have a loyal following who has become accustomed to you covering a specific set of topics, this kind of post can surprise people and evoke a great response.

Rant post

The rant post shows your human side by revealing your passion and anger about a topic that's relevant to your audience in an op-ed style. Although the rant post isn't for everyone, the right blog and audience can respond well to a rant.

Getting promotional

Some organizations use their blogs in a promotional way; that is, the blog clearly sells the company and its products or services. Although this type of blog might come across as pushy in some industries, promotional content can work very well for the right company. Here are eight instances of promotional blog content.

Comparison post

As the name suggests, the comparison post is an article that compares the features and benefits of your product to a competitor's solutions. For best results and to build trust, include cases for which your product is *not* the best solution.

Project showcase post

Similar to the behind-the-scenes post, the project showcase post explains how the company completed a project. Use your blog to outline a specific project that you or your organization is working on or has completed. Detail the process and strategy behind the project, and if possible, share the results.

Income report post

In the income report post, open the books and show your audience a breakdown of the money you and your organization are making. Show people exactly how much you've earned, where it came from, and (most important) the lessons you've been learning in and around your business. This sort of transparency builds trust with your audience.

Company update post

You can use your blog to let your customers and prospects know of new employee hires, acquisitions, major contracts under way, or other changes at your company. As with the income report post, this is a great way to build trust with your readers.

Product update post

Similar to the company update post, for a product update post, you create content around new products or services that you're offering or the updates coming to existing products or services. If you have rabid fans of your products and services, you might be surprised by how well an announcement post of a new product or a new feature will do on your blog.

Presentation post

You can publish presentations given by employees that contain interesting and valuable content for your audience. Within the post, consider embedding the video from the presentation to accompany the text. Be sure to include the slide deck from the presentation so that readers can follow along.

Best-of post

Unlike the previous best-of post, here you create a blog article that pulls together and links to the most popular blog posts you have published over a period of time. Select content that has really resonated with your audience, driven lots of traffic to your site, or sparked good comments.

Products tip post

Create content that helps your customers be more successful with your product or service by offering tips and how-tos about one of your products or services. This post type is both promotional and useful as well as very powerful for the right blog and audience.

Prospects read product tip posts, too, which can help to convert them.

TIP

Stirring the pot

If it fits your brand, you can take a stand and turn out controversial articles. You can get a lot of traffic on controversial posts — nothing goes viral as quickly as rousing posts that encourage debate. Just make sure that this type of post fits with your brand's personality. Here are the six ways for you to be controversial on your blog.

What-if post

This type of blog post speculates on potential events or circumstances. The success of this type of post rests on your ability to choose a "what if" that is interesting and debatable.

Debatable post

Many people enjoy sparring. With this post, use your blog to present one side of a debatable argument. You might also find someone who disagrees with you and present both sides in the same post.

Attack post

In your post, pick a fight. Starting an argument with the right person or organization forces your audience to choose sides and can draw a great deal of attention. Be careful with this one, though, because you're likely to create enemies with the attack post. When done right, however, the attack post can also produce die-hard fans.

Predict post

Post about what you think will happen on a given topic or situation. If you take a debatable and speculative approach, a prediction post can get a great response.

Reaction post

Use your blog to react to content created by someone else. The content you react to might be a blog post, book, or presentation. Post your feelings on this subject.

Embed reaction post

In this post, embed a resource such as a video, presentation, or infographic, and then provide a reaction or a rebuttal to that content. You can find videos to embed on YouTube, presentations on SlideShare, and infographics on Visual.ly. Although this one is similar to the reaction post, the content you are reacting to is embedded in this post, which may not be the case with the reaction post — a subtle but notable difference.

Start with a quick intro to set the stage. Then give your reaction underneath the embedded resource. The titles of these posts are usually a variation of the title of the resource you are embedding.

TIP

When choosing the embeddable resource to which you will react, look for a video with lots of views or an infographic or presentation with lots of social shares on Facebook, Pinterest, or Twitter. Then add your reaction to this popular piece of content below the embedded content. When you do this, you practically guarantee that your post will be well received.

Engaging the audience

It pays to create an engaged audience who regularly tunes in to your content. Although engagement isn't necessarily the end goal, it's hard to deny the power of content that pulls a reader in. Here are the final six blog post ideas that help to create a captivated audience.

Question post

Similarly to the FAQ post, the question post answers questions that your audience asks in social media, on forums, or in the comments section of your blog. In contrast to the FAQ post, though, the question post may be about something that isn't commonly asked yet is an engaging question to build an article around.

Answer post

The answer post is the sister of the question post. In this post type, you simply ask a question and allow your audience to answer it in your comments section. This type of post is generally very short, allowing your audience to create the bulk of the content through a discussion in the comments. This type of article works well if you have a blog with an engaged readership that comments often.

Challenge post

Use a blog post to pose a challenge to your audience. As you can see in Figure 6-6, BuzzFeed challenges its readers to eat cleanly for two weeks and posts the steps and recipes to follow to reach that goal. This post can work well as a series, with periodic updates that feature participating audience members.

Customer showcase post

Use your blog to feature a customer or project that you and a customer have worked on. Although this type of blog post type is partly promotional, it also builds engagement.

Here's A Two-Week Clean Eating Challenge That's Actually Delicious

This is a delicious two-week meal plan that will teach you to cook and eat healthy, feel awesome, and stay that way. Just like last year's, but better.

posted on May 1, 2015, at 10:08 a.m.

Christine Byrne
BuzzFeed Staff

FIGURE 6-6:
BuzzFeed creates a challenge post to engage its audience.

Source: https://www.buzzfeed.com/christinebyrne/clean-eating-2015?utm_term=.skwm7PgOB#.scbm31a5W

Freebie post

Use a blog post to allow your audience to access a relevant giveaway. The giveaway can include a free download, case study, or one of your products or services, for example. Center your blog post around this promotion.

Contest post

Announce a contest on your blog and then list the rules, tell how readers can enter, and describe what people can win. A contest post can work well as a series with updates featuring contest results.

Multiplying your blog ideas

There you have it: Fifty-seven blog post ideas (described in the previous sections of this chapter) that you can start using today. And you can develop these blog post ideas to deliver even more content. These 57 ideas actually become 228 ideas when you realize you can deliver them in four different ways:

>> **Text:** Text articles are the traditional form that blogs take, and they're still the most common format for delivering content on the web.

- » **Images:** Content can appear solely in the form of images. You can distribute image posts via infographics, cartoons, drawings, charts, graphs, or still photography.
- » **Video:** You can circulate video blog posts in numerous ways, including in a presentation-like style or using the familiar interview style in which only the person's head and shoulders are visible to the camera.
- » **Audio:** Deliver audio blog posts via podcast or simply by embedding an audio player on a web page.

These 57 ideas with their four types of formats make it easy to get started creating blog content. Simply choose a blog post idea (such as a series, an interview, a what-if, or something else) and then decide on the best delivery format (text, images, video, or audio). For example, you might choose an FAQ post (idea) delivered via video (format). Or, you might choose a people-to-follow post (idea) delivered via image (format).

With this list of 228 blog ideas at your disposal, you'll never run out of ideas for blog posts again.

Creating Stellar Content without All the Fuss

Creating content that people actually like and share takes a lot of work. Coming up with the idea is only half of the battle. Writing the content takes a lot of time. In this section, you learn a few methods of creating high-quality content, very quickly.

Previously in this chapter, some of the blog post ideas we bring you are the link roundup post, the embed reactor post, and the crowdsourced post. In the following sections, we take a closer look at why these three types of content are so effective and easy to produce.

Curating and aggregating content

The link roundup post involves curating information from multiple sources and pulling it all together into one article. The content you aggregate does not have to be produced by you or your organization. The link roundup works well as a list post because it is a very easy and effective way to present the content.

For instance, a food blogger might go out and find, or aggregate, guacamole recipes for an article. All the recipes don't have to be the blogger's personal recipes but can be pulled from around the web. The author then lists each recipe, states why the recipe is worthwhile, and attributes and links to the source.

The advantage of the link roundup is that you don't have to create the content yourself. None of the guacamole recipes you use have to be yours. You can therefore post much quicker than if you had to create all the content yourself. Also, readers appreciate that you've done the research and the work for them and gathered all those recipes in one place on your blog. An article like this may serve as a resource for readers to return to, so they bookmark your content and continually return to you.

Although you can produce the link roundup post quickly and create goodwill with your readers, a challenge on your end is finding quality outside content that doesn't reflect poorly on your brand. Typically, link roundup posts are not text heavy. They provide brief descriptions that introduce the post you reference before you link to it. Even if the post has little text, it should have big, beautiful pictures for a visually engaging post. You can acquire the images from the article you link to.

Figure 6-7 shows a link roundup blog post, and the following paragraphs give some tips about writing your post.

FIGURE 6-7:
An excerpt of a link roundup of detox water recipes from DIY Ready.

Source: http://diyready.com/diy-recipes-detox-waters/

Pique interest with your headline

If your headline falls flat, no one will read your article. Spend time creating a headline that both piques interest and explains the benefit of reading the article. We cover headline creation strategies in Chapter 5.

Introduce your topic

Quickly introduce the topic of the post and explain why people should read it by conveying the benefit they can derive from it. Your introduction doesn't need to be complex because you're sending the reader to other articles where the topic is explained in greater detail.

Write the body

The body of this post is often minimal, requiring only a quick summary of each piece of content that you have aggregated. Consider including an image and be sure to link to each resource you have aggregated. No magic number of resources to aggregate exists, but the more posts you aggregate, the better your post typically performs.

Reacting to popular content

The embed reaction post type is one of the fastest ways to produce high-quality blog content. Websites like YouTube (see Figure 6-8) and SlideShare provide a piece of code that allows you to embed a piece of content on your own website. The embed reaction post begins with locating a popular piece of content that you can embed on your blog.

You can embed one piece or multiple pieces of content, depending on the complexity of the topic. The more popular the piece of content you embed is, the more likely it is that your audience will engage with and share your post. You can determine the popularity of the piece of content by looking at things like the number of views or number of times it has been shared.

After you have found relevant and engaging content to embed, you react to the content in the body of the post. In your reaction, you can agree or disagree with the embedded piece, much as you would in an op-ed article, or you can expand upon the content. How much text you need for the embed reactor post will vary depending on the complexity of the topic and how long it takes to explain your reaction.

Of course, you want to ensure that the content you embed is of high quality and fits your brand. But as with the link roundup post, you don't have to create all the content yourself, which is a major time saver.

When you're looking for content to embed, YouTube is an obvious choice, but many other places offer quality content for this post type. For instance, visit Visual.ly for professional infographics that you can share, or SlideShare for presentations and documents that make for stellar embed reactor content.

You can see an example of an embed reactor post in Figure 6-8, with tips on how to put this type of post together in the following paragraphs.

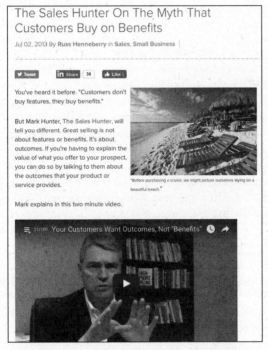

FIGURE 6-8:
A sample of an embed reactor blog post from Salesforce.com.

Source: https://www.salesforce.com/blog/2013/07/sales-myth-customers-buy-on-benefits.html

Create an engaging headline

As always, focus on creating an engaging headline, and give yourself ample time to craft it (turn to Chapter 5 for more on headlines). Indicate what the reader will gain from reading your article. The headline of an embed reaction post is usually a variation of the title of the resource you are embedding.

Write the introduction

As with the curating and aggregating post, your introduction needs to indicate the value readers can gain from this post. You can keep it simple because the embedded content further explains the topic at hand. Simply provide the context in your intro.

Embed your content

Embed text, audio, video, or an image that is relevant to your audience. Bonus points if the embedded content is popular.

Write your reaction

Add your analysis or reaction to the content. You can explain what provoked this response in as little or as much text as you deem necessary to adequately describe the topic.

Crowdsourcing content

The crowdsourced post is another fast and engaging article to put together. In this post, you gather three or more experts and have them answer the same question. You then combine the answers into a single post: the crowdsourced post. You're sourcing the crowd for answers and bringing them all together.

For example, your post might be about social media tools. You can reach out to professionals and ask them to answer what their favorite social media tool is and briefly describe why. Then succinctly introduce the post and state the question you asked before stating each expert's answer. This approach makes for a very rich post because you're pulling in many different responses and insights that provide value for your readers.

Source the highest-profile experts you can or simply include colleagues you want to be featured with. Display answers from people who both understand your industry and can provide a solid answer to your question. Chances are, your friends or colleagues can answer this question or know someone who can; reach out to them.

Another great aspect of the crowdsource post is its likelihood to be distributed. The experts you include in the article have an incentive to share the article with their audience, which in turn helps you expand your audience base. With that in mind, make sure that those featured in the article know when it's published to increase the chance that they'll share the post.

TIP

When you reach out to experts, don't ask just one question; ask several questions. For instance, if you email ten experts in your market five different questions and each expert responds, you have the makings of five different crowdsource articles. The number of questions you ask is equal to the number of posts that you'll get and the number of times the expert will be exposed to your audience, making this mutually beneficial for you both.

Figure 6-9 shows an example of a crowdsourced post, and the following paragraphs give you the steps for writing it.

FIGURE 6-9: A crowdsourced post from robbierichards.com.

Source: `http://www.robbierichards.com/seo/best-keyword-research-tool/`

Write the headline

The headline could be the question you asked experts or you could specify the number of experts featured in the article, such as, "9 Physical Trainers Reveal Their Favorite Cardiovascular Workout." Find more on headlines in Chapter 5.

Write the introduction

Your intro does not need to be long for the crowdsource post. State the question that was proposed to the experts, as well as any context or backstory that is necessary for the reader.

Provide the answer to the question you asked

For each expert's answer, provide the expert's name, company, title, and headshot. Then state the answer the expert provided verbatim, editing only for grammar. This makes for a great article with many points of view. You're not looking for your experts to write you a book, so imposing a word limit on them is okay. Where applicable, provide links to the expert's website and social media channels, such as Twitter and LinkedIn.

REMEMBER

Contact or tag experts in social media or via email to let them know that your post is live on your blog. This way, you help ensure that the expert shares your post, which brings traffic to your blog.

3

Generating Website Traffic

Discover the various types of landing pages and when to use them. Learn what types of content gets prospects to visit your landing page and buy your product.

Determine what your market is searching for on sites like Google and Bing, and position your business to reap the benefits of search traffic.

Take advantage of social media to build your brand, handle customer service issues, and interact with prospects, customers, and partners.

Create paid traffic campaigns and effectively drive traffic to your website or landing page by using the Big Six traffic sources: Facebook, Twitter, Google, YouTube, Pinterest, and LinkedIn.

Launch email marketing campaigns that move people through the customer journey, build relationships, and drive traffic to your website.

Chapter **7**

Building High-Converting Landing Pages

anding pages are fundamental to digital marketing. The broadest way to define a landing page is as any page where a visitor enters your website. For the purposes of this book, we use a more specific definition: A *landing page* is a web page designed to persuade a visitor to take a specific action. Your website should contain a landing page for each offer you make to prospects and customers. These are the pages toward which savvy digital marketers funnel traffic from all sources both internal and external to their website.

The performance of your landing pages will make or break your digital marketing campaigns. You can master the art of driving web traffic, but if the landing page fails to do its job, the campaign is doomed. In this chapter, we examine the elements of a winning landing page. We also tell you about the different types of landing pages and when to use each kind, how to assess the success of your landing pages, and how to convert customers into buyers.

Exploring the Types of Landing Pages

You categorize landing pages by the specific action you want the site visitor to take. For example, some landing pages are designed to persuade visitors to enter their contact information, whereas others ask the visitor to buy a product or service. The campaigns that most digital marketers run fall into one of two landing page categories:

>> **Lead capture page:** Sometimes called a *squeeze page,* this page's goal is to persuade site visitors to enter their contact information so that they become leads.

>> **Sales page:** This page is designed to persuade a visitor to purchase a physical product, information product, or service.

There are many ways to design and lay out a good landing page, but they all have one thing in common: focus. A solid landing page has a singular goal and as few distractions as possible. The focal point of the page should be the action you want the visitor to take.

The typical website home page is, for example, a page designed to allow the visitor to make a variety of choices. From the home page, a visitor can click a link to visit a product page, learn more about the company, or visit the company blog. For this reason, the home page of the website is a poor landing page in almost every circumstance. A home page simply presents visitors with too many choices.

A landing page should strive to plug as many "leaks" from the page as possible. This means removing links to other offers, more information, and anything else that isn't absolutely necessary to achieve the goal for that page. Figure 7-1 shows a landing page with as few links as possible to minimize distractions and increase the chances of prospects opting in.

WARNING Some sources of traffic, such as Facebook advertising and the Google AdWords network, require you to have links to some pertinent pages, such as a Privacy Policy and Terms of Use page. Check the Terms of Service of each traffic platform before you run traffic to a landing page.

Source: http://www.digitalmarketer.com/lp/fb-ad-templates/

SHOULD YOU USE A LANDING PAGE BUILDER?

Building landing pages from scratch can be intimidating. How do you construct a page with a design and layout designed to persuade site visitors to take action? How do you produce a page with a clear focus on the desired action and as few distractions or "leaks" from the page as possible? One option is to hire a web page designer and developer who understands how to build custom web pages that convert visitors into leads and sales.

For most businesses, creating custom landing pages is unnecessary. Much more cost effective is to use an application that provides proven landing page templates. These applications provide templates for virtually any circumstance in lead capture or sales. Look for a landing page builder that fits your budget and provides you with the templates that fit your circumstances. For example, if you expect to capture leads using webinars, you want to use a landing page application that provides a webinar registration template and integrates well with the webinar delivery application you're using. We make recommendations for both landing page and webinar applications in Chapter 16.

Creating a Lead Capture Page

The lead capture page, sometimes called a *squeeze page*, is an important landing page type to any business that benefits from lead generation. As demonstrated in Figure 7-1, the lead capture page is an extremely focused page containing the following:

>> **A gated offer:** A small "chunk" of value that solves a *specific* problem for a *specific* market that is offered in exchange for their contact information. You can learn more about gated offers in Chapter 3.

>> **Headline/subheadline:** Text at the top of the page that compels the site visitor to read the bullets and consider taking the gated offer on the page. We cover headline strategies in Chapter 5. Although the headline tactics discussed in Chapter 5 focus on blogs, you can also apply them to the headline of your landing page.

>> **Bullets:** Strong statements that outline the benefits of the gated offer.

>> **Product image:** If you can show a visual representation of the gated offer, do so. This approach may not be applicable to all offers.

>> **Proof:** Include trust icons such as logos of associations you are a member of, reputable brands you are associated with, or testimonials from satisfied customers.

>> **Lead form:** The form is the mechanism that actually collects the contact information.

REMEMBER

Ask only for information that you plan to use in your marketing. In general, the more information you ask for in your form, the lower your conversion rate will be. So if, for example, you don't plan to follow up via telephone, don't ask for a phone number in the lead form.

Creating a Sales Page

The sales page is designed to persuade the site visitor to take a specific action: make a purchase. Sales pages come in many forms, but most digital marketing campaigns require one of two types of sales page:

>> **Sales letter:** You can sell services, information products, and even physical products using a sales letter. For decades, marketers have crafted long-form text

and video pitches aiming to persuade the prospective customer to buy. Sales letters are typically very long. A person reading a sales letter is deciding to buy and should therefore receive as much information as possible. The sales letter should demonstrate why the product or service on the sales page provides value, as well as help to overcome any last-minute objections the person may have. These objectives usually result in a lot of copy. Figure 7-2 shows an excerpt of a DigitalMarketer sales letter landing page for one of our products.

FIGURE 7-2:
An example of a landing page for a product.

Source: http://www.digitalmarketer.com/lp/
sbp/get-content-engine/

>> **Product detail page:** Unique to e-commerce businesses, the product detail page is a staple landing page for the digital marketer selling physical products and, in rarer cases, information products or services. Figure 7-3 pictures a classic product detail page from retailer, Crate & Barrel. This product detail page includes everything the prospect needs to make a purchase decision:

- **Product name:** The product name is descriptive and specific about what is being offered.

- **Call to action:** The "Add to Cart" button is easy to find.

- **Product price:** The price is in an intuitive location and is shown side by side with the suggested price.

- **Product images/video:** Multiple, high-quality photographs of the product showing everything you'll receive.

- **Product description:** Product description including the overview, details, and dimensions of the product.

- **Quantity option:** The capability to select more than one product.

- **Product reviews:** Easy to locate reviews from previous customers who have purchased the product.

- **Wish list:** The capability to add the product to a list to be purchased later. Crate & Barrel's call to action for this feature is "Add to Registry" and "Add to Favorites."

- **Social media buttons:** The capability to share the product page on social sites like Facebook and Pinterest.

- **Shipping information:** Shipping information is easy to locate and the policy is easy to understand.

- **Product videos:** A video demonstrating the product in action.

- **Upsells/Cross-sells:** Additional products this prospect might be interested in. Crate & Barrel refers to this as "People who viewed this item also bought."

FIGURE 7-3:
A classic product detail page from e-commerce behemoth Crate & Barrel.

Source: http://www.crateandbarrel.com/w%C3%BCsthof-classic-ikon-12-piece-knife-block-set/s532597

Writing a sales letter

Mastering copywriting is a bit like mastering a craft such as pottery or oil painting: It involves a tremendous amount of art. That said, writing persuasive copy starts with understanding the fundamental components of a sales letter. In truth, you can apply the principles that comprise a persuasive sales letter to all your communications, including emails, blog posts, presentation titles, and more.

A beginner can use the process we describe here verbatim, but as you become more comfortable with the process, feel free to change it to meet your circumstances. A sales letter, above all else, should be truthful and therefore might not contain some of the elements outlined in this process simply because they don't apply to your offer.

Here are the steps of the process required to write a well-crafted sales letter. You can refer to this as a checklist to ensure that you've included all the essential elements of a persuasive letter:

1. Craft the headline.
2. Write the subheadline.
3. Write the opening.
4. Show ease of use.
5. Forecast the future.
6. Establish credibility.
7. Write bullets that sell.
8. Show proof.
9. Make the offer.
10. Sweeten the deal.
11. Communicate urgency.
12. Reverse risk.
13. Make the call to action.

The following sections explain each part of the sales letter.

Step 1: Craft the headline

The headline is the first thing that people read and is therefore the most critical piece of copy on the page. If you're just getting started, use a "How To" headline because they are simple to write and very effective. The How To headline will apply to 99 percent of the offers you are promoting. Of course, your offer may require a different kind of headline. If that's the case, use a search engine such as Google to search for a list of proven headlines. You can find dozens of blog post articles that provide fantastic headline formulas.

Don't start with a clever headline. Start with clear, simple, and direct language that communicates the benefit to reading the sales letter copy. Clear and direct almost always converts better than clever and confusing. Later, when you get more comfortable with copywriting, you can get clever.

Take a look at the following How To headline formulas and feel free to use them (filling in the blanks with your pertinent information) or to provide inspiration:

How to Get *[desired result]* in *[time period]*

How to Turn *[blank]* into *[desired result]*

How to *[desired result]* When You're Not *[blank]*

How to Fast-Track *[desired result]*

How to *[desired result]* Even If *[something challenging]*

For example, this last headline formula might be used to write a headline at the top of a sales letter that reads: How to Buy a Home Even if You've Declared Bankruptcy.

Step 2: Write the subheadline

The subheadline is optional but is often needed to elaborate on the headline. Once again, you can find dozens of articles online that provide lists of classic headline formulas. Here are a few to get you started:

Discover How Quickly You Can *[desired result]*

Learn How Easily You Can *[desired result]*

You, Too, Can Have *[desired result]* in *[desirable time period]*

What Everybody Ought to Know about *[blank]*

How *[authoritative person]* Got *[desired result]* in *[time period]*

For example, the last headline formula might be used to write a subheadline that reads: How Serena Williams Got in The Best Shape of Her Life in 14 Days.

REMEMBER

You made a claim or promise in the headline you created in Step 1. Your subheadline should support the headline. It shouldn't introduce a new claim or promise, and it certainly shouldn't conflict with it.

Step 3: Write the opening

By the time your landing page visitors are reading your opening, they have read the headline and subheadline. Some readers have even scrolled to the bottom of your letter to see the price and offer. In other words, they are interested.

If you're just getting started, try the classic "Problem/Solution" opening to a sales letter. In the first step of the opening, you identify the problem that the prospective buyer has.

TIP

Your visitors are wondering whether you truly understand their problem. As the marketer, your job is to establish common ground between you and your visitors. Show empathy for the problem and be specific about their state of discontent.

Next, you want to reveal that a solution to this problem exists, and it is your product or service (of course!). You don't need to go into great detail about the product or service at this point; you do that later.

For example, if you're selling tax preparation services, you might open your sales letter with the following:

> It's that time of year again. April 15th is drawing near, and you've got an entire weekend circled on your calendar to dig up all those receipts and tax documents.
>
> Let's face it, preparing your own taxes is frustrating at best.
>
> If you'd rather spend that beautiful spring weekend with friends and family, let our firm handle your taxes this year.

Step 4: Show ease of use

The key to this part of your sales letter is to communicate (if applicable) that your solution is easy to do or quick to deliver results (or both). Now more than ever, prospective customers want results quickly and easily. If you can demonstrate ease of use or speed of results through text, images, or video, do it.

Step 5: Forecast the future

In this part of the sales letter page, you paint a picture in the minds of your readers of what it will look like if they solve their problem. You want your readers to imagine and feel the sense of being free of their problem.

The easiest way to start this section of the sales letter is by filling in the following blank:

> Imagine what it would be like to _____.

For example, Ford Motor Company might write the following to sell the Mustang GT:

Imagine pressing the gas pedal and feeling the thrill of the Mustang's 435 horsepower engine.

TIP

What problem does buying a Mustang GT solve, anyway? It won't cure customers of the flu or get them out of credit card debt. In Chapter 1, we talk about articulating the customer's movement from the Before state to the After state. In your sales copy, you must be able to articulate the value of that After state. In the case of the Mustang, you're freeing people from their boring, old, and slow car of the Before state and delivering to them a new, beautiful, and exhilarating car.

Step 6: Establish credibility

In this step of putting together your sales letter, you need to address a question in your visitors' minds: Why you?

That is, why are you or your organization qualified to solve their problem? You need to establish why the solution you have is credible. You have a number of ways to demonstrate your credibility, including the following:

» **Use a testimonial:** If you have a broad testimonial from a happy customer that fortifies your credibility, you can place it here.

» **Give your credentials:** Provide any credentials that give people a reason to believe in you as a solution — for example, you're a doctor, earned your MBA, served as an Air Force pilot, or other credential that relates to the type of solution you're offering.

» **Borrow credentials:** If you know someone whose credentials are worthy and who endorses you and your product, identify that person here (and include his or her endorsement, if possible).

» **Tell your story:** Have you had an experience that makes you qualified to solve this problem? (Gotten over your stage fright, taught yourself to walk again, lost 50 pounds?) Tell that story.

» **Use impressive numbers:** If you have impressive data, years' worth of experience, or numbers of successful customers, use them here.

Remember that at this point, no one who doesn't have the problem you're describing is reading this copy. At this point in the sales letter, you must explain why you're qualified to solve the problem.

Step 7: Write bullets that sell

Although you hope that the reader of your sales letter will read every word you write, the truth is that most people will only skim your letter. Adding bullets to your sales letter breaks up the text and often causes even the most hurried skimmer to pause and read. You should include three to five bullets that explain the benefits of your offer. Take your time on this step, but don't get bogged down. For your first draft, this step should take no longer than 30 minutes. You can come back and spend more time on these benefits after you have created this first draft.

TIP

This is not the time to explain the product or service you are offering. This is the time to outline the benefits your reader will receive if they buy your product or service.

Remember that people don't buy products and services; rather, they buy a desired outcome:

>> They don't buy cold medicine; they buy a good night's sleep.

>> They don't buy a gym membership; they buy a shapely or healthier body.

>> They don't buy pest control; they buy a clean, safe home for their children.

Step 8: Show proof

In this step of writing your sales letter, you create the most important element of your copy: proof. Proof isn't the same thing as credibility or the credibility of your organization, which you established in an earlier step. Establishing your credibility creates trust, but throughout your copy, you've started to introduce promises to your readers. Now you need to substantiate those promises by providing proof of your claims. If you're selling a physical product, this is a good time to demonstrate, through video or images, how the product works and show it doing the things you described in the bullets you wrote earlier.

Infomercials have mastered the concept of showing proof. They show knives cutting through nails and then easily slicing a tomato, or they demonstrate a cleanser removing a red wine stain. Proof appears in many forms, including:

>> **Demonstration:** If you can show that it works, do it.

>> **Social proof:** If you have testimonials that fortify the claims you've made, include them here. Mention how many other people have benefited from your solution.

>> **Data or research:** Use data and research that you have conducted yourself or from reputable sources.

> » **Borrowed credibility:** Find and use information from reputable sources such as *The New York Times, Harvard Business Review,* or trade associations.

The higher the risk involved in your offer, the more proof your buyers will need to feel comfortable in making a purchase with you.

If you can't properly substantiate a claim you've made, consider removing it. A claim or promise with no proof can do more harm than good.

Step 9: Make the offer

The offer you make to your readers should include exactly what they can expect to receive if they give you money. Most important is for your offer to be clear and not at all confusing. If your readers have even a shadow of a doubt as to what they will get, they won't buy. Here are some examples of information to include for the sake of clarity:

- » Will you ship a product? How long will it take to get there?

- » What are the dimensions of the product? What is the weight?

- » How much does it cost? Are payment terms available? Do you accept American Express?

Think through the questions that your readers might have about the offer and be sure to answer all those questions.

Step 10: Sweeten the deal

You may find that bonuses are not applicable to your offer. However, if you can add bonuses, you will almost certainly increase response. Perhaps you can add, at no additional cost to your buyers, a bonus product to the first 100 people who respond. Or give those who buy before a specified date an additional discount.

Adding a bonus is a great way to increase urgency (covered in Step 11) by taking those bonuses away after a certain date, or after a certain quantity has been sold.

Step 11: Communicate urgency

Adding urgency to your offer, if appropriate to your product or service, gets your readers to take action now, which is what you want. If they decide to think about it or to do it later, they're unlikely to return.

You can persuade people to take action now by communicating the urgency of taking the offer now. If they believe they could come back tomorrow, next week, or next year and get the same offer, they're less likely to take action now.

Don't manufacture scarcity or urgency, but if you have a real reason that people should take action now, be sure to communicate it. Here are some examples:

>> Register for this event now; there are only 32 seats remaining.

>> Buy now: This offer is available only until midnight, January 26.

>> Only 1,000 of these coins were created by the U.S. mint.

Another way of creating urgency in your sales letter is with a simple statement, such as, "Think how much it is costing you every day that you don't take action on this problem."

Step 12: Reverse risk

In this step of the sales letter, you add *risk reversal*, which provides people with a feeling of security about the purchase. You have numerous ways to reduce risk, including by

>> Providing a guarantee

>> Offering a free trial

>> Providing a return policy

>> Using trust seals, including association membership logos, BBB insignia, secure checkout seals, and so on

Step 13: Make the call to action

A call to action tells people exactly what you want them to do and how to do it. It's a simple command statement, such as "Click the Add to Cart button below."

Understanding the elements of a product detail page

Product detail pages, also known simply as product pages, are the most important pages on an e-commerce website. When prospects visit your product page and look at the images, read the descriptions, and consume the customer reviews, they are showing interest and thinking about purchasing your product. The product page is the make-or-break point that determines how successful your e-commerce store is. Your product page needs to get people to ascend to the next level: conversion. So pay extra attention to your product page or pages. The following sections describe the elements of successful product pages.

Product images

Although buying online is convenient, it can be a detriment because people can't physically pick up and examine the product the way they do in a brick-and-mortar store. People don't buy products on the Internet; rather, they buy pictures of products. To overcome the fact that the prospects can't hold or touch your product, include as many high-quality images of the product as is necessary to fully convey its features and attributes.

REMEMBER

People buy based on what the product looks like, and the more complex or expensive the product is, the more pictures are necessary to successfully show the product.

Image zoom

Give people the ability to zoom in on your product image so that they can get a close look at the product, its texture or features, and how it's used. Image zoom can also help overcome doubts potential customers may have because it gives people a chance to examine a product before they put it in their shopping cart.

Product description

Be sure to include a well-written product description that is immediately visible on the page so that prospects can quickly learn about the product's features without having to dig through the page for more information. Don't skimp on the product description. Describe its unique selling points and how it solves people's problems or improves their lives. Aim to create product descriptions with 250 words or more, and include the keywords that you're targeting within the description. Including those keywords improves the product's search marketing, which we discuss in Chapter 8. Similar to product images, the more complex or expensive a product is, the more detail is required. To improve readability and user experience, organize the product description with headlines, bullets, and step lists.

Product sales video

The product sales video is a great medium to demonstrate the product in use and is an extremely effective tool to make your sales pitch. Products that are expensive or complex do well with a sales video. Also, the product sales video is a fantastic way to overcome objections a potential customer may have. If you do include a sales video, make it easy to find rather than buried at the bottom of the page.

Third-party pitch video

This type of video is also called an endorsement or press video, and it's basically a second product sales video. Although not essential, third-party endorsements can significantly increase conversion on a product page. This type of video features someone who's not associated with your brand actively recommending your brand and product. This is similar to a celebrity endorsement, although you don't need a celebrity for this video to be effective. Third-party pitch videos are often scripted and professionally shot.

Call to action

The call to action on a product page is the Add to Cart button. This button must be highly visible and accessible to the consumer. The Add to Cart button should be easy to locate on both desktop and mobile devices. In Figure 7-4, you can see two highly visible Add to Cart buttons on a product page for Best Buy — the cart icon in the top-right corner and the Add to Cart call-to-action button right above the price. Depending on the length of your product page, consider adding multiple Add to Cart buttons so that people can add your product to their cart no matter where they are on your page.

FIGURE 7-4: Bust Buy has two Add to Cart buttons in the first half of the page.

Source: http://www.bestbuy.com/site/insignia-39-class-38-5-diag--led-1080p-
smart-hdtv-roku-tv-black/4863802.p?skuId=4863802

Reviews

Include reviews, user-submitted content, and a frequently asked questions (FAQ) section within your product page. Reviews in particular serve as a form of social proof and are like a personal recommendation. Customer reviews don't have to exist in only written form; they can also be videos. Customer video reviews are one of the best forms of proof you can include on a product page because the video gives potential customers someone to relate to while reviewing your product.

People regard review videos as harder to fake or manipulate than text testimonials, so they carry more weight. The main difference between customer video reviews and third-party pitch videos is that the third-party videos are professionally produced by the business, whereas a customer review video is shot by the customer, likely with his or her cell phone camera. To get more reviews, both in written and video form, follow up with past customers via email and ask for an honest review; you can incentive your customers to leave reviews by offering coupons and contests.

Cross-sells

Amazon.com does cross-selling well with its Customers Who Bought This Item Also Bought section, as shown in Figure 7-5, where the site suggests other products that a customer may want to add to his or her cart based on the product that is currently being viewed. Cross-sells are an effective way to increase your basket size, or offer an alternative, related product that may better suit potential customers' needs, thus ensuring a sale.

Source: https://www.amazon.com

Grading a Landing Page

In the previous sections of this chapter, we tell you about the most common landing pages and their essential elements, and in this section, we give you some criteria by which to evaluate the effectiveness of your pages. Landing pages come in many shapes and sizes, from short-form lead capture pages to long-form sales letters, so some of the elements included in the following sections may not apply to the landing page you're evaluating. For example, a long-form sales letter that sells a service is unlikely to use a lead-capture form.

Evaluate your landing pages based on the criteria that apply to *your* pages. The most important thing to keep in mind is that improving each factor in the following list that is relevant to your landing page will have a substantial impact on the conversion rate of your landing page.

>> **Clarity:** You have a matter of seconds to convince new visitors to your landing page that they should stick around. Use the headline, subheadline, images, and anything else immediately visible on the page to answer the following questions for them: "What is it?" and "What does it do for me?"

>> **Congruence:** Nothing sends landing page visitors scurrying away faster than a lack of congruence between wherever they came from and your landing page. The text, offer, and imagery on the landing page should match (ideally exactly) the text and imagery that was in whatever ad or referring traffic source that brought the visitor to the landing page. For example, if you click an ad that states "10% off of winter apparel" and you arrive on a page offering summer apparel, you're going to lose most of your traffic. Keep the visuals (colors, images, fonts, and so on) and offer congruent from the traffic source to the landing page and you'll keep more traffic on your offer.

>> **Visualization:** Typically, an image or graphical representation of the offer increases conversions. Avoid using overused stock and royalty-free imagery that might make your offer appear cheap. Instead, wherever possible, use custom photography or graphics to depict your offer.

>> **Number of fields:** The number of form fields should be appropriate for the offer. For example, high-commitment offers have longer forms, and lower-commitment offers have fewer form fields.

Don't ask for information that you don't need! If you plan to follow up only via email, just ask for a name and email, at most. In fact, test dropping the name field, too, if you don't plan to personalize your follow-up messages by including the person's name. In general, having fewer form fields leads to a higher conversion rate.

>> **Visible and compelling call-to-action button:** People frequently debate button colors, but one constant is that the button color should contrast (not blend in) with the surrounding design elements. For example, if the background color of your website is sky blue, don't use that sky-blue color as your call-to-action button color.

Second, use a compelling statement as the text on your call-to-action button. "Submit" is not good enough. Test button text that gives a specific command or speaks to the end result (such as "Get Free Instant Access").

>> **Professional design:** The design of your landing page should be of professional quality. If you're using a quality landing page builder tool, the templates provided will take care of most of the design and layout. (We offer recommendations for landing page builder tools in Chapter 16.) Avoid making major changes to these tested layouts and designs until you get more comfortable building landing pages that convert.

>> **Relevant trust icons:** Reputable brands that you do business with or are affiliated with, "As Seen On" logos, and testimonials let your visitors know that they're making a smart decision to give you their contact information or make a purchase.

>> **Clear privacy policies:** Not only are privacy policies and terms of service required to advertise on some sites (including Google), they're also good for conversions.

>> **Visual cues:** The landing page should incorporate arrows, boxes, and other visual devices to draw the eye to the call-to-action area.

Chapter 8

Capturing Traffic with Search Marketing

No discipline in digital marketing has evolved over the years quite as dramatically as search marketing. In the early days of the Internet, search engines like Alta Vista, Lycos, and Yahoo! were fairly unsophisticated. Search marketers who understood the simple factors these sites used to rank websites could drive search engine traffic to a page regardless of its quality.

Today, search engines like Google consider hundreds of factors in deciding which web page to display for a search. In the current search marketing landscape, the best web pages usually win. Sure, loopholes still exist, exploited by less-than-reputable search marketers, but the scales have tipped toward those who play by the rules. In this chapter, you discover those rules and put yourself in a great position to receive traffic from the billions of searches that take place each day.

Search isn't limited to big search engines like Google and Bing. Social media sites such as Facebook and Pinterest also have search capabilities. Also, Amazon, iTunes, TripAdvisor, and thousands of other sites provide search to their users. Depending on your business, it can be more valuable to understand how search operates on YouTube or Amazon than on Google or Bing.

Knowing the Three Key Players in Search Marketing

Three main players make up the search marketing landscape, each with a different motivation. Understanding who the players are and what they want gives you a better understanding of how to make search marketing work for your business. The important players in search marketing are

- **Searchers:** People who type search queries into search engines
- **Search engines:** Programs that searchers use to find products, services, content, and more on the Internet
- **Marketers:** The owners of websites and other channels that publish content and make offers to people on the Internet

As a marketer and business owner, you want to maximize the amount of traffic, leads, and sales you get from search marketing. To do this, you must give searchers and search engines what they want.

Understanding searchers' needs

The key for both marketers and search engines is understanding the mindset of searchers. By understanding what motivates searchers, marketers and search engines can serve them better.

People use search engines every day for everything from researching a school project to looking for reviews for a big-ticket purchase like a car or home. What motivates searchers is simple: They want to find the most relevant, highest-quality web pages about anything and everything they're searching for, and they want to find those pages *now*.

If marketers and search engines can satisfy searchers, everyone wins. Searchers find what they want; marketers get traffic, leads, and sales; and search engines gain users.

Knowing what search engines want

A search engine company, such as Google, is a business, and like any other business, it must generate revenue to survive. As a result, it's useful to understand how search engines generate that revenue. If you understand what motivates the search engine, you can plan your search strategy accordingly.

Most search engines generate most of their revenue by selling advertising. Figure 8-1 shows a typical set of advertisements in a Google search results page.

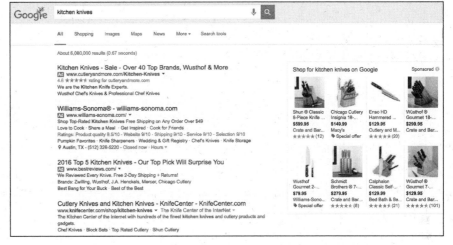

Source: www.google.com

FIGURE 8-1:
Google displays ads at the top and in the top-right corners of search result pages.

As a result, it's in a search engine's best interest to serve the best, most popular, most relevant content to searchers. Failure to deliver what searchers want sends those searchers elsewhere to find what they're looking for, which means less opportunity to show ads.

WARNING

BLACK HATS AND WHITE HATS

If you want to build a successful search marketing campaign, you need to stay within the borders of each search engine's terms of service. Search marketing tactics that violate those terms of service are called *black-hat;* those that play within the rules are called *white-hat.*

Black-hat search marketing tactics are not only unethical (and sometimes illegal), but also bad for business. Violating the terms of a search engine may create short-term results, but those results won't be sustainable. Search engines like Google continuously update the algorithms they use to rank websites in an effort to squash black-hat methods such as link buying and keyword stuffing.

Marketers who use white-hat search marketing strategies — those who follow the search engine's terms of service and build a better user experience for searchers — are rewarded with higher rankings and more traffic, leads, and sales from search engines.

Other search engines generate revenue by establishing affiliate relationships with the businesses to which they refer traffic. When a searcher visits one of these affiliate partners and makes a purchase, the search engine makes a commission on that sale.

Targeting Search Queries

One way that people discover your business, brands, products, and services is by using search queries typed in search engines. A searcher navigates to a search engine, types a keyword or phrase, and taps or clicks a search button, and the search engine returns popular, relevant results. The searcher clicks or taps one of those results, and he's off to the races.

To help make your brand discoverable and available to a searcher, marketers have two broad categories of search queries to keep in mind:

» **Branded queries:** Keywords or keyword phrases that searchers type in search engines when they're looking for a specific business, brand, product, or service. The search query "Southwest Airlines," for example, is a branded query that Southwest Airlines should target.

» **Nonbranded queries:** Keywords or keyword phrases that searchers type in to search engines when they're not looking for a specific business, brand, product, or service. The search query "fly to Chicago," for example, is a nonbranded query that Southwest Airlines should target.

By understanding the preceding two categories, marketers can target keywords or keyword phrases to help make their brand discoverable and available to searchers.

Suppose that a searcher is looking for a bed-and-breakfast inn, and she types the search query "historic bed and breakfast near me" in Google (see Figure 8-2). This query is a nonbranded search query. The searcher isn't looking for a particular bed-and-breakfast; she's simply researching and discovering historic bed-and-breakfasts nearby.

On the other hand, the searcher might be searching for a specific bed-and-breakfast, such as Austin's Inn at Pearl Street, in which case she types a query such as "reviews of Austin's Inn at Pearl Street." This query is a branded search query (see Figure 8-3).

FIGURE 8-2:
A discoverable search query for local bed-and-breakfast inns.

FIGURE 8-3:
A branded search query for Austin's Inn at Pearl Street.

Defining a search query

Each of the billions of search queries entered in search engines each day contain the intent and context of an individual searcher. *Intent*, as it relates to search marketing, involves understanding what the searcher is looking for. The *context* of the query is made up of the reason why the searcher has that intent. In other words, intent is the "what" of a search query, and context is the "why."

Following are examples of intent and context of three people who might be searching the Internet:

>> **Person 1:** I want to start a vegetable garden because I want to add organic food to my diet.

- *Intent:* Want to start a vegetable garden.

- *Context:* Add organic food to my diet.

>> **Person 2:** I want to start a vegetable garden because I want to spend more time outdoors.

- *Intent:* Want to start a vegetable garden.

- *Context:* Spend more time outdoors.

>> **Person 3:** I want to start a vegetable garden because I want to save money on grocery bills.

- *Intent:* Want to start a vegetable garden.

- *Context:* Save money on groceries.

Each searcher in these examples has the same intent: start a vegetable garden. But each person has a slightly different reason for wanting to start that vegetable garden. In other words, the context behind the intent is different in each case.

A search marketer should focus on satisfying both the intent and context of searchers. Each intent and context represents a query worth targeting. In the preceding examples, searchers might type any of the following queries in a search engine:

>> "start a vegetable garden" (intent only)

>> "add organic food to my diet" (context only)

>> "start an organic vegetable garden" (intent and context)

A business that sells vegetable gardening products or services would do well to target all these keywords based on the intent and context of its ideal customer.

TIP

Refer to the customer avatar described in Chapter 1 of this book. Pay particular attention to the sections about goals, values, challenges, pain points, and objections to the sale. These sections contain clues to the intent and context of the terms that your ideal customer might be typing into search engines.

Choosing the right queries to target

Each query typed in a search engine contains the searcher's intent and context, or both. To determine the intent and context that your ideal customer is typing in search engines, you need to do keyword research, using tools such as Google AdWords Keyword Planner (https://adwords.google.com/KeywordPlanner).

Coming up with keywords the "old-fashioned" way

But before you start using keyword tools, one of the best ways to do keyword research is to brainstorm ideas with anyone who comes into contact with your customers. After all, you know your customers' wants, needs, and pain points better than a keyword tool does. Gather the appropriate members of your team to answer questions about your customers. This will help you come up with relevant and specific keywords and keyword phrases to research with a keywords tool. After you have completed the brainstorming phase, move on to your respective keyword tool to see what keywords and phrases will work best for your search marketing campaign.

To help with your brainstorming, answer questions like these in the subsequent example. Following are examples of how online shoe retailer Zappos might answer questions to sell shoes to people who plan to run a marathon:

>> **Q:** What is our ideal customer researching before he buys our product or service?

A: The ideal diet for a marathon runner.

>> **Q:** What is our ideal customer interested in that's related to our product or service?

A: Treating sore leg muscles.

>> **Q:** What barriers does our ideal customer need to overcome before she buys our product or service?

A: Finding time to train for a marathon.

>> **Q:** What does our ideal customer hope to accomplish with our product or service?

A: Running a marathon.

>> **Q:** What information does our ideal customer need to evaluate our product or service against our competitors' products or services?

A: Compare the weight of Nike and Adidas marathon running shoes.

Using keyword research tools

After brainstorming, you move on to your chosen keyword research tool. Dozens of good keyword research tools are available for purchase, but the free Google AdWords Keyword Planner (https://adwords.google.com/KeywordPlanner) meets the needs of most search marketers. Google provides this free tool to allow advertisers to research the behavior of searchers who use its search engine. Advertisers use the information provided by this tool to choose keywords they bid on.

Typing a keyword phrase like "run a marathon" in the Keyword Planner tool (see Figure 8-4) returns several keywords to target:

>> "running event"

>> "marathon runner"

>> "marathon tips"

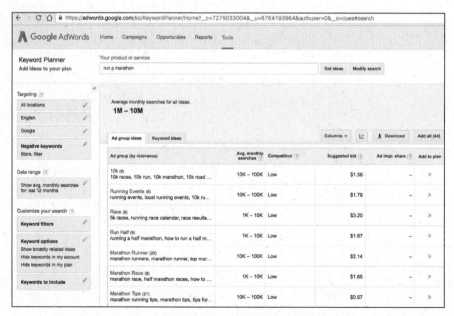

FIGURE 8-4:
Planning keywords with Google AdWords Keyword Planner.

Source: https://adwords.google.com/ko/KeywordPlanner/Home?_c=7275033004&_
u=6764193964&authuser=0&_o=cues#search

The Google AdWords Keyword Planner gives you the following information about each query:

>> **Average monthly searchers:** The average number of times people have searched for this exact keyword based on the date range and targeting settings that you select.

>> **Competition:** The number of advertisers bidding on this keyword or keyword phrase for a paid traffic campaign (turn to Chapter 10 for information about paid traffic). In the Competition column, you can see whether the competition for a keyword idea is low, medium, or high.

REMEMBER

Don't be discouraged if you research keywords and find that the Google AdWords Keyword Planner has no information to report. The main reason to use this tool is to research keywords to target on Google's advertising platform. Keywords that may be absolutely relevant to your business, and thus good keywords to target, may not appear in this tool, particularly for branded queries such as the names of your products, services, or brands.

Satisfying searchers

Much like bloodhounds on a hunt, people often search the web until they satisfy their intent, context, or both. To compete for a search query, a marketer needs to create a web page or asset that satisfies the searcher's query. That web page or asset could be anything from a blog post to a product demonstration video.

The web page shown in Figure 8-5 satisfies the intent of any searcher who enters the query "mojito recipe" in the Google search engine, and the web page shown in Figure 8-6 satisfies the intent of a searcher who enters the query "buy canon eos 70d" in the Amazon search engine.

Other assets you might create to satisfy the intent of a searcher include podcasts, videos, and social media updates.

REMEMBER

The web page or asset needs to be discoverable by the search engine that the marketer is targeting. The Pinterest search engine, for example, discovers new Pinterest pins added to your Pinterest boards, and the Google search engine discovers new web pages and blog posts added to your website (assuming that you haven't created any technical barriers for the search engine). We talk more about technical barriers in the "Optimizing for search engine robots" section, later in this chapter.

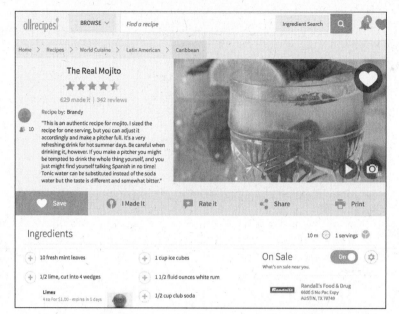

FIGURE 8-5:
Allrecipes.com
satisfies a
searcher's intent
for a mojito
recipe.

Source: http://allrecipes.com/recipe/147363/the-real-mojito/

FIGURE 8-6:
A search query in
Amazon satisfies
a search for the
Canon EOS 70D.

Source: https://www.amazon.com/s/ref=nb_sb_noss?url=search-alias%3Daps&field-keywords=buy+canon+eos+70d

If the web page or asset you create satisfies the intent, context, or both of a searcher, it has a chance to be shown to that searcher. That said, many factors determine which web pages and assets are shown for any given query. In the following sections, we go into more detail about these factors and how to optimize your assets so that they are more likely to appear in front of your ideal searcher.

CONVERTING PROSPECTS TO CUSTOMERS

Don't fall into the trap of thinking that the goal of your search marketing is to get better rankings in search engines. Also, don't make the mistake of thinking that search marketing is just about getting traffic. The goal of search marketing, as with all marketing, is to move your customer from one stage of the customer journey to the next (covered in Chapter 1).

For every searcher who visits your blog, YouTube channel, or Pinterest home page, you need to provide a call to action to take the next step.

Suppose that a searcher types a query indicating that he's looking for a demonstration of your product. He lands on your product page and finds a product-demonstration video. Great job! You anticipated the intent of your ideal customer and created a page that satisfies that intent on an appropriate channel. Don't squander this visit by failing to make a call to action to the next logical step in the customer journey. In this case, the appropriate next step is to buy the product. Failing to make a clear call to action to this logical next step isn't just bad marketing but also a bad user experience. This person is looking for a demonstration of your product, which means he may also be looking to buy it. Provide a call to action that will help to move him to the next step in his customer journey with you.

Optimizing Your Assets for Specific Channels

After you've built a web page or asset that targets a specific intent, context, or both, you need to determine where that asset will "live." We refer to the various places you can house your web pages or assets as *channels*. Starting with a searcher's intent and context helps you determine the correct channel to use to deliver the web page or asset. If you want to satisfy searchers with the intent of understanding how your product works, for example, you might create a product–demonstration video, so it would make sense to choose YouTube as the channel for this asset.

In this section, we discuss strategies to use in optimizing your assets for several popular channels.

Optimizing for Google

Your website is a channel that can get traffic from search engines such as Google. This section lays out the steps for optimizing a web page for Google.

Step 1: Write the <title> tag

The <title> tag is the most critical search ranking element on any web page. This tag is displayed on search engine results pages and is meant to be an accurate and concise description of a page's content, telling search engines and searchers what the page is about. The <title> tag appears in blue on search engine results pages and is the link that users click to access the related content (see Figure 8-7).

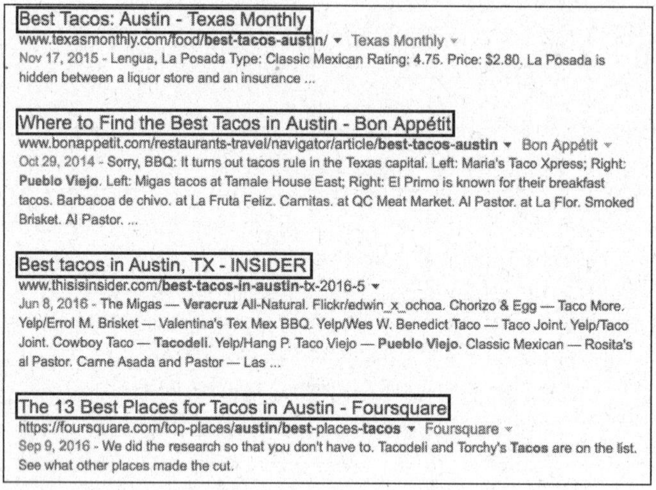

Best Tacos: Austin - Texas Monthly
www.texasmonthly.com/food/best-tacos-austin/ ▼ Texas Monthly ▼
Nov 17, 2015 - Lengua, La Posada Type: Classic Mexican Rating: 4.75. Price: $2.80. La Posada is hidden between a liquor store and an insurance ...

Where to Find the Best Tacos in Austin - Bon Appétit
www.bonappetit.com/restaurants-travel/navigator/article/best-tacos-austin ▼ Bon Appétit ▼
Oct 29, 2014 - Sorry, BBQ: It turns out tacos rule in the Texas capital. Left: Maria's Taco Xpress; Right: **Pueblo Viejo**. Left: Migas tacos at Tamale House East; Right: El Primo is known for their breakfast tacos. Barbacoa de chivo. at La Fruta Feliz. Carnitas. at QC Meat Market. Al Pastor. at La Flor. Smoked Brisket. Al Pastor. ...

Best tacos in Austin, TX - INSIDER
www.thisisinsider.com/best-tacos-in-austin-tx-2016-5 ▼
Jun 8, 2016 - The Migas — **Veracruz** All-Natural. Flickr/edwin_x_ochoa. Chorizo & Egg — Taco More. Yelp/Errol M. Brisket — Valentina's Tex Mex BBQ. Yelp/Wes W. Benedict Taco — Taco Joint. Yelp/Taco Joint. Cowboy Taco — **Tacodeli**. Yelp/Hang P. Taco Viejo — **Pueblo Viejo**. Classic Mexican — Rosita's al Pastor. Carne Asada and Pastor — Las ...

The 13 Best Places for Tacos in Austin - Foursquare
https://foursquare.com/top-places/**austin**/best-places-**tacos** ▼ Foursquare ▼
Sep 9, 2016 - We did the research so that you don't have to. Tacodeli and Torchy's **Tacos** are on the list. See what other places made the cut.

FIGURE 8-7: Examples of <title> tags.

Keywords are essential for <title> tags, so start those tags with your most important keywords for that page. Using the keywords you've chosen for the page you're optimizing, create a title for your piece that's no more than 70 characters long; otherwise, the search engine may truncate it. The <title> tag should read well because it is displayed prominently on the search results page.

Step 2: Write a meta description

The meta description, often displayed directly below the <title> tag, further describes the content of the page. Typically, searched keywords appear in boldface in the meta description. Although search engines don't use your meta descriptions to determine your ranking for a search query, searchers read these descriptions to determine whether they want to click your results.

The meta description is the elevator pitch for your page, so make it compelling. Include words that describe the content of the page in a way that entices searchers to click your result.

Keep your meta description shorter than 150 characters; otherwise, it's likely to be truncated on the search result page. Consider using a call to action in your meta description, such as "Shop now!" "Click here for free shipping," or "Browse the latest trends."

Figure 8-8 shows some examples of meta descriptions.

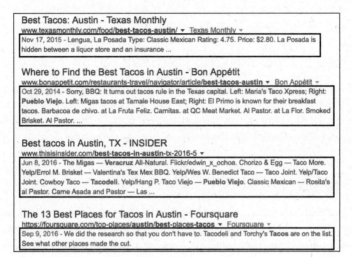

FIGURE 8-8:
Examples of meta descriptions.

Step 3: Optimize the URL

A URL (Uniform Resource Locator) describes a site or page to visitors and search engines, so it's important to keep the URL relevant and accurate so that the content ranks well. A URL (also referred to as a *slug*) is set up like this:

```
www.YourSiteNameHere.com/keywords-that-describe-this-page
```

Include your keywords in the URL after the forward slash (/). Search engines use the keywords in this section of the URL to further determine what the page is about and where it should rank. Although the keywords in your URL don't play as big of a role in your search rankings as your title tag does, keywords are still important elements to optimize.

Step 4: Write body copy

Text on a page, also called content or copy, gives the search engine information about what search queries your page will satisfy, so it's important for every page on your site to have text. Having content on a web page is also very helpful in getting the page to rank in search. Aim for 500 words or more on each page, but don't fill your web pages with low-quality content just to get words on the page. On video- or image-heavy pages, of course, you may have very few words on a page, and that's okay. Always err on the side of satisfying the intent of searchers by giving them enough information to make sense of the page.

Throughout the body, use relevant keywords or keyword phrases that describe the page. Include your keywords and variations on those keywords in the body titles or headings. In short, use the keywords you're targeting and variations on those keywords anywhere it seems natural to do so.

Step 5: Optimize the <alt> tag

The <alt> tag provides alternative information for an image on your page, in the form of text, for users who can't view the image (because of a slow Internet connection or an image error, for example). In the <alt> tag, describe the image while using the keyword phrase you've chosen for your piece.

Optimizing for YouTube

YouTube is a search engine and, therefore, is interested in keeping searchers within its network so that it can show those searchers ads. As a result, YouTube sends traffic to videos that are keeping YouTube visitors engaged on its site.

Here's how to get more search traffic to your videos on YouTube.

Step 1: Create engaging thumbnails

The YouTube search engine measures how many people see your video in their search results against the number who play your video. If your videos get played often, YouTube rewards them with higher rankings.

The most important factor in increasing the number of plays that a video gets is the video thumbnail, which is the image searchers see for the video (see Figure 8-9) in the YouTube search results. A compelling thumbnail can have a big effect on your click-through rate and, thus, your rankings in YouTube.

To engage your audience, make sure that your thumbnails are bright, vibrant, and crisp. Include compelling text for each thumbnail to tell viewers about the content and to entice them to click or tap it.

TIP

If you don't have a graphic designer, you can create professional-looking thumbnails with a tool called Canva (https://www.canva.com/). This tool offers many free and paid templates you can use. Also, you can import your own images into Canva to create thumbnails that set your videos apart.

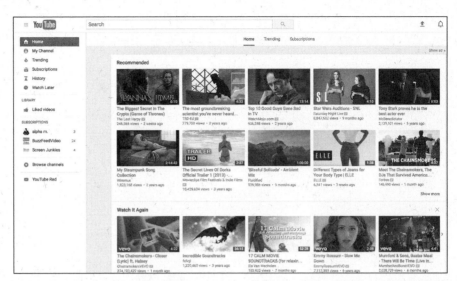

Source: https://www.youtube.com/

FIGURE 8-9: Each video image is a thumbnail.

Step 2: Ask for engagement

YouTube's goal is to keep searchers within the confines of YouTube so that it can show ads to those searchers. The number of shares, views, and comments your videos receive indicates to YouTube how well your videos are keeping searchers engaged.

In addition, a video with lots of views, more likes than dislikes, and favorable comments proves to new viewers the quality of the content. Good quality leads to more likes and shares. In the description and in the video itself, be sure to ask viewers to like, comment, share, and check out more of your videos.

Step 3: Optimize content for keywords

Like your website, your YouTube videos need to be optimized for keywords. Make sure you include the keyword(s) or keyword phrase(s) in the video's title, the description, the tags, the filename of the video file you upload, and the video you create. This practice helps users find your video and improves your rankings and relevancy on the YouTube platform.

TIP

To gain more insight into your score, as well as other metrics, you can use a tool like vidIQ (`http://vidiq.com/`) to track and manage your channel.

Step 4: Look at retention

How long people watch your video is known as *audience retention*, which is an important metric to measure. The YouTube reporting suite allows you to view retention metrics, as shown in Figure 8-10.

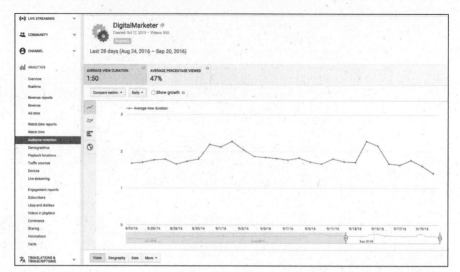

Source: https://www.youtube.com/analytics?o=U#r=retention

FIGURE 8-10: Examining video retention in YouTube.

It's normal for a video to gradually lose viewers; not everyone watches a video the whole way through. That said, pay attention to audience retention on outlier videos that do very well or very poorly. Attempt to determine why some videos have high retention while others have trouble holding people's attention. Then optimize and change your video content accordingly.

Optimizing for Pinterest

Believe it or not, Pinterest is a search engine. In fact, it's an important search engine to understand if you sell physical products. Follow three steps to optimize search for your Pinterest channel.

Step 1: Enhance your images

Pinterest is all about the pictures. You want big, beautiful, crisp pictures to grab people's attention. Next, include a text overlay on your image. The text overlay serves as the pin's headline, providing context and further describing the pin.

The size and shape of your images matter on Pinterest. The platform is vertically oriented, so make sure that the images you use are vertical with an aspect ratio of 2:3 to 1:3.5 and a minimum width of 600 pixels. You can use horizontal images for your pins, of course, but vertical images tend to do better.

WARNING

Pins with an aspect ratio greater than 1:3.5 are truncated.

TIP

As mentioned in the YouTube section, you can use Canva (https://www.canva.com/) to craft engaging pins with professional images and eye-catching fonts.

Step 2: Optimize board covers

Pinterest pins are categorized and housed in boards. You can find your boards on your profile page. Like the images you use for your pins, your board covers should be optimized with engaging, professional pictures that have text overlays to further describe the board. Figure 8-11 shows a Pinterest profile page with keyword-optimized boards that have text overlays.

FIGURE 8-11:
A keyword-optimized board from DIY Ready's Pinterest profile page.

Step 3: Target keywords

Creativity is important in Pinterest, but avoid being cute, creative, or punny. The Pinterest search engine is less sophisticated than search engines such as Google, so your search results will improve if you use your target keywords verbatim when naming pins and boards and when adding descriptions.

To discover the best keywords for your pin, board, or description, use the Pinterest platform to research your keywords, as follows:

1. **Type a keyword or keyword phrase in the Pinterest search engine.**

2. **Make note of the suggested keywords Pinterest provides below the keyword.**

When you search in Pinterest, it gives prompts for keyword and keyword phrases related to what you're searching for. This can be used to provide inspiration for keywords and phrases to optimize for in Pinterest. See Figure 8-12 for an example of searching for "wedding ideas" in the Pinterest platform.

Source: https://www.pinterest.com/

FIGURE 8-12:
An example of prompts Pinterest gives when searching the platform.

3. **Create new pins and boards for any relevant keywords suggested by Pinterest, and include these keywords in the descriptions of those pins and boards.**

Optimizing for Amazon

If you're selling on Amazon, you need to understand how its search engine operates. To get a product page to rank on Amazon, follow these four steps.

Step 1: Build sales with promotions and launches

To Amazon, lots of sales in a short amount of time indicate that a product is hot and that it should be moved up in the search rankings. Use periodic promotions, sales, and launches to increase sales velocity, and watch your rankings soar.

Step 2: Increase reviews

Reviews are extremely important on the Amazon platform, and lots of positive reviews indicate to Amazon that your product should be moved up in the search rankings. Even if people love your product, they may not take the time to review it. Remind and encourage people who have bought your product to write a review with tools such as Feedback Genius, which helps you message customers while staying within Amazon's terms of use.

Step 3: Create a compelling product name

If you want people to click your product, you need to have a compelling product name. A cute or clever name may sound cool, but it can be vague, causing people to overlook it because they don't know what the product is. To increase the click-through rate, make sure that your product's name accurately describes what the product is and does. Look to your competitors for inspiration; see how they present their names on Amazon.

REMEMBER

People don't buy products on Amazon; they buy pictures of products. Include as many clear, crisp product images as necessary to satisfy the needs of a prospective customer. When buying on Amazon, your buyer can't hold your product in his hand or examine it, so you need to include quality pictures that demonstrate exactly what the buyer will get. The more expensive or complex the product, the more images you're likely to need.

Step 4: Create keyword-targeted product pages

Your Amazon product page contains text, and every one of those words helps determine your rankings. Include the keyword or phrase you're targeting in the title of the page and throughout the product description. Aim for a product description of 250 words or more. Don't stuff the description with keywords, though, and keep user experience in mind. Favor quality over quantity. As with product images, the more expensive or complex a product is, the more detailed a product description you need.

Optimizing for iTunes

Podcasting is an effective and affordable way to distribute content on the Internet. If you're podcasting, you need to understand how iTunes ranks podcasts so that you can get more exposure to iTunes users. Take three steps to improve your search rankings within iTunes.

Step 1: Solicit reviews

Positive reviews tell iTunes that your podcast is worthwhile and should be rewarded with high search rankings. To generate reviews, use the podcast itself to ask people to leave reviews. At least once per episode, have a call to action to remind people to review your podcast.

Step 2: Create a clear title and a clean cover design

You want a specific title and a sharp cover design not only to describe your podcast, but also to attract an audience. A cute title is likely to get lost or passed over because people won't know what your show is about. Therefore, be precise in your title, and include keywords that improve your rankings and help searchers find you. In that same vein, include keywords within the episode's title and description.

Next, include a sleek cover design for your podcast — one that demonstrates the theme of your podcast but isn't too busy. Keep in mind that your podcast cover is the size of a thumbnail. Keep the cover simple; otherwise, your message is likely to get lost.

Step 3: Grow downloads

Like reviews, the number of downloads your podcast receives indicates the quality of that podcast. As a result, download velocity has a direct effect on your search results in iTunes. Steady, consistent increases in downloads improve your rankings.

TIP

To increase downloads as you launch your podcast, publish three to five episodes at the same time, because the more times you publish in the beginning, the more episodes people have access to and the more downloads you're going to see as people subscribe. As you gain subscribers after the first couple of weeks, you can publish on a consistent date, such as one episode every Tuesday, to let your audience know when to expect your latest episode.

Optimizing for review sites

If you're marketing a local business such as a restaurant, hotel, or retail store, you need to focus some of your search optimization efforts on review sites such as Yelp and TripAdvisor. Following are two steps to take to optimize for those sites.

Step 1: Gain legitimate reviews

You don't want to "game" reviews; reviews that aren't legitimate can result in backlash from both your customers and the review site. Instead, you want to encourage honest reviews by making sure that the customer experience is top-notch and deserving of a good review.

That said, you can certainly encourage your customers to submit legitimate reviews with tools such as TripAdvisor's Review Express. A second method is to ask customers for their email addresses and for product or service reviews at the point of sale. Later, you can follow up with people and remind them to review by sending them an email, and you can entice people to review by offering giveaways or contests.

After someone gives you a review, respond by thanking the person for his time and letting him know that he's been heard. If someone gives you a negative review, respond to that person with empathy so that she knows that she's been heard. Explain your side of the story, and if the review requires more attention, move it to a private channel such as email or phone. It's best to handle customer-service issues outside public channels like review sites.

REMEMBER

On most review sites, review scores outweigh the number of reviews. Focus on getting fantastic reviews from satisfied customers. Sure, the sheer number of reviews you receive is important, but only if those reviews indicate that your customers are happy with your business.

Step 2: Claim your profile

If you've been in business for a while, you're likely listed on virtually every review site, whether you know it or not. Visit the relevant review sites, and search for your business. Then claim your business (or start a profile if needed) on the review site by answering questions and performing verification checks that prove the business is yours. By claiming your business, you can manage your profile, make edits, and add information to your profile on the review site.

Fix any inaccuracies in your profile, and add information that current and potential customers may find helpful, such as hours of operation, location, contact information, and company history. Within the description, include keywords wherever it makes sense to do so, and use categorization appropriately to improve your search rankings within the review site platform.

Optimizing for search engine robots

Search engine *robots* are programs that visit web pages and "crawl" or index the content on those pages. However, if barriers have been placed, the robot can't crawl the page, so that page doesn't get indexed or served to searchers. One of your search marketing goals should be to make it as easy as possible for search robots to access and index your pages.

At this point, search marketing can become extremely technical. If your website is unintentionally creating barriers and "speed bumps" for search engines, you may need to involve a search engine optimization (SEO) professional who understands the technical side of search marketing.

To determine whether your website has robot optimization issues, install Google Search Console (https://www.google.com/webmasters/tools/home) on your website. Google Search Console (formerly Google Webmaster Tools) is a free tool that allows you to see your website as the Google search engine sees it. You can view important technical information about search robots' capability to index your website, including the following:

>> **Index status:** The total number of URLs from your site that have been added to Google's index. If your website has 100 pages, for example, you should see that number of pages in the index-status report.

>> **URL errors:** Pages that Google is having difficulty accessing. Investigate the reasons why pages have errors, and repair them.

>> **Security issues:** If your site contains malware, it will appear in the Google Search Console. A site with security issues is very unlikely to be served traffic by search engines like Google. Address malware issues immediately.

Earning Links

A search marketer must create a website that earns links from external sources. Links are the Internet equivalent of positive word of mouth about your business. For instance, if a blog about personal finance links to the personal finance site Quicken.com, that link from the blog is saying that Quicken has quality content that the blogger considers trustworthy and relevant; it's the Internet equivalent of a referral in the physical world. Pages with more links pointing to them generally get better search results than pages with fewer links.

Links that point to a web page are considered to be votes for that page. Search engines take into account the volume and, more important, the quality of the links to a page to determine which pages to serve in their results for a particular keyword search query.

In the following sections, we discuss how to earn links by using search marketing tactics that stay within the search engine's terms of service and avoid black-hat tactics, as stated in the "Black hats and white hats" sidebar, earlier in this chapter.

Step 1: Cross-link your own content

The method of building links that's most under your control is cross-linking on your own site. If a financial planning website publishes a blog post titled "Ten Mistakes to Avoid When Planning for Retirement," it would make sense, for both the reader and the search engine, to find a cross-link from this blog post to a page explaining the company's retirement-planning services.

Linking within your own website improves user experience and sends signals to search engines about what pages are important on your website. Cross-link to important pages on your website wherever and whenever it makes sense to do so, while keeping user experience in mind.

Step 2: Study your competitors' links

The next step is doing some competitive research. Using a tool such as Open Site Explorer (`https://moz.com/researchtools/ose/`), you can research your major competitors to see what sites are linking to them. Then reach out to those sites to see whether they're interested in linking to your site as well.

Step 3: Create generous content

You can earn links by creating so-called *generous content:* content that mentions other people, especially influential people who could link back to you or share your content on their social networks. One way to create generous content is to write an article about a specific person or brand and then link to the appropriate site. This article may take the form of a biography or an interview.

Another way to build generous content is to create a crowdsourced post that asks experts to write 100 words or so on the same topic and then links to each expert's site. We cover creating generous content, such as the crowdsourced post, in detail in Chapter 6.

The bottom line is that to earn links to your website, you need to start giving out some "link love" of your own. Be generous with your website by quoting others and referring your visitors to pages you like. Make sure that you let people know when you link to them.

Step 4: Create content worthy of a link

Great content provides assets that people want to share with their network. Create outstanding content, particularly on your blog, that people link to because it provides tremendous value. For example, a bank that wants to attract prospective homebuyers might build a free and easy-to-use monthly mortgage calculator. If others find this tool useful, they will link to it and improve that bank website's standing in the search engines.

Step 5: Publish primary research

One powerful way to generate links is to publish *primary research:* new research that you collected yourself. Because primary research can be difficult and time-consuming to create, it's valuable and rare. Solid primary research is in great demand and often leads to high-quality links as people cite that research on their web pages.

Step 6: Keep up with the news

The last step is creating newsworthy content and publishing it as the topic in question is trending. To do this effectively, keep an eye on industry news. One of the best ways to do that is to use social media, particularly Twitter, because Twitter tends to be the nervous system of the Internet.

Be ready to produce content about your industry at a moment's notice or find creative ways to relate trending, newsworthy topics to your industry. This is tough work, but being one of the first people to create content can have a big payoff: You'll be one of only a few sources of information about something, causing other people to link to you as the story develops. But before you jump the gun, make sure that you can verify the news story or risk the embarrassment and damage to your reputation for publishing inaccurate information.

BUILDING LINKS IN A POST-PENGUIN WORLD

The number of links pointing to a web page has been a factor in garnering search traffic for nearly two decades. In that time, less-than-reputable search marketers have developed ways to manipulate the number of links a web page receives. In 2012, Google launched the Penguin update to stop sites deemed to be spamming its search results, particularly sites buying links or obtaining links through link networks in an effort to boost their Google search rankings.

Today, black-hat search marketing tactics such as link buying violate Google's terms of service, and updates like Penguin make it difficult to execute those tactics. The only sustainable way to build links to your web pages is the old-fashioned way: Build something worth linking to.

All links aren't created equal. Links from high-quality, authoritative sites have a greater effect than links from low-quality sites. A link from *The New York Times* or University of Southern California website, for example, carries more weight than a link from a brand-new blog with no authority. Search engines have deemed reputable publications and college sites, like the *Times* and USC sites, to be unlikely to link to a low-quality page or a page that infringes upon the search engine's terms of service.

Chapter 9

Leveraging the Social Web

Social media is an affordable and efficient way to reach prospects, leads, and customers. But social media communication is a vast discipline, encompassing everything from social networking on sites like Facebook and Twitter to content-publishing platforms like YouTube and Medium. And that's just to mention a few of the hundreds of social channels to choose from — each with its own brand of processes, procedures, and protocols. The opportunities in social media are exciting, but they can seem intimidating at times.

At its core, social media marketing is no different from other forms of marketing. It's essentially just a new way to interact with customers, prospects, influencers, and partners. In this chapter, we help you sort through the madness, make a plan, and start using social media to create value for your company. We tell you how to generate leads and sales, practices to expand your exposure, the powerful uses of "listening" tools, ways to sharpen your skills for gaining the trust of your prospects, and how to avoid social media mistakes.

The Social Success Cycle

Most businesses treat social media marketing as a single discipline, but it's actually composed of four equally important parts:

>> **Social listening:** Monitoring and responding to customer service and reputation management issues on the social web

>> **Social influencing:** Establishing authority on the social web, often through distributing and sharing valuable content

>> **Social networking:** Finding and associating with authoritative and influential individuals and brands on the social web

>> **Social selling:** Generating leads and sales from existing customers and prospects on the social web

Understanding why and how to employ each component of the social success cycle is the key to making sense of what can look like chaos on the social web.

As a marketer, it's hard to know where to start with all the different avenues you can take with social media. The good news is that all major social media channels fall into only two categories — and recognizing these categories is key to effectively harnessing social media channels as part of a comprehensive marketing strategy.

Seeker channels are social media platforms that users go to when seeking specific content. Think of these channels as modified search engines like Bing or Google. Users generally go to the channel to search for and discover content, and they consume that content on that channel. The two big players in this category are YouTube and Pinterest. When users visit YouTube, they are generally in "seeker" mode. They use YouTube's search bar for a specific inquiry and consume the video right on the platform. Similarly, people use the Pinterest search bar to get specific information on topics like recipes, crafts, or fashion. Though it's image-based, Pinterest also operates like a search engine.

These seeker channels are perfect for social influencing. Strategically placing content on these sites provides a way to share valuable information with your target audience and works to build authority and trust with your brand. Seeker channels are also perfect for social selling. You can optimize videos on YouTube or images on Pinterest with calls to action that serve to transform leads into customers — or at the very least, encourage your prospect to consume even more content on your website. Figure 9-1 shows a GoPro YouTube video with a clear call to action at the end of the video to submit images and videos to GoPro.

FIGURE 9-1:
GoPro makes a call to action to get its audience to engage with the brand.

Source: https://www.youtube.com/watch?v=svNfpnEr-wY

On the opposite side of the coin are *engagement channels*. On these social media outlets, users primarily engage and connect with others. This is the place where user-to-user conversations are commonplace. Users carry on conversations and share short-form content that links to longer-form content elsewhere. A great engagement channel example is Twitter. Because of Twitter's 140-character limit, you often see tweets bearing a snippet of information with an accompanying link that takes you off the platform and to another site. Engagement channels are best for social listening, because conversation is paramount. You find conversations going on between brand and customer, customer and customer, customer and prospect. These back-and-forth conversations are perfect places to monitor and respond to your customers and prospects, or even to see how your competitors are communicating. Because conversation is a native experience, engagement channels are also perfect places for social networking. Major engagement channels available on the social web are Twitter, Facebook, and LinkedIn.

Not every social media channel falls into these two categories, but most of those with widespread usage do. As a marketer on a seeker channel, your priority is to make sure that users can discover your content when they are performing searches. Engagement channels are all about listening, sharing content, and networking. Be sure to focus on social customer service and how often you engage in active conversations with your customers, prospects, and influencers on engagement channels.

Listening to the Social Web

Social listening involves strategically monitoring and responding to mentions on the social web (whether it's praise or criticism) about your brand, key members of your organization, your products or services, or anything that falls into your industry niche. This role can be filled by a single individual or, depending on the size of your organization, an entire team tasked with monitoring mentions. Regardless of whether you're the only employee of your business or employed at a Fortune 100 company, social listening concepts apply across the board.

These days, a business can fail at social media in many ways. Sometimes, social media seems like something that was forced on the business world. As a result, many businesses have resisted participating in social media channels. On occasion, employees with access to official social channels post questionable status updates that can have an embarrassing impact on companies and their principal members. But the biggest failure of all is ignoring social media conversations altogether.

The fact of the matter is that prospects, leads, and customers are actively talking about you, your brand, and your industry on the social web. If companies are not actively listening for these conversations, someone may as well have installed a telephone in your customer care department that is ringing off the hook with no one picking up the phone. There lies the biggest social media sin. It's not posting something embarrassing or angering the masses with less than politically correct statements — it's ignoring the social telephone.

When we think about users posting complaints and praise on the social web, we tend to think of Twitter and Facebook as the place to find these mentions. The truth is that, depending on the type of business you have, people are likely talking about you on all sorts of channels, from demonstration videos on YouTube to reviews on sites like Yelp and Amazon. These conversations are the mentions that your company needs to be aware of and actively listening for on the social web, and they're what makes a social listening program so essential.

Social listening is a foundational concept in the social success cycle. Today, people expect organizations to engage in social listening, and your prospects, customers, and clients expect your participation in the conversations they initiate over the social web. If you're just getting started in social media, don't begin by networking, influencing, or selling — begin with listening. Use social media as the customer-service and reputation-management channel that it already is for your brand. For an example of responsive social listening, see Figure 9-2, which shows the grocery store chain Save-A-Lot responding to a customer complaint and letting him know he's been heard on the Facebook network.

FIGURE 9-2:
Save-A-Lot lets a customer know that he's been heard.

Source: https://www.facebook.com/savealot/posts_to_page/

Social listening goes far beyond customer service. Also, listening to the social web informs all other aspects of your social success cycle:

>> **Social influencing:** Social listening impacts social influencing by letting you know what sort of content you should share that your audience finds most valuable.

>> **Partnerships:** By paying attention to who on the social web is sharing influential information in your industry, your social listening can inform you about potential partnerships and journalists who might give your brand earned media mentions.

>> **Social selling:** Social listening plays an important part in *social selling*, which is when a brand uses social media to generate leads and sales. The brand will answer prospect questions and offer insight until the prospect is ready to make a buying decision. Therefore, social listening can inform social selling by telling you what people are likely to respond to, what they desire, and what they are asking for on the social web so that your products and services can best meet the prospects' needs.

Choosing a social listening tool

Many social listening tools are available for conducting your social listening campaigns. These tools require various levels of financial commitment and feature options that can help you initiate an effective social listening program. Luckily, whether you work solo or have a large team of social listeners, lots of help is available to help you meet your social listening goals.

If you don't have the bandwidth or budget to dive into more advanced social listening tools, you can use Google Alerts (https://www.google.com/alerts) as part of your social listening strategy. Google Alerts is a free option for social media marketers on a shoestring budget. As you might be aware, Google constantly crawls the web looking for new content. The Google Alerts feature lets you set up email alerts whenever the search engine finds mentions of preselected keywords, such as company names, product names, or names of the public-facing members of your organization. It's a viable option if yours is a very small business that doesn't generate many mentions, and ones that don't require complex feedback loops.

Small businesses with one or two dedicated social listeners can graduate up to a tool like Mention (`https://mention.com`), which uses a more sophisticated keyword search and can pull mentions directly from all aspects of the social web, including social media channels, blogs, and new sites. Also, an entire suite of similar tools exists that competes with Mention, so if you do your research, you can find the tool that best suits your needs. Social listening tools like Mention are mid-level in price and features. They won't break the bank, but they provide helpful features like metrics, sentiment, and reporting.

Going beyond the mid-level tools, enterprise-level businesses can use a much more sophisticated (and expensive) listening tool such as Radian6 (`https://www.marketingcloud.com/products/social-media-marketing/radian6/`). This platform offers more advanced reporting features, integrations with CRMs, and help-desk software. It's ideal for advanced workflows of larger social listening teams as well.

Planning to listen

Earlier in this chapter, we discuss how important social listening is as a strategy, but how exactly does one execute on social listening? Make no mistake: Social listening doesn't happen by accident; it's a tactical endeavor. You execute social listening campaigns by using tools that "listen" for keywords. Before you begin implementing your social listening campaign, you need to determine exactly what keywords you need to listen for. Five keyword categories apply to virtually any business (see Figure 9-3):

>> **Brands:** This category includes your company name, brands, subbrands, and products.

>> **Topics:** Determine the industry-related topics people in your industry discuss and how you can contribute and build your authority on these topics.

>> **Competitors:** Establish who your competitors are, find out what people say about them, and ascertain what needs and problems your competitors' customers and prospects are voicing on the social web.

>> **Influencers:** Settle upon the influential brands and individuals who have an impact on your industry. Be aware of what they are saying about your shared industry on the social web.

>> **People:** Pay attention to what customers, prospects, and others are saying about the high-profile, public-facing individuals who are a part of your organization.

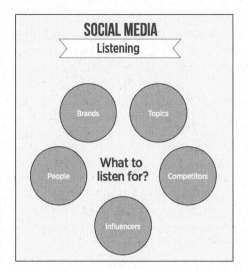

FIGURE 9-3:
The five keywords
that apply to
virtually any
business.

Apple, Inc., one of the world's largest technology companies, can serve as an example of a company that possibly engages heavily in social listening. Apple likely listens for all its brands, such as iOS and the Apple Watch (and many, many more of its creations). Alerts for conversations about industry-related topics also apply — think mentions of "smartphone camera" or "wearable tech." The company also probably pays close attention to what people say about its competitors, such as Android and Jeff Bezos, the CEO of Amazon. Major blogs and individuals influence the public's opinion about Apple, such as Gigaom and John Gruber, a producer of a technology-focused blog called Daring Fireball. Of course, Apple would want to be aware of conversations concerning its CEO Tim Cook and Arthur Levinson, the Chairman of the Board. If all this seems like a lot to be listening for, you're right; it is. In an organization the size of Apple, an enterprise-level social listening tool like Radian6 informs entire teams of people who are listening for conversations about all these examples — and many, many more.

Listening without paid tools

As we discuss earlier in the chapter, you can use Google Alerts as a free option for a social listening tool. However, sometimes you may need more sophisticated tools but still lack the budget to manage the cost. For example, your business might be a startup with a small team that's attracting a good deal of conversation on the social web. Or perhaps your brand name isn't specific enough to pull relevant mentions through the Google Alerts algorithm. The good news is that two tools are available for you to use in lieu of a paid social listening tool that can assist you much better than Google Alerts: Hootsuite and the Google search engine.

Hootsuite (https://hootsuite.com/) is a free social media management platform that provides a dashboard for social media management. It integrates with most major social media platforms including Twitter, Facebook, Instagram, LinkedIn, and YouTube. The dashboard allows you to set up "streams" of notifications such as mentions of specific Twitter handles and Facebook accounts. You can monitor social media updates in which you are tagged and set up streams around the specific keywords you select. Hootsuite gives you a low-budget way to find mentions of keywords you might otherwise have missed.

In addition to using Hootsuite, also consider running your keywords through a regular Google search. As you know, conversations about you aren't just happening on big social media sites. They also show up on places like Tumblr and Medium, as well as forums and blogs. Put your keywords in quotation marks so that Google searches for only the entire term, and voilà! You have a curated list of content that mentions your phrase. You don't have to scroll through the pages forever, but take a hard look at the first 10 to 20 links that come up; these are most essential to your reputation management.

Utilizing the feedback loop

After you locate mentions of your brand on the social web, it's best to respond inside your social listening campaign, which you do by creating and implementing various feedback loops. Generally speaking, a *feedback loop* is a procedure that helps businesses respond and address customer issues on the social web. It often works behind the scenes of the public-facing social media, but it's an important step in making sure that your prospects and customers feel valued and heard. Feedback loops (pictured in Figure 9-4) seek to accomplish a communicated resolution to customer issues with a predetermined period of time.

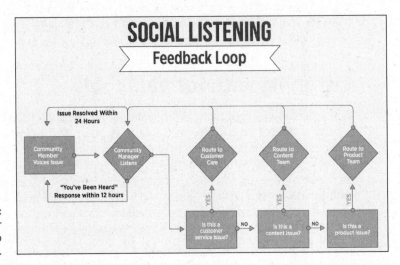

FIGURE 9-4: A flow chart for setting up feedback loops.

Say that a customer raises a concern that directly or indirectly involves your company, products, or services and posts on Twitter, for all the world to see. In the age of social media and digital communication, this is a common occurrence. That's why the first line of defense in the feedback loop is your community manager, the person at your company who monitors the conversations happening on the social web. Your company might use a paid tool like Mention or Radian6, described earlier, to listen for these complaints as they happen. You might have multiple community managers, or *you* might be the community manager. In any case, someone must be listening to the social web when your customer voices the issue.

Sometimes issues simply can't be resolved immediately, and that's okay. Just letting customers know that their message has been received is enough to make them feel respected and appreciated, and will buy you some time to find the resolution. Imagine being a waiter at a busy restaurant during happy hour and an unexpected table of ten walks into your section. At the moment, you don't have time to take this table's order or even drop off water. What can you do to buy yourself some time? You stop by the table, verbally acknowledge your customers' arrival, and inform them that you will be with them shortly.

We call this the "You've Been Heard" response, and it's a powerful way to de-escalate situations — both for busy restaurants and on the social web. The social media universe moves lightning fast. Twenty-four hours might as well be a thousand years, especially when unhappy customers are involved. That's why having someone in your company who is listening to what's being said and responding to issues quickly is crucial. We try to respond within 12 hours to Facebook messages and even quicker on Twitter, a channel with even less patience. This first-response time depends on the size of your company, so it's important to sit down and think about how quickly your organization can respond and what your feedback-loop time frame looks like — just be sure that customer service issues are addressed the same business day that the issue was raised.

After you've identified an issue and made the first response, your next step is to determine who in your company's hierarchy is equipped to resolve the issue. Most important is to realize that many different kinds of feedback loops exist, so where you route a concern relates to the size and organization of your company. One of the most common feedback loops is the customer service loop. When someone raises a customer service issue on social media, the community manager can route that issue to the customer care department. But you can structure all sorts of feedback loops. Perhaps a customer informs you of a broken video on your blog. In this case, the community manager routes the issue to your content team or, perhaps more specifically, to the managing editor of your blog. Customers can have all sorts of technical issues with your products and often take to social media with their frustrations. Addressing the concerns quickly and making sure that the right people in your company know about the problem are the most important actions to take.

By no means are feedback loops limited to the categories just mentioned. Perhaps your legal team needs to be in the know on certain issues. Maybe your CEO wants to address particular issues that people voice on social media. Or your products team may want to know how customers are describing and feel about the characteristics of your products.

Regardless of the type of feedback loop that your community manager identifies, putting a consistent response procedure in place is crucial. If a resolution is required to resolve the issue, who responds to the customer — the community manager? The customer care team? Or should you assign particular people in each department to handle responses? Ultimately, the decision depends on what makes sense for your team. Just remember that in a perfect world, a resolution should be presented to the customer within 24 hours of the original complaint.

Many social listening tools are available to make this process much easier. Tools that we mention earlier in this chapter, like Mention and Radian6, can equip your community manager with live streams of social media alerts based on specialized keywords. These platforms can also assign individual comments and tweets to specific members of your team, making the feedback loop process easier to implement.

Handling customer service issues

The Internet makes it easy for upset customers to vent their frustrations publicly in the heat of the moment. Whoever on your team is designated as social listener should be trained in how to communicate with upset customers on the web. Here are three steps for a social listener to follow when dealing with an upset customer on a public social media channel:

1. **Respond in a timely manner.**

   Reply to the issue within a designated amount of time. If you can communicate a resolution immediately, do so. Often, however, other people in your organization need to get involved in the conversation. Meanwhile, the customer should at least receive the "You've Been Heard" response in a reasonable time frame. Your business should decide what that time frame is, but remember that if you wait beyond 12 hours for any contact with the customer, you risk causing even more frustration.

2. **Empathize.**

   Empathy is agreeing that you'd feel the same way in someone else's shoes. It means you are not a robot, so canned or overly scripted responses won't cut it here. Making a statement of empathy — simply communicating that you realize the situation is frustrating — can go a long way in easing tension. An example of an empathy statement is, "We are so sorry to have caused you an inconvenience."

3. **Move the conversation to a private channel.**

Don't try to troubleshoot a customer-care issue on a public forum like Twitter or a public-facing Facebook page. Issues are much easier to address one-on-one. Giving customers individual attention also makes them feel appreciated and heard. Many customer-care issues also involve private information like email addresses and credit card info, so you want to be discreet about your customer's private details. Your company decides where this private conversation takes place, whether by phone, support ticket, or a private message on the social channel.

Any company with solid social customer service in place uses this three-step plan. Figure 9-5 shows an example of the hotel chain Best Western responding to a customer service issue posted on Facebook and moving the conversation to a private channel to be addressed.

FIGURE 9-5: Best Western moves a customer complaint to a private channel.

Source: https://www.facebook.com/BestWestern/posts_to_page/

Influencing and Building Brand Authority

REMEMBER

Social influencing is the act of establishing authority on the social web, often by distributing and sharing valuable content. Although social influencing may not have a direct effect on revenue or cost in your business, it does have a tremendous indirect effect on your business's value.

How does establishing authority on the social web indirectly affect the bottom line? The answer lies in the discipline of content marketing. Sharing descriptions and links to authoritative content created by your brand leads to more traffic to your website from social channels. Most important, social influencing increases "mind share." In other words, the more powerful your social influencing campaign is, the more your audience will understand what your organization does, the products you sell, and the solutions you offer. When you influence others, you start to occupy a space in their minds. Social influencing is all about using the social web to brand yourself with the people you're connected to.

For an example of social influencing, see Figure 9-6, which shows the home improvement company Lowe's linking to content on its website via Twitter. Consistently sharing authoritative content like this increases awareness for what Lowe's offers, establishes Lowe's as an authority in the home improvement space, and teaches the company's customers and prospects how to be successful with the products Lowe's sells.

FIGURE 9-6:
Lowe's uses Twitter to link to its website and build brand awareness and authority.

Source: https://twitter.com/Lowes/status/780098549962928128

Growing your social following

You can get more fans, followers, or connections for your social media channels by applying the same principles to all your social media channels in your effort to expand your following. Social sharing plug-ins, profile optimization, and indoctrination email series are all tactics that will grow your social channels.

Most content management systems (CMS) tools, such as WordPress, Shopify, or Squarespace, offer the capability to add social sharing plug-ins to many different places on your site. Use these plug-ins to make it easy for users to share your content on the major social media channels with a click of a button. Anytime you see something on your pages that can be social, be sure that social sharing functionality has been applied.

Optimizing your social media profiles also helps you to gain followers. Search engines on social media channels are notoriously weak and often rely on the information you provide on your profile to improve search functions. Make sure to use proper image sizes on your cover and profile pages, and complete every relevant field in your profile so that the channel's search engine can find you easily when potential connections are searching for you, your brands, and the topics you discuss and share content about. Include keywords where appropriate, but remember that you are on social media to relate to humans first, so make sure it's readable. Certainly include the names of your brands, relevant people, and location if that's an important aspect of your business. Add relevant links where appropriate. Also important is to be approachable by having active conversations with prospects, customers, and influencers.

If your business is implementing an email marketing strategy, your initial welcome email to new subscribers is another perfect avenue for growing your social media following. New subscribers are never more engaged and excited about you and your brand as when they first sign up, so use this email as an opportunity to ask them to connect with your social channels as well. For more on creating effective email campaigns, see Chapter 11.

Bouncing followers

Increasing the frequency of your marketing message increases intimacy with customers and prospects more quickly. The more often your prospects or customers come in contact with your message, the more familiar they become with your brand. Luckily, you don't need a huge marketing budget to increase frequency. You can use social media to bounce people from one social channel to another, building intimacy with your brand as they go.

For example, you can send an email to your list that bounces your subscribers to a blog post. The blog post then links to a YouTube video. The idea here is that some percentage of your audience will react in specific ways — such as by subscribing to your YouTube channel. This increases how often they see your marketing message because now, in addition to receiving your emails, they're also getting your updates via YouTube. Instead of investing in expensive ads via TV, radio, print, or billboards, you leverage relatively low-cost digital channels to increase frequency. Have a look at your current assets and see how you can bounce your audience from one channel to another to reach your audience more frequently.

Keeping your content interesting

The content you share on social media doesn't have to map directly back to the products and services you offer. In fact, incredibly boring social channels are those that broadcast marketing messages about products or services that don't involve conversation-worthy topics. Instead, the exceptional social media marketer discusses satellite topics that their existing market finds interesting.

Rosetta Stone, a language learning software, is particularly adept at this strategy. The company doesn't just talk about its language learning software. Instead, it offers an entire range of topics that various segments of its audience enjoy discussing. Because Rosetta Stone is in the language-learning business, it posts social media updates about international travel and culture, research on learning theory, and information about famous multilingual people. Rosetta Stone realizes that its audience doesn't want to talk about its software on the social web; its followers are much more likely to discuss German music, Celtic culture, or how the brain works.

Think about how your own business can expand conversation beyond the confines of the products and services that you sell. Research and map the topics that are relevant to your audience and what interests them outside your specific niche. Revisit the customer avatar discussed in Chapter 1 if needed.

Socializing blog content

Most blog posts have a short life span. Even if you're sending them to your email subscribers, most blog posts experience the bulk of their traffic in the first 24 to 48 hours. But how can you use social media to maximize the long-term impact of your blog content? Through the process of social distribution, your blog post can live a long, happy life. This process not only notifies social connections as soon as a post is published but also ensures that the post continues to cycle through your social feeds for days, weeks, and months afterward.

In the following sections, we describe six ways to properly share a new blog post on social media.

Splinter

Splintering your content is the process of breaking off bits and pieces of it and posting those pieces a là carte. When a piece of content is published and ready for sharing, you have all the source material needed to splinter shareable content for social media posts. You can splinter headlines, quotes, images, questions, and statistics found in your content and distribute them across your social media channels.

Visualize

Visual content is necessary to drive engagement and clicks on social media. Buffer, a software application company designed to manage accounts on social networks, saw an 18 percent increase of clicks, 89 percent increase in favorites, and 150 percent increase in retweets by using images, which goes to show that you're leaving a lot of distribution reach on the table if you don't incorporate images into your social strategy. The feature image (which usually appears at the top of your blog posts) is typically the first visual asset that you should share on social media channels. But one image isn't enough; you need to create a visual asset for every splinter. Quote images, a visual device with a simple picture and a standalone quote, for example, are perfect for Facebook and Twitter. Don't think you're hindered if you can't afford a graphic designer. Canva (`https://www.canva.com/`) is a free tool for creating images that you can share on social networks. Just make sure that your images fall within your social media channel's guidelines. Figure 9-7 shows a quote from a DigitalMarketer blog post that was turned into a quote image and then tweeted on Twitter.

Broadcast

After creating your splinters and visual assets, you need to broadcast your content on your social media channels. Focus your copy on the benefits and point of the article, and maintain a consistent personality and tone on your pages whenever possible. Then, how do you address your audience on your social channels? Do you usually address your audience in a light-hearted, bantering way, or do you typically use more serious and direct language? Appeal to your audience by maintaining that tone in your social media updates.

When broadcasting your content on Facebook, Twitter, LinkedIn, and others, use images from the article. For broadcasting on Twitter in particular, you can use several social media management tools to schedule posts for you (we recommend Hootsuite). Because Twitter posts have a shorter life span than other social media channels, you distribute your article more frequently. Create three tweets set to publish every three to four hours:

>> **Tweet 1 — Title:** Simply tweet the title of the blog post and a link to the blog post.

>> **Tweet 2 — Quote:** Splinter a quote from the blog post and tweet it, followed by a link to the blog post.

>> **Tweet 3 — Question:** Ask a question that the blog post will answer in this tweet and, as always, include a link to the blog post.

FIGURE 9-7:
Using a quote from a blog post and turning it into a visual tweet.

Source: https://twitter.com/DigitalMktr/status/
780361297116495872

Tag

When broadcasting a post, tag people and brands whenever it makes sense. You can tag the author or any companies and brands mentioned in your blog as you create the copy for your social media update. By doing so, you drive traffic to your post and draw attention from your social influencers and their followers. Also, use hashtags wherever appropriate — particularly on networks like Twitter. A hashtag is a simple way for people to search for tweets with a common topic. Figure 9-8 shows Hilton Hotels tweeting a contest with the hashtag #ATL (for Atlanta, Georgia) and #MusicMonday. Anyone who monitors these hashtags or topics has a chance to see these tweets.

FIGURE 9-8:
Hilton promotes
a contest by
using hashtags.

Source: https://twitter.com/HiltonHotels/status/
757613891610406913

Monitor

Most of the social media action occurs in the first 24 to 48 hours of a blog post's
life. During this time, you need to monitor the performance of that blog post on
the social web. One tool you can use for this monitoring is a URL shortener called
Bitly. URL shorteners like Bitly create shorter links that are easier to remember
and, more important, provide analytics. For example, Bitly reports on who's clicking from what channel, where people share your content, and which broadcast
and social media platform performed the best. It can also tell you what time your
post performed at its peak, where in the world your content is reaching, and even
which tweets performed best so that you can determine the best copy for your
audience on Twitter. In Figure 9-9, you see the reporting dashboard available for
a Bitly link.

Schedule

A normal, undistributed piece of content usually creates a spike in clicks before it
vanishes off the face of the social earth. That's why long-term automated distribution (or scheduling) is necessary. Scheduling your content into a social media
management tool results in perpetual sharing and content distribution with no
action needed from you after loading it into your library.

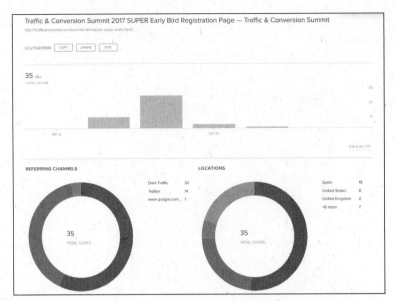

FIGURE 9-9:
Reporting data on a link from Bitly.

Source: *https://app.bitly.com/default/bitlinks/2d6HMtC#*

Tools like Edgar (www.meetedgar.com) are perfect for scheduling and automation across Twitter and LinkedIn. Edgar allows you to make categories and choose what time content publishes using those categories. Then the library randomizes itself and posts content in rotation so that you're not bombarding your audience with the same tweets day after day. Keep in mind that when you're broadcasting your content, you already have everything you need to schedule. After you've set up your three broadcasting tweets (see the "Broadcast" section, earlier in this chapter) the first day your content is published, take those same tweets and load them into a tool like Edgar. Doing so puts your tweets into automated rotation and keeps social traffic flowing to your blog posts.

WARNING

Use your best judgment when automating your social updates. For instance, you may want to pause your automation schedule during a crisis or a natural disaster. Your audience may view you as disrespectful or oblivious if your automation schedule keeps you tweeting about your latest sale when a hurricane has just devastated the coast.

Networking That Moves the Needle

You've probably heard the old adage, "It's not what you know, it's who you know," which, of course, means that you have to engage in networking. Networking is all about the public relations side of your business. In traditional public relations (PR) endeavors, you seek out third parties such as newspaper journalists who can amplify your marketing message. Social networking accomplishes this same goal by finding and associating with authoritative and influential individuals and brands on the social web.

Although social influencing is about distributing your own content such as blog posts, podcasts, and videos to establish authority, you can connect with others via social networking by sharing other people's content with your audience. As with person-to-person networking, in social networking you use social media to look for and to establish connections in the hopes of creating mutually beneficial partnerships with an individual or a brand. This mutually beneficial partnership can involve writing guest posts for each other's respective blogs or gaining a speaker for an event that your company is putting on.

You can use social networking to reach out to journalists, bloggers, and podcasters who hang out on social media channels. Brands that have authority in print publications or radio stations also fall into this category. Social networking is a high-impact activity that can move the needle for your business in leaps and bounds.

Tapping into niche media

Consider a startup software company with a great product and a desire to earn media mentions to grow awareness for the business. This company could target big players like the NBC network, with the potential to reach millions. Or it could target mid-sized blogs that specialize in startups like TechCrunch, an online publisher that primarily covers businesses ranging from startups to established firms. The reach on TechCrunch is lower than that of NBC, but still significant. It would be wonderful to be featured in outlets that have enormous reach; however, as a general rule, the difficulty of earning a media mention on a platform increases as the amount of reach increases.

The good news is that thousands of niche media players are running blogs, podcasts, YouTube channels, and more. Although you sacrifice the amount of reach you can attain with any one niche media outlet, securing media mentions on these niche properties is much easier than on the large outlets. Enough niche media mentions can, in the aggregate, exceed the reach of even major networks like NBC, however.

Reaching niche media

Niche media companies are small- to medium-sized firms that also focus on and publish content on a specific topic. These small publishers may be creating great content but often aren't well-known nationally or even within their field. To reach niche media properties en masse, you have to understand what these properties want. That's not difficult, though, because it's the same thing that every media property needs: great content from reliable sources. A small, niche media player, however, doesn't have access to teams of journalists and content creators working around the clock to produce new content. It's constantly searching for more content to serve to its audience.

When you reach out to niche media properties, you have to speak their language and address their pain points. Let them know that you are a reliable, authoritative resource who can contribute great content to their audience — and all you need in return is a byline that links to your website or landing page. Remember that great content educates, inspires, or entertains an audience, and that is exactly what these niche media properties are searching for.

Networking by topic

As you work to earn media mentions and build partnerships through social networking, brainstorm satellite topics that relate to your company, and use those topics as a way to network with others. Chances are, you'll determine plenty of topics from your brainstorming session that are outside your organization's expertise. You can take the opportunity to locate brands and individuals who are authorities in those topics and use social networking strategies to form connections and partnerships with those people. Share their content with your audience often, and tag authors or brands as you go. By doing so, you associate and potentially partner with these brands and individuals as part of the networking phase of your social media marketing mix.

For example, if the language learning software company Rosetta Stone wants to share content about traveling to Spain on its Facebook page, it might share an article about that topic from a reliable travel brand like Lonely Planet or TripAdvisor. By sharing content about something that interests potential customers, Rosetta Stone would simultaneously be networking with influential brands.

Creating a social media "short list"

Creating a "short list" of this nature involves a specific process that uses Twitter to organize the people and brands you want to network with. If there is one thing that is more valuable to media properties than new content sources, it's gaining more exposure to the content that they already have. This means that sharing your influencers' content with your audience on the social web is a surefire way to build goodwill and increase the likelihood that the influencer will notice you and return the favor in kind. However, the firehose of content on Twitter makes tracking down and organizing your influencers' content challenging. You need a way to easily identify and share their content. That's where short lists come into play.

Several tools are available to help you identify the key players in your industry, niche, and other topics relevant to your audience. Paid tools like GroupHigh and Inkybee allow you to track down influential bloggers, organized by topic. Free resources like Klout (`https://klout.com/home`) or Kred (`http://home.kred/`) are social scoring platforms that score social media users based on how influential they are around particular topics.

More likely than not, however, you already have an idea of the people and brands who can move the needle for your business! Find their Twitter profiles and create a Twitter list with their handles. Next, set up a stream for your new short list using Hootsuite. You can then sort out the people and brands to network with from the general noise of Twitter. You can easily reference the content they are sharing, join the conversation, and create some goodwill by sharing their content with your audience. Start with 10 to 20 influencers and then keep an eye on who they are networking with so that you can grow and curate your list. Keep your list up to date. If an influencer starts to wander outside the realm of your topic, remove him and start the search all over again.

Flipping the script on media outreach

The web holds such an abundance of information that a phenomenon in digital public relations has been developing: reverse media outreach. Not only are you working to reach out to long-tail media but the media, in general, are also using the Internet to find reliable sources for their content. Media properties use search engines like Google to find experts they can interview, quote, and otherwise use to create content for their media properties. To take advantage of this phenomenon, you need to position yourself as an expert and make yourself available to these media players.

To attract the media to your business, create authoritative, relevant content on a regular schedule and distribute it on your social channels. By becoming a content creator yourself, you increase the likelihood of contact by both traditional and niche publishers to get information for the content they produce for their audience. Second, accept interviews. If you show a little inclination to provide blurbs for blogs or appear as a guest on a podcast, you won't be asked to do so very often. Allow media to contact you, accept the interviews, and more requests will follow.

Third, learn the basics of SEO for the content you create. Media are using search engines like Google to locate their sources, so you need to understand how a search engine finds you, your information, and your products or services. To learn more about search engine optimization, turn to Chapter 8.

Staying compliant with the law

The Federal Trade Commission regulates how businesses use earned or paid media mentions for promotion. If you give any sort of incentive or reward to a media property in exchange for a mention — be it a blog, video, podcast, or other type of media — make sure to disclose that information in the content. Incentives can include money, free samples, or anything else you've given in exchange for the mention. To stay current on the FTC Endorsement Guidelines, visit www.ftc.gov.

Selling on Social Channels

How do you generate sales on social media channels? The answer is that you don't — at least not directly. Instead, use a value-first strategy to generate leads and sales. The ultimate goal with social selling is to move prospects and leads from channels that you don't own, such as Twitter, Facebook, and YouTube, to channels that you do own, such as your email list. By doing so, you position your prospects and leads to engage with you on a channel you control.

REMEMBER

Leading with content is the first rule of the value-first strategy on social media. Content is the native communication medium on the social web; everyone wants information that entertains, inspires, or educates. Use this content in your social selling strategy to move people from social channels like Facebook to your website and, ultimately, onto your email list.

Leading with value

The primary concept to understand about social selling is that it is contingent on consistent implementation of the social listening, influencing, and networking. Prospects are much more likely to become loyal, repeat customers if they know, like, and trust your brand. Providing value first means that you frequently give your social media followers a reason to know, like, and trust you by providing social customer care, solid content, and participating in conversations with your prospects, customers, and influencers. After you give your social media followers a reason to trust you, only then do you see results from your social selling efforts.

Designing "value first" offers

Approach social selling with care; high-dollar and complex offers not only go against protocol on most social channels but also just don't perform well. Instead, focus on offers that provide value before you ask your prospect or customer to make huge commitments. You can place three different offers on any of your social media channels that allow you to sell without moving your prospects along the customer journey too quickly:

» **Ungated offers:** Asking someone to read your blog post is considered an offer. Reading a blog post may not cost money, but it does cost time. The majority of your offers on social media should be ungated.

» **Gated offers:** This is content that requires contact information (name, email address, and other information) to access. Keep in mind that you're not asking for money at this stage; you're asking for permission to contact a lead.

» **Deep discounts:** Flash sales or offers at 50 percent off or greater are value-first offers and are appropriate for social media marketing.

We discuss ungated, gated, and deep-discount offers in greater detail in Chapter 3.

Avoiding Social Media Mistakes

No discussion about social media marketing would be complete without acknowledging some big mistakes to avoid on the social web:

» **Don't respond when you're angry.** Some social media users try to bait you into responding unprofessionally. If someone makes you angry, give yourself time to cool off before responding, or assign someone else you trust to handle the situation. Always be professional in your response.

» **Don't buy followers/connections.** It doesn't make ethical or business sense to have robots or fake accounts follow your social channels. Focus these resources on creating a great experience for the followers you do have, and your social channels will grow naturally.

» **Don't try to be everywhere.** The social web is far too large to have a presence everywhere. Master a few channels where you can have influence, network with people, and sell your products and services. Use a tool (discussed in this chapter and also in Chapter 16) to conduct social listening on channels where you don't have an active presence.

» **Don't be a salesperson.** There is a time and place for social selling. Be strategic and intentional with offers that are appropriate for social media channels.

» **Don't automate everything.** Your social channels should be personable and approachable. Avoid automating every update, and leave room for your users to connect with you on a human level.

Knowing When to Automate

Although we end the previous section by cautioning you not to automate every-thing, there are times when automating your social media content is acceptable. In fact, you can greatly enhance your social influencing efforts by using automa-tion tools. We can say the same for social selling. Automated tools can keep your gated offers and deep discount offers in front of your followers without manual effort. On the flip side, you can appear very disingenuous if you attempt to automate the conversations that take place in the social listening and social networking stage. These conversations require an actual person responding in real time, whether you're handling social customer care issues or participating in discussions with influencers on the social web.

Chapter **10**

Tapping into Paid Traffic

How do you get traffic to your website? This is the number one question that business owners ask about digital marketing. The truth is that getting traffic to a website is not a problem. In fact, thousands of traffic platforms, including Google, Facebook, and Twitter, allow you to buy advertising and would love nothing more than to send traffic to your website. The question isn't how to get traffic; rather, it's what to do with the traffic when you get it. What product or service should you offer? What content should you show your visitors? Should you ask them to give you their contact information or come right out and ask them to buy a product or service?

Paid traffic is available in many forms, such as pay-per-click advertising using platforms like Google AdWords, banner ads, and paid ads on social networks that include Facebook and Twitter. Paid traffic is a powerful tool because it helps to build your brand, makes people aware of your products or services, and generates leads and sales for your products and services.

In this chapter, we discuss the major advertising platforms and when you should choose to use each one. We also show you how to set up a powerful form of advertising called retargeting and how to troubleshoot your ad campaigns to get the most out of every campaign you run.

Visiting the Traffic Store

Imagine that you and your sweetheart are browsing through recipes, deciding what to have for dinner tonight. You settle on a rice dish that you've been wanting to try for a while. The only issue is that you have no rice on hand.

How should you proceed? Should you grow the rice for your dinner tonight? That would be ridiculous, right? Instead, you head to the supermarket and buy a package of rice.

Rice is a commodity that is bought and sold every day — and so is website traffic. If you want traffic, you need to go to the traffic store.

After you understand paid traffic, you can quickly test content and offers by turning traffic on and off like a water faucet. This capability is important because it allows you to quickly test new offers, landing pages, and content without waiting on slower traffic sources like SEO and social media. When you start treating website traffic like the commodity it is, you finally have a predictable and reliable source of website traffic.

REMEMBER

No perfect traffic store exists. For instance, your audience may not use certain platforms or your brand may face advertising restrictions on certain platforms (industries such as electronic cigarettes, dating, and dieting encounter such situations). To determine the proper store, you must do research, as we discuss. Also, the strategy and the system we examine throughout this chapter apply to whatever traffic store from which you choose to purchase.

Understanding Traffic Temperature

You move people toward a conversion by creating relationships with them. As you run paid traffic campaigns, you need to understand where you stand in your relationship with your leads and customers. Are they just now learning about you; are they aware of you but haven't bought from you; have they bought from you and now you're working to turn them into lifelong customers and raving fans?

At our company, we refer to where we are in the relationship with a prospect or customer as traffic temperature. To build an effective traffic system, the strategy you need to employ is knowing who you're talking to by defining your target audience, and the stage of your relationship, so that you make the appropriate offer at the right time. Traffic temperature consists of three different levels (see Figure 10-1):

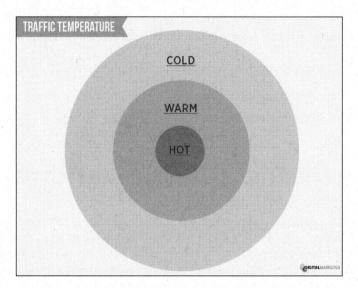

TRAFFIC TEMPERATURE

FIGURE 10-1:
The three stages
of traffic
temperature.

>> **Cold traffic:** These are people who have never heard of you, your brands, or your products or services. You have no relationship with these people, but they are important because they bring new leads and sales to your business. You must build trust, credibility, and authority with your cold traffic. Before they agree to buy from you, they need to prove that your brand is a worthy investment of their time and money. Make ungated offers to valuable content on your blog, podcast, or YouTube channel to cold traffic. Turn to Chapter 3 for more information about ungated offers.

>> **Warm traffic:** These are people who have heard about you or engaged with your brand but haven't bought from you. They may have read your blog, listened to your podcast, or joined your email newsletter. People in the warm traffic stage are evaluating whether they like what you say, and are interested in learning more and possibly purchasing from you. They're deciding whether your company is the best option to solve their problem. They're also evaluating your competitors to see whether they do it better or more cheaply. Make entry point offers and gated offers to these folks to get them in the door without much risk. See Chapter 3 for more information about entry point offers and gated offers.

>> **Hot traffic:** As you've probably guessed, these are people who have bought from you. They may be first-time buyers to repeat buyers. These are the customers you have already spent time, money, and energy to acquire. The biggest mistake that advertisers make is concentrating only on bringing in new leads and sales. The savvy marketer also uses paid traffic to sell more and more often to the customers he already has. Make profit maximizer offers to hot traffic. For more information about profit maximizers, turn to Chapter 3.

In summary, you want to follow these steps for traffic temperature:

1. Introduce yourself to cold traffic with valuable content.

2. Convert warm traffic to leads and low dollar buyers.

3. Sell more and more often to existing buyers.

Choosing the Right Traffic Platform

Before you craft a marketing message, decide what traffic platform your audience is using, which you do by determining where your market is "hanging out" online. The traffic platform you make your offer on is essential to the success of your campaign. Even with the perfect marketing message, if your ad is placed on the wrong traffic platform, your entire campaign will fail. For instance, if your target audience doesn't use Twitter, you shouldn't be spending money advertising on it.

You have thousands of traffic stores to choose from, but what traffic store is the best match for your business? If you're looking to buy traffic, do so from a source that can help you reach your market. To reach your market, you must first define your customer avatar (see Chapter 1 to learn more about creating your customer avatar).

Traffic stores such as Twitter, Pinterest, YouTube, and others have aggregated millions of users, and each platform has slightly different demographics. Use broad demographic information (such as age, gender, and income) to help determine the correct traffic store that your audiences use, and thus the best store to reach them on. To help create your customer avatar, use research tools, such as the analytics software company Alexa. This type of tool gives the user demographics of traffic stores and websites. Also, research your audiences' specific interests (such as their hobbies, the books and blogs they read, authority figures they follow, and the pain points they have) to determine how to target your audiences after you're on the platform.

This research takes time, but when done correctly, it helps you determine both the correct traffic store to advertise on and the message you use to reach out to your audiences. The next section examines the Big Six traffic stores that you can reach your audiences on.

Introducing the Big Six traffic platforms

We say it earlier, but it's worth saying again here: You have thousands of traffic stores for businesses and marketers to choose from. In this section, however, we discuss the six main traffic stores on the web today:

- » Facebook
- » Twitter
- » Google
- » YouTube
- » Pinterest
- » LinkedIn

Chances are, your market hangs out on one or more of these traffic stores, allowing you to effectively reach out to your target audience. The Big Six are effective traffic stores because

- » They experience a large volume of users and have the necessary resources that give you the capability to scale campaigns.
- » Their ad interfaces are user friendly and easy to use.
- » Their targeting options are (usually) better than other traffic stores on the web. These traffic platforms allow you to target ads to people based on everything from their demographics, interests, the keywords they've typed into a search engine, and the pages they've visited on your website. For example, if you sell swimming pools in San Diego, you might target your ads based on any of the following criteria:
  - People who live in San Diego.
  - People who are interested in water sports.
  - People who typed the query "in ground swimming pool san diego" into a search engine.
  - People who have visited the in-ground swimming pool product page on your website.

You can, in fact, combine these targeting options to, for example, target people living in San Diego who have an interest in water sports.

No matter the experience level or the industry of your business, the Big Six give you effective platforms for reaching almost any market, in almost every part of the globe. In the following sections, we cover the best uses and nuances related to dealing with these traffic stores.

Facebook

With well over 1.7 billion monthly active users (users who have logged in to Facebook within the last 30 days), Facebook allows you to reach almost any market. The Facebook Ads Manager is user friendly and offers a multitude of targeting options, so you can get really specific when targeting your market, thereby making your ads more personal and effective. Because Facebook is easy to use and fairly inexpensive to buy traffic on, it's a good place to start if you're new to paid traffic or are testing a new strategy. Plus, you can apply many strategies used in Facebook on other advertising platforms.

Ads on Facebook are like commercials on TV or the radio: You're displaying your message in front of your audiences, but you're also interrupting those audiences. So you need to make sure to put your ads in front of the right people and to give your audiences a reason to click your ad, which is what the domain registrar and web hosting company GoDaddy does in the Facebook ad shown in Figure 10-2.

Source: https://adespresso.com/academy/ads-examples/41161-godaddy/?_sf_s=ford&lang=en

FIGURE 10-2:
GoDaddy gives a reason to click its Facebook ad.

Facebook provides many objectives for marketers to select from. Choosing your objective is the most important part when setting up your campaign because it's your way of telling Facebook exactly what you want your campaign to accomplish. Therefore, before you launch your campaign, know your end goal (such as to send people to your website, promote your company Facebook page, increase conversions on your website, get video views, or any of many more possibilities), and align that goal with your Facebook objective. To determine your objective, ask yourself: Who am I targeting and where do I want to send them?

After you complete the first step of setting up your campaign (choosing your objective), you move on to setting up the audience you intend to reach. This step is essential. If you choose the wrong audience, your Facebook ad is likely to fail or, at the very least, not reach its full potential. To ensure that you reach the right audience, your targeting needs to be specific. The more specific your campaign is, the better it will perform. To improve your campaign's specificity, answer the following questions about your target market for *every* ad you plan to run on Facebook:

>> **Who are the figures, thought leaders, or big brands in your niche?** Chances are, members of your audience follow these influencers on Facebook.

>> **What books, magazines, newspapers do your ideal customers read?**

>> **What events do they attend?**

>> **What websites do they frequent?**

>> **Where do they live?**

>> **What tools do they use?** These tools can range from programs such as Photoshop or Evernote to physical tools such as fishing rods or lawn care equipment.

>> **What's specifically unique about this audience?**

By knowing the answers to these questions, you can specifically target your audiences' likes, behaviors, and locations on Facebook, making your ad more personal and more likely to be placed in front of an audience who is open to your message. Also, targeting specific likes and interests helps to narrow down your potential audience size, which is good because you don't want it to be too broad; if it is, your ad can be less effective.

At our company, we have found the most success, in terms of conversions and high Relevance Scores (the algorithm that Facebook uses to judge the quality of your ad; similar to Google's Quality Score) with our Facebook ads when the audience size is made up of 500,000–1,000,000 people (plus or minus several thousand — it doesn't have to be *exactly* 500,000, for instance; there's wiggle room). This way, you're showing your ad to not only a large enough audience but also a specific one that will find your ad relevant.

If your business is local (as opposed to a national or international company) and you're targeting a specific town, city, state, or region, you don't have to worry about the size of your audience. Often, the audience size for local ads on Facebook doesn't reach half a million to a million people; the town you're targeting may not even have a population of that size. Local businesses don't need to worry about audience size but instead should be concerned with how you're targeting that audience. All other businesses that aren't local should focus on how you're targeting your audience *and* the size of your audience.

The next step is to create your ad copy. When writing your ad's copy, speak to your audience based on the pain point you're targeting and where you are in the relationship. For instance, you don't talk to someone you've just met the way you speak to someone you've known for ten years, and the same goes for your copy writing. Think of your ads in the context of where you are in the relationship with your lead or customer.

Next, follow these tips when writing your ad's copy:

>> Grab your target audience's attention by calling out to it. For instance, you might call out to your target city, such as, "Hey, Seattle!" or use what residents call themselves, such as, "Hey, Austinites!" or even call to people by their interests, such as "Hey, amateur wrestling fans!"

>> Within the copy, hit upon a pain point your target audience deals with and then give people a solution (your offer, of course).

>> If you have the room, add a sentence to eliminate doubt and overcome a reason the customer may have for choosing not to buy.

>> Finally, consider what you want people to do after they've finished reading your ad. Include a strong call to action to help move them to the next level.

Next, make sure that the image accompanying your copy portrays and backs up your marketing message. The image ties the ad together and makes the ad feel congruent. You don't want an image that feels as though it came out of left field and has nothing to do with the copy or the offer. The image should stand out and be eye catching but not spammy-looking, so avoid too many arrows or obnoxious colors. Ultimately, you want the image to resonate with your market. If making images isn't your strong suit, or you don't have a graphic designer, consider using tools such as Canva (https://www.canva.com/) or outsourcing your graphics with services such as Fiverr (https://www.fiverr.com/) or Upwork (https://www.upwork.com/) to create professional images for your ads.

Figure 10-3 depicts the elements that make up a Facebook ad and what to include.

TIP

For cold audiences in particular, you don't want your Facebook ad to "scream" that it's an ad; rather, you want the ad to be informative and provide value. Remember that you're building credibility with your audiences. Ad copy that targets cold audiences is often longer than ads for warm or hot audiences. It also contains more information about the offer and what happens when people click the ad. In contrast, your language can be a little more informal and your copy shorter with warm and hot audiences.

You can find more details and how-to guides from Facebook Blueprint (www.facebook.com/blueprint), an educational resource created by Facebook that offers free online courses to help people take their Facebook campaigns to the next level.

Twitter

With Twitter, you can reach almost any market, and targeting on Twitter is very similar to Facebook. People use Twitter to consume content and expect to find content in their Twitter feed, which makes this a great platform to run traffic to cold audiences. Use your tweets to introduce yourself and drive people to content, such as your blog, that provides value, establishes your brand as an authority, and starts building a relationship with your audiences.

You can create many different paid ads on Twitter, whether you seek to gain more Twitter followers or to generate website clicks and conversions. As with your efforts on Facebook, your Twitter campaign objectives should align with your overall campaign objective or end goal. Figure 10-3 depicts a promoted tweet from Liberty Mutual that clearly states its benefit and includes a call to action. Notice how the image the company uses is congruent with the copy of the tweet.

FIGURE 10-3:
A promoted tweet from Liberty Mutual.

Source: https://twitter.com/LibertyMutual/status/738760608796053504

To encourage engagement with your tweets (that is, to cause retweets and likes), link to something of value and don't make your tweets super "salesy." The most effective sponsored tweets are the ones with the same look and feel of a regular tweet. They don't mention a product or sell anything. These tweets are less invasive and are known as *native ads*. Native ads follow the form and function of the medium in which they are placed. A native ad is not exclusive to Twitter and can be found on other paid traffic platforms. Native Twitter ads look like any other tweet and consist of good copy that piques interest and links to informative content that drives traffic off the Twitter platform to your predetermined landing page (see Chapter 7 for more on landing pages).

With Twitter, you typically target cold traffic with content to drive awareness for your brands, products and services. Therefore, rather than drive traffic to a traditional sales landing page for your product, drive traffic to informative blog articles that provide value and build credibility. Then, in your article, weave calls to action to a relevant offer that lead people to the next traffic temperature. Return to Chapters 5 and 6 for blogging strategies to use for your Twitter landing pages.

REMEMBER

To be effective, each landing page article needs to have standalone value. In other words, readers derive value from the landing page regardless of whether they take your offer. To avoid having a negative impact on your relationship with a prospect and harming your chances of gaining a customer, be sure that your landing page delivers on the promise you made within your tweet. For instance, if you tweet about bridal shower ideas and the link you provide doesn't deliver, people will view you as less trustworthy and associate your content with negative click bait.

TIP

When using Twitter, look for tweets that perform exceptionally well. If one of your tweets results in high engagement, the tweet will likely do well as an advertisement. Consider investing money in that tweet and promoting it to your cold audiences.

Google

Google AdWords is a great traffic platform because you can present ads to people when they are actively looking for a solution. Google's AdWords program shows ads to people based on the keywords they type into the Google search engine. For example, if a searcher types "buy dog treats" into Google, a company that sells dog treats can place a bid to show an ad on the results page, as shown in Figure 10-4. People use Google to research products and services, and the search queries they type in offer insight into the pain points they face and the solutions and benefits they are looking for.

In comparison to other platforms, Google ads are seen as less interruptive and invasive, and they require less of an introduction to your prospects because people are actively searching for a solution. Although AdWords is generally more expensive than other traffic stores, it is very effective at generating high-quality leads and customers: Even though they may never have heard of you, these potential customers actively seek solutions and are often more open to becoming leads and customers.

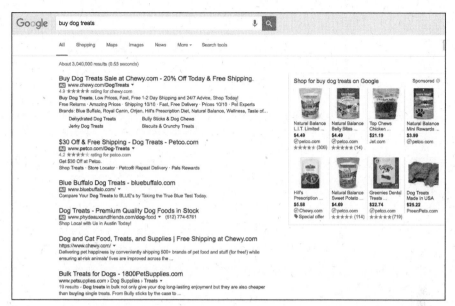

FIGURE 10-4:
Ads appear for
the search query
"buy dog treats"
on the Google
platform.

Source: https://www.google.com/webhp?sourceid=chrome-instant&ion=1&espv=2&ie=UTF-
8#q=buy%20dog%20treats

Here are some aspects to note about Google AdWords:

» **You need a goal:** AdWords isn't a platform you just get on to run some traffic and test your market. Deciding on a goal before you begin your campaign is imperative. If you're new to this, you may want to start with another traffic store that is cheaper, such as Facebook, to test the market before you graduate to AdWords.

» **You pay based on clicks:** You pay only when someone actually clicks your ad (which helps to control your budget).

» **You can target by location:** There's a big opportunity for geo-targeting for local businesses, so you can specifically "speak" to local markets. This feature works well for both local businesses and larger companies looking to segment a national or international campaign.

You should begin with researching the keywords that you intend to bid on for your ad. When conducting keyword research, remember these tips:

» Use tools to help you find keyword ideas and estimate how the keywords may perform. Google Keyword Planner (https://adwords.google.com/KeywordPlanner) is such a tool and is a free service provided by Google AdWords.

» Enter keywords and keyword phrases related to your business.

>> Use spy tools such as iSpionage (`https://www.ispionage.com/`), SEMrush (`https://www.semrush.com/`) or SpyFu (`https://www.spyfu.com/`) to research your competitors or other companies in your niche to gain insight on the keywords they're targeting.

As you conduct your keyword research, be aware that you can set four types of parameters on your keywords within AdWords. These are known as keyword match types. You use them to set and control which searchers trigger your ad to appear after they've typed in a search query. Here are the keyword match types, along with examples for each:

>> **Exact match:** This match type means that someone has to type your keyword or keyword phrase *exactly* as it appears in your campaign in order for your ad to be displayed. You designate exact match by putting square brackets around a keyword. For example:

[lawn service]

If you have the exact-match keyword [lawn service] in your AdWords campaign, the only time your ad appears is when someone types the search query *lawn service* into Google.

>> **Phrase match:** Your keyword must appear in the *same order* as it appears in your campaign to trigger your ad. Phrase match is designated by quotation marks around the keyword, as in the following:

"lawn service"

If you have the phrase *"lawn service"* in your AdWords campaign, your ad could be triggered for the following search queries:

- Best lawn service

- Lawn service Austin

- Dan's lawn service and landscaping

The preceding terms trigger your phrase match ad because the words *lawn* and *service* appear next to each other in the search query. However, with phrase match, your ad would *not* be triggered by the following search queries:

- Lawn mowing service

- Lawn and landscaping service

Your ad would not be triggered by those search queries because the words *lawn* and *service* do *not* appear in the *same order* as they do in the campaign.

>> **Broad match:** With broad match, Google shows your ad for similar phrases to and relevant variations from the keyword. This includes plurals, synonyms,

misspellings, and related searched and relevant variations. In contrast to the other keyword match types, broad match has no symbol designation.

If your broad match keyword is *lawn service*, Google may trigger your ad for search queries that include

- Lawn mowing service prices

- Lawn services near me

- Lawn service name ideas

- Creative lawn service names

While this can place your ad in front of a large audience, it may not place it in front of the *right* audience. Because broad match can trigger so much, we don't recommend it for someone just starting out in AdWords.

» **Broad match modifier (BMM):** This keyword type triggers your ad for close variations, such as misspellings (but not synonyms), in any order. BMM falls between broad match and phrase match in that you have more control than broad match, but it's not quite as restrictive as phrase match. You designate a BMM with a plus sign (+) in front of your keywords:

+lawn +service

Google knows keywords with the plus sign in front of them *must* appear some- where within the search query, but not necessarily in the order they appear in the campaign. Search queries that may trigger this ad include the following:

- Lawn mowing service

- Lawn and landscaping service

- Professional lawn care services

After you research your keywords and decide on the keyword match type to use in your campaign, you select how much to bid for your keywords. Remember these tips when choosing your bidding strategy in AdWords:

- Select the Manually Set My Bid For Clicks option, which allows you to be in control of your budget. Otherwise, your budget is automated by Google AdWords.

- When first starting a campaign, use a default bid of $2– $3 until you can see how competitive your keywords are.

- Set a daily budget, again to keep your budget under your control.

When you're finally ready to write your ad, follow these tips and tricks to create copy for Google ads:

» **Include a call to action.** What is the ultimate action you want your target audience to take after people have read your ad? Tell them what you want them to do in your ad. Calls to action can include "call now," "download your free report," and "order today," among other possibilities.

>> **Use your keywords.** Include the keywords you are bidding on within the ad's copy. Not only does this help with your Quality Score (the algorithm that Google uses to determine how much you ultimately pay for a click), it also bolds the keywords that match a person's search query, which makes your ad stand out more.

>> **Ask a question.** Consider using questions to call out to your audience. Questions often capture people's attention more than a statement does. For instance, instead of the copy "Get rid of termites" try "Termite infestation?" Or instead of "Experienced and insured plumber in St. Louis" try "Looking for a reliable St. Louis plumber?"

>> **Reference holidays or local events.** When your ad mentions upcoming events or holidays, it seems more timely and relevant to searchers.

>> **Focus on benefits and speak to your prospects' pain points.** Don't include your product's specifications, such as size, color, or even what the product does, within your ad. That doesn't entice people to click; rather, people want to know how your product can make their lives better. Within your ad, focus on the emotional outcomes your product provides, not the technical specs. (You include tech specs within the product description on your sales landing page, as we describe in great detail in Chapter 7.)

YouTube

YouTube is great traffic platform for building relationships with customers and prospects. Because of the different kinds of ads you can create with this traffic platform, you can build relationships and move people from cold prospects to hot repeat buyers, all within the YouTube platform. For instance, you can use YouTube to establish yourself as an authority and give value to your market, and then send people to more content to learn from, such as another video or a blog post, after which you retarget them (we detail retargeting in the latter half of this chapter) with video ads to make an entry point offer. See Chapter 3 for more information about entry point offers.

Note that people are conditioned to skip YouTube ads. With the advertisements that play before someone else's video, like the one from GoPro camera company pictured in Figure 10-5, you have only five seconds to grab your audience's attention before people click the Skip button.

After the five-second threshold, people often have the chance to skip your ad, and if you haven't given them a reason to stay, your audiences will likely skip your ad to view the content they originally came to watch. To keep them from skipping, do one or more of the following within the first five seconds:

FIGURE 10-5:
A GoPro YouTube
ad with a Skip
button.

» Call out to your audience to grab people's attention. For instance, you can call out to your market based on where people live (city or state) or address one of their interests.

» Ask them a question they can relate to and identify with. For example, a home improvement company might place an advertisement on a video about replacing a bathroom sink and open that video ad with the question, "Are you updating your bathroom?"

» Speak to a pain point they are facing or a benefit they are seeking.

» Entertain them.

» Give your target audience a reason to stay by immediately providing value so that people want to visit your channel or website to learn more.

Other ways to ensure that your ad grabs your target audience's attention is to include an enticing thumbnail image (the static image overlaying your video before someone plays it) and a strong video title, also called a headline. The title and the thumbnail explain and demonstrate what your video is about. Your thumbnail image is one of the first things people see, so you want to make sure that your first impression is appealing and eye catching. If creating professional-looking images is outside your skill set, use services such as Fiverr or tools such as Canva to make high-quality thumbnail images. Then back up your image with an engaging title or headline. Include your targeted keywords within the headline (and within the video's description) to improve your targeting.

Pinterest

This social network has more than 100 million active users, with 47 million-plus of those users living in the United States. It's therefore an ideal traffic store for those advertising in America. Pinterest users are heavily female: Women make up about 85 percent of Pinterest (and of those, 42 percent are adult women with spending power). Although Pinterest is an ideal platform to target women living in America, Pinterest is growing both internationally and among adult male users: Pinterest is the fastest-growing social network by percentage, and one-third of new accounts are created by men.

Pinterest users are in an open-to-buy mindset. In fact, 93 percent of Pinterest users plan purchases by using Pinterest. Studies have also found that when Pinterest traffic was referred to Shopify, it resulted in an average purchase of $50 from Shopify. As a traffic store, Pinterest has a lot of potential, to say the least.

To advertise on Pinterest, you create what is known as a *promoted pin*, which is an advertisement that allows you to target your market based on demographics, locations, and devices used, as well as people's interests and the search queries that people type in. Pinterest, like Google, is run on a cost-per-click (CPC) basis with a budget that you can specify, and you pay only when someone clicks through the pin to your website. Similar to Twitter, Pinterest is a native advertising system; create advertisements that blend in with the platform so that the ad follows the form and function of any other piece of content on the platform. Figure 10-6 depicts a promoted pin from Kraft, in the right half of the figure, for its recipes board.

FIGURE 10-6:
A promoted pin from Kraft.

Source: https://www.pinterest.com/pin

Before you create your promoted pin, research the keywords you intend to target. You can do your keyword research right on the Pinterest platform. Start by typing in the main keyword for your market in the Pinterest search bar. As you type, Pinterest gives you suggested searches, which are the most commonly searched queries that include your keyword on Pinterest. This technique helps you focus in on the keywords to target on Pinterest. You can also use online tools, such as SpinKeywords, to research keywords for your promoted pin campaign.

Each promoted pin is allowed only up to 20 keywords, so when selecting the keywords you want to target, choose the most relevant keywords. If you choose to target more than 20 keywords, your promoted pin may be denied by Pinterest. Therefore, aim for 15 to 20 keywords per promoted pin.

Next, when creating your promoted pin, select your image with care. The Pinterest platform is all about big, beautiful images, and for your promoted pin to stand out, you must use an image that is both eye catching and of high quality. Within your image, consider adding a simple, clear text overlay to your image that can serve as a headline and provide context to the image. The size and shape of your image matters on Pinterest; this platform is vertically oriented, so although horizontal images can work for promoted pins, strive to use vertical images whenever possible. An image size of 600 pixels by 900 pixels is a good place to start for your pin image.

You want your promoted pin to be helpful, beautiful, and actionable. After you select an image that helps you create such a pin, write a detailed description that gives value to your market, addresses a pain point, and demonstrates the benefit of the product you're featuring in your promoted pin. Remember that people don't care about the product's unique selling points (USP) at this point; rather, they care about what the product does for them and how it can make their life better. Address these concerns within your promoted pin's description.

TIP

Within the first 75–100 characters of your pin's description, include the link to the product's landing page (see Chapter 7 for more on landing pages). Including this link early in your text ensures that your link appears above the fold, allowing your landing page to be one click away from the Pinterest platform.

WARNING

Don't use more than four individual images per pin. You want the images to be big and beautiful so that your promoted pin stands out, and having more than four images creates a busy pin with small images. If you decide to have more than one image in a promoted pin, be sure that each image has a clear focus and a theme. You don't want to sell an assortment of random products in a pin; instead, the products should complement each other.

LinkedIn

LinkedIn stands out from other traffic stores because it's geared toward a specific market. LinkedIn is professionally focused and business-to-business (B2B) centric.

It's a powerful resource to employ for lead generation and running ads to cold traffic, though, just as Twitter and Facebook are.

You can choose among a multitude of ways to target your audience within LinkedIn, from demographics, such as age and gender, to job title, to skills that users have listed in their profiles, such as "customer service" or "social media marketing." And with more than 450 million users and counting, LinkedIn offers a large market to reach.

How large should your audience size be when running traffic on LinkedIn? Some marketers argue that 300,000 is the sweet spot. However, in contrast to your Facebook audience, your audience size on LinkedIn doesn't need to be an issue. The market is smaller and more specified on the LinkedIn platform, and the target is business professionals. Other traffic stores, such as Facebook and Twitter, encompass a much broader audience. When you advertise on LinkedIn, the size of the audience is less important. The main concern, just as with all traffic stores, is putting the right message in front of the right audience. For instance, if you want to target CEOs, don't worry about the audience size, but focus instead on creating an ad and an offer that CEOs will find relevant.

As with the other traffic stores, your LinkedIn ad needs the following:

>> Specific copy that calls out to your audience and is relevant to it

>> A professional, captivating image

>> A call to action that moves the audience to the next step

One way to drive traffic on LinkedIn is to sponsor content and send people to your content, such as your blog posts. To be effective, the content you're sending traffic to should educate and give value to your audience. Then, within the blog, provide calls to action or banner ads for an offer that your LinkedIn audience finds relevant. This strategy is one way for you to obtain a return on investment (ROI) from your LinkedIn campaigns.

Although LinkedIn is one of the more expensive platforms, the specific nature of this traffic store makes it generate high-quality leads that are open to your message.

Choosing the right traffic platform

You have many traffic stores to choose from, and each one has its strengths. In summary, here are the scenarios in which to consider using one or more of the Big Six:

>> **Facebook:** This platform can work in almost any market, unless the market isn't approved by the Facebook TOS (terms of service), such as the vaping

industry (visit Facebook's advertising policies for more details on its TOS at https://www.facebook.com/policies/ads/). With Facebook, you want to utilize a process known as retargeting, which we define and explain in the next section.

>> **Twitter:** Advertise on Twitter when you want to target a younger market or one that is highly tech savvy. Twitter is a large platform with a lot of users, so it can work in almost any market.

>> **Google:** Use Google if you have a proven offer that has performed well on other traffic sources, or an offer that is difficult to target in terms of prospects' interests or demographics and thus requires keyword targeting. With Google, you want to engage in retargeting.

>> **YouTube:** This traffic store can work in almost any market, especially if you have an offer that requires demonstration or keyword targeting. Again, with this platform, you want to engage in retargeting.

>> **Pinterest:** Think about using promoted pins when you're selling physical products, particularly to women, or if you're creating content with lots of original or curated images.

>> **LinkedIn:** Go to LinkedIn when you're selling high-dollar B2B products or services. Consider also advertising on this platform when you're promoting a webinar to a B2B audience or want to reach people by their job title.

Setting up Boomerang Traffic

Needless to say, not everyone who comes to your site will convert on the first visit; in fact, for most sites, only 2 percent of web traffic converts on the first visit. So how do you get the other 98 percent to "boomerang" and come back to your site? You do it through a strategy known as ad retargeting.

For instance, say that you go to the online shoe and clothing store Zappos. You look at a pair of shoes and then leave Zappos without buying. Next you visit the *Huffington Post* to read an article and notice an ad for the same pair of shoes that you were just considering on Zappos.com. You are being retargeted. In this section, we go into more detail about what retargeting is and how to employ it in the following sections.

Defining ad retargeting

After people have visited your site, sales page, or social media page, you can safely assume that they're interested in learning more. Even if they left without buying, you can also assume that they didn't say no; they just didn't have time to take action right then or needed more time to think about your offer. To encourage people to return to your site (like a boomerang), you use the paid traffic strategy of retargeting.

The goal of retargeting (sometimes called remarketing) is to bring people back to your site and get them one step closer to converting. You do this by serving former visitors ads based on their prior engagement with your site. With retargeting, you don't try to change prior visitors' minds; rather, you remind them about your offer.

Although other forms of retargeting exist, we focus on the most frequently used: site-based retargeting. *Site-based retargeting* uses tracking pixels and cookies to serve your ad to previous site visitors, as we explain in the next section.

Setting cookies and pixels

A *tracking pixel* (simply referred to as a pixel) is a piece of code that you place on your website to trigger a *cookie*, which is the text file that stores information about the user's visit to your site. The cookie uses a simple JavaScript code and allows ad networks and traffic platforms to identify users when they visit another site, and then serves them targeted ads based on your preferences as an advertiser. Simply put, the tracking pixel delivers information to a server, and the cookie stores information in a user's browser so that the server can read it again later. The cookie stores the site visit but does not store any sensitive information, such as the site visitor's name, address, or any information that might personally identify the visitor.

When people come to your site, a cookie is placed, and eventually, users leave and visit other sites. The cookie lets your retargeting platform, such as Facebook or Google, know when one of these "cookied" visitors goes to a site where retarget-ing ads can be shown. If ad space is available, your retargeting ad may be shown. This entire process is automated and occurs within a fraction of a second.

When done right, retargeting allows you to make relevant offers to specific audi-ences, and the more specific and relevant the offer, the more likely the offer is to resonate with your audience and lead to a conversion. The next section tells you how to create specific retargeting offers.

Segmenting with content

The biggest mistake that a digital marketer can make with retargeting campaigns is to assume that all visitors are alike and show every visitor the same ad. The key to successful retargeting is audience segmentation (we also discuss content segmentation in Chapter 4). Failing to segment your visitors can lead to poor campaign results and the waste of many of your impressions (the views on your ads) and ad spend. For instance, you wouldn't want to retarget a user who has viewed vegan recipes with a banner ad for a steakhouse restaurant.

When you segment your audiences, you can identify and understand their intent. Segmentation allows you to retarget and send offers based on a person's interests, thereby personalizing the retargeting experience and making the ad that much more compelling.

To segment your audience, examine your website or blog and divide its content into like categories or topics. For example, a food blog might separate its content by types of lifestyles such as vegan, gluten-free, and vegetarian. When people visit content about vegetarian food, they are showing interest in vegetarian food. Do you have an offer that is relevant to a vegetarian? If so, retarget those that visit your vegetarian content with that relevant and specific offer.

Troubleshooting Paid Traffic Campaigns

After you've set up a paid traffic campaign, let it run for three to five days so that you can start collecting data. When that time is up, you should assess and trouble-shoot your campaign. Although you're looking for problems or why goals aren't being met, troubleshooting doesn't necessarily mean that something is wrong with the campaign. The goal of troubleshooting a campaign is to fix any problems that may have arisen since its launch, but also to look for ways to optimize the campaign and possibly, if justifiable, to scale the campaign.

We examine four areas to focus on and the steps to take when troubleshooting a paid traffic campaign, as follows:

>> The offer

>> The targeting

>> The ad copy and creative

>> The ad's congruency

With paid traffic, a lot of trial and error is involved in a campaign, even if you've done everything right. At our company, for example, for every ten paid campaigns that we run, only one to two break even or turn a profit. But that doesn't mean that you should throw away an underperforming campaign and start all over. With some digging, you can find what's holding back the campaign and get it back on track.

Make sure to examine each of the following areas one at a time so that you can isolate the specific issue of your campaign. If you try to assess all the areas at one time, you won't understand the root cause or what ultimately fixed your campaign, so you may end up facing the same problem in the future. Implement one step, run your ad for an additional five days and collect more data, and then move on to the next steps if necessary.

Read on for more details about troubleshooting each of these areas.

Strengthening your offer

The first aspect to focus on when your campaign isn't performing as expected is your offer. Ask yourself: Do people want what you're selling? If you don't offer something that your market actually wants or needs, you won't get conversions. To see whether your offer is appealing, answer these three questions:

>> Are you solving a problem for a specific group of people?

>> Does a specific need exist for what you're offering?

>> Are you offering your market value?

If your answer is "No" to any of these questions, you've already found your problem.

No matter how compelling your landing page copy is or how attention grabbing your image may be, the best marketing campaign in the world can't solve an offer issue. This is why your offer is so crucial and is the key to the success or failure of any marketing campaign. A poorly executed marketing campaign with a great offer usually outperforms a great marketing campaign with a poor offer. If a poor offer is your problem, you need to come up with a new and better offer before you run traffic to it. See Chapter 3 for more on crafting winning offers.

Tweaking your targeting

Another big culprit of a struggling ad campaign is your targeting. If you've concluded that your offer isn't the problem and have proof to back that up, examine whether you're targeting the right people. Regardless of whether you have the best offer and marketing message, putting your offer in front of the wrong audience means that your campaign will fail. Are you targeting people who will actually buy?

The biggest targeting mistake you can make is to go too broad in fear of missing out on potential prospects. When starting your campaign, you want your market to be as specific as possible. If you're in doubt about the size of the audience you're targeting, go a bit smaller. Then, if the campaign meets or exceeds expectations for this smaller audience, you can scale it and make your audience a little broader.

If you believe that your targeting is off, reassess your customer avatar. You might have a misconception of your audience. Go back and make sure that you're being specific enough and that your information on your audience is correct.

Another big issue that can impede your targeting is to advertise on the wrong traffic platform. You might be placing ads on a platform where your market doesn't hang out online. Return to the "Choosing the Right Traffic Platform" section, earlier in this chapter, to help make sure that you're putting your ad on a platform where your market is active.

Scrutinizing your ad copy and creative

After confirming that your offer is enticing and you're putting your offer in front of the right people, examine your marketing message. The ad copy and the creative (the image) are the segue between your offer and your target market. The copy and creative ensures that people can see the end benefit of your offer. If your marketing message doesn't catch your target audience's attention and give people a reason to click, your campaign will fail because you aren't generating traffic.

Inspect your ad copy to make sure that it does the following:

>> Calls out to your audience

>> Hits a pain point that your audience experiences

>> Gives your market a solution or a benefit (a reason to click)

Next, the image needs

>> To be eye catching

>> To correspond with your marketing message

Overall, verify that your creative and your copy don't say different things. They need to match or you risk confusing your audience. In addition, this matchup helps make your ad copy and your creative more compelling, which also leads to the next area to troubleshoot.

Checking the congruency of your campaign

Finally, you need to troubleshoot the congruency of your ad as you move prospects to the next step of your marketing funnel. For instance, after people click your ad and visit your landing page, do they get what they expected? If your landing page doesn't have the same look and feel as your ad, people may think they've landed in the wrong place or that you won't deliver on the benefit promised in the ad. Something seems wrong to site visitors, causing them to click the Back button in their browser.

So not only do you want each step of the campaign to build off the previous, you also want the campaign to remain congruent throughout. To maintain congruence, consider keeping the following elements in your ad design consistent throughout the campaign's path:

>> Color scheme

>> Layout

>> Imagery

>> Font type, size, and color

Next, if you make an offer or touch on a pain point or benefit within the ad, reference that again on the landing page. Make sure that these items appear quickly and aren't buried down the page or you risk losing the prospect. The easiest way to assure the prominence of these items is with the copy: Use the exact same language from your ad to your landing page headline, subheadline, and body copy. Also include the same images from the ad within the landing page.

By ensuring that your ad and your landing page both reflect the same benefit, pain point, offer, and design, you can maintain familiarity and preserve congruency.

Chapter **11**

Following Up with Email Marketing

magine that it's seven o'clock on a Tuesday morning. You wake up to the beeping of your alarm, roll out of bed, and stumble to the kitchen, where the coffee that you programmed to brew last night is just finishing its drip cycle. You grab a mug, add some cream and a tiny sprinkle of sugar, and sit down at the kitchen table. Then you check your email.

If you're anything like most adult Americans, this routine may be familiar. Email is not only part of our daily routines, but also one of our primary sources of information. It probably isn't a surprise to you that email has a higher return on investment than any other channel by far. In fact, email returns an average 4,300 percent return on investment for businesses in the United States.

Email plays an important role in digital marketing because it helps move customers from one stage of the customer journey (see Chapter 1 for more on the customer journey) to the next in a way that yields high return on investment. Because email is both cost effective and time effective, not to mention one of the first channels that most customers turn to, this channel often yields the best results.

In this chapter, we show you how to create an email plan that gives your customers a reason to come to you again and again as you grow your business through dynamic, relationship-based marketing.

Understanding Marketing Emails

To start, it's important to understand the types of marketing emails that businesses send. The key to success in email marketing is employing the right type of email at the right time.

Figure 11-1 shows the goals of three types of emails — promotional, relational, and transactional — and how they're used in marketing strategy.

PRIMARY GOAL BY EMAIL TYPE					
CUSTOMER SERVICE	BRAND AWARENESS	LEAD GENERATION	RETENTION & LOYALTY	ENGAGEMENT & NURTURING	SALES & UPSELLS
TRANSACTIONAL: ✓	✓	✓	✓	✓	✓
RELATIONAL:	✓	✓	✓	✓	✓
PROMOTIONAL:		✓	✓	✓	✓

FIGURE 11-1:
The primary goals of each email type.

Promotional emails

Promotional emails present the leads and customers on your email list with an offer. The offers could be promotional content, a gated offer like a white paper or webinar (see Chapter 3 for more on gated offers), a brand announcement, product release, event announcements, or trial offers, just to name a few.

Promotional emails are the most common marketing emails. This isn't surprising. Because 66 percent of consumers have made a purchase as a direct result of an email marketing message, we know that promotional emails work.

REMEMBER

Promotional emails provide value and help tee up sales. They're great for lead generation, retention, loyalty, engagement, nurturing, sales, and upsells. They should be part of any email marketing strategy. The problem is that many companies use them as the only part of their email marketing strategy, so they miss out on opportunities to relate to customers in diverse ways that are often more effective.

Relational emails

Relational emails deliver value to your customers by providing free content and information such as subscriber welcomes, newsletters, blog articles, webinar guides, surveys, social updates, contest announcements, and more.

Relational emails may not sell a product or brand directly, but they build relationships with the customer by adding value upfront. For example, when your email subscriber receives a piece of high-quality content in an email newsletter, he or she is interacting with your brand in a deeper, more meaningful way.

Transactional emails

Transactional emails are sent in response to an action that a customer has taken with your brand. They include messages such as order confirmations, receipts, coupon codes, shipping notifications, account creation and product return confirmations, support tickets, password reminders, and unsubscribe confirmations.

These emails reengage customers who have engaged with your business in some way (see "Reengagement campaigns," later in this chapter) and give the customer an idea of the voice behind your brand.

Do you follow up quickly and deliver what you promised? Do you have systems in place that give the customer true value? Do you respect your customers' wishes? The leads and customers on your email list are observing how you conduct business, and your transactional email is a big part of that.

THE CHEMISTRY OF TRANSACTIONAL EMAILS

Think about the last time you purchased something you loved — a pair of boots you'd wanted for years, a new snowboard, a great bottle of wine, or dinner at your favorite restaurant. Now consider the way you felt when you made that purchase. You were excited, right?

As you purchase a product that you've been wanting, your brain is flooded with feel-good endorphins. You're happy about that product. Perhaps an hour later, you get a shipping confirmation with information about the key features of that snowboard or an email listing recipes for dishes that go with that wine. You've already made a feel-good purchase, and when the marketer reengages you when you're still on that high, you move farther along on your customer journey.

TURNING NEGATIVES TO POSITIVES

Many businesses tend to minimize contact when a customer takes a negative action, such as returning a product or unsubscribing from an email list. But we believe that these events are perfect times to follow up with transactional emails, for these reasons:

- **Product returns:** Nordstrom, for example, allows customers to return any item at any time for any reason. This return policy is highly compelling and makes purchases feel less risky. When Nordstrom follows up with customers who make returns, it confirms the positive experience that those customers had with its return policy.

- **Unsubscriptions:** When a customer unsubscribes from your email list, first respond to his negative action by unsubscribing him (give him what he wants). Then send him an unsubscribe confirmation that lists other ways he can engage with your brand, such as social media or bricks-and-mortar stores. Remind him that you're happy to communicate with him in the place that best fits his needs.

Transactional emails meet all the primary goals of marketing (refer to Figure 1-2). They offer a customer service experience, tell customers about your brand, generate leads, increase customer retention and loyalty, engage customers, and even help with sales. Yet most businesses rarely use transactional emails properly, mistakenly assuming that promotional and relational emails are more effective.

Research shows, however, that transactional emails have the highest open rates of the three types and produce 2 percent to 5 percent more revenue than standard bulk email does. We've come to a fascinating conclusion: Transactional emails are chemically more likely to be successful (see the nearby sidebar "The chemistry of transactional emails").

Sending Broadcast and Triggered Emails

Email best practices say that you shouldn't just send every email to every subscriber on your list, and time management best practices say you can't spend every day manually sending emails to customers. For these reasons, your emails should be divided into two types: broadcast and triggered.

Broadcast emails

Broadcast emails are emails that you manually send to your entire list at a given time. They aren't responses to customer actions; you send them at a specific time and for a specific purpose. What we're going to say next may make you a bit upset, but we'll say it anyway: Overusing broadcast emails can hurt your customer relationships and cause customers to stop proceeding on the customer journey. Broadcast emails should be used for only three purposes:

>> **Newsletters:** You should send your regular daily, weekly, or monthly email newsletter to your entire list as promised when your subscribers subscribed.

>> **Promotions:** Not all promotions should be broadcasted to your entire audience. Only major promotions that you feel deliver value to your entire customer base should be sent to everyone. The rest should be sent to a segmented list (see the next paragraph).

>> **Segmentation:** Send a broadcast email to your entire list to determine the specific interests of certain customers and then segment your email lists.

Triggered emails

Most of the emails that you send should be *triggered emails*, which are fully automated. After you get the content honed and ready, you can let your email service provider do the work for you.

Triggered emails automatically go out after customers take a specific action. But there's a catch: Just because you can trigger something doesn't mean you should. In this day of detailed digital automation, you can probably get data to trigger an email every time your customer logs on to a computer or pours a cup of coffee. But that would just annoy your customers. Specific actions that trigger an automated email for each customer action might include

>> New subscriber welcome email

>> Gated offer email (see Chapter 3 for more on gated offers)

>> Registration confirmations

>> Purchase receipts

>> Segmented promotion

>> Referral requests after customers leave a review

>> Abandonment of a shopping cart

>> Reengagement after a subscriber has ignored your brand emails for a specific period

Building a Promotional Calendar

The first question many business owners ask us is when to send email. This question is a good one because a great email campaign will engage customers like never before if it's sent at the right time. Conversely, if an email is sent at the wrong time, it won't be as effective as it could be.

The first thing you should do as a business owner or marketer after you decide to start an email marketing strategy is come up with a promotional calendar. That way, you'll know when to send the messaging your customers need when they want to receive it.

REMEMBER

Using a promotional calendar gives you the opportunity to elicit action. It mobilizes your subscribers to do something that you want them to do — buy something, ask for information, call you, or come to a store, for example. The right message delivered at the right time elicits action.

Cataloging your products and services

Before you can build an accurate, all-encompassing promotional calendar, you have to know exactly what you're promoting. Spend some time carefully cataloging every product and service that your business offers and taking some time to understand how to promote it best. At DigitalMarketer, we use a promotional asset sheet (see Figure 11-2) to keep a detailed record of our assets. Every time we release a new asset, we add an asset sheet to our list. And every time we update our promotional calendar or run an email campaign, we spend some time updating these asset sheets.

Be sure that whatever record you keep of your promotional assets contains the following information:

>> Name of the product or service

>> Price (both full price and sale price)

>> Where the transaction occurs

>> Whether you've sold this product or service via email before

>> Whether past marketing efforts worked (and why or why not)

>> When you last promoted this product or service

>> How many emails you sent about this product

>> Whether the product is currently available to promote (and if not, why not)

FIGURE 11-2:
A promotional
asset sheet.

> **Promotional Asset Sheet**
>
> Product/Service _____
> Price $ _____
>
> Transaction Occurs:
> ☐ On-line   ☐ Over Phone   ☐ In Person
>
> Previously Sold with Email?
> ☐ Yes   ☐ No
>
> If Yes, what were the results?
> _____
> _____
> _____
> _____
>
> Last Email Promotion: _____   Number of Emails Sent: _____
>
> Currently Available to Promote?
> ☐ Yes   ☐ No
>
> If No, why?
> _____
> _____

You may be wondering why you should spend so much time cataloging your marketing efforts. Wouldn't that time be better spent, perhaps, marketing those assets? The truth is that by carefully tracking the sales of your products, as well as the marketing campaigns that correspond with your sales, the job of marketing those assets becomes much easier. When you know what you have available to sell and the results of the promotions you've employed in the past, you can simply do more of what's working and less of what isn't.

The time you spend cataloging and analyzing these assets and the campaigns surrounding them is valuable marketing time. We believe that all marketers should gather the promotional assets from all the products and services they offered so that they know exactly what they can sell, how they can sell it, whom to sell it to, and (perhaps most important) when to sell it.

Creating an annual promotional plan

After you catalog your assets, create an annual promotional plan. This plan aligns your 12-month revenue goals with your annual promotions and marketing efforts to help you reach your goals. Figure 11-3 shows a sample worksheet.

You can download your own 12-Month Promotional Planning Worksheet at `http://www.digitalmarketer.com/email-planning`.

TIP

MONTH	GOALS	SET PROMOS	REVENUE GOALS		POTENTIAL PROMOTIONS
1 JAN.			TARGET: $ _____ EXPECTED: $ _____ REMAINING: $ _____		
2 FEB.			TARGET: $ _____ EXPECTED: $ _____ REMAINING: $ _____		
3 MAR.			TARGET: $ _____ EXPECTED: $ _____ REMAINING: $ _____		
4 APR.			TARGET: $ _____ EXPECTED: $ _____ REMAINING: $ _____		
5 MAY			TARGET: $ _____ EXPECTED: $ _____ REMAINING: $ _____		
6 JUNE			TARGET: $ _____ EXPECTED: $ _____ REMAINING: $ _____		
7 JULY			TARGET: $ _____ EXPECTED: $ _____ REMAINING: $ _____		
8 AUG.			TARGET: $ _____ EXPECTED: $ _____ REMAINING: $ _____		
9 SEPT.			TARGET: $ _____ EXPECTED: $ _____ REMAINING: $ _____		
10 OCT.			TARGET: $ _____ EXPECTED: $ _____ REMAINING: $ _____		
11 NOV.			TARGET: $ _____ EXPECTED: $ _____ REMAINING: $ _____		
12 DEC.			TARGET: $ _____ EXPECTED: $ _____ REMAINING: $ _____		

FIGURE 11-3: An annual promotional planning worksheet.

Developing a marketing plan

Creating and developing an annual marketing plan takes some time, but after it's done, you have a solid framework for building your promotional calendar. Follow these steps:

1. **Write your 12-month revenue goals.**

   Consider your target revenue goals, and figure out where you want to be each month to reach those goals.

2. **List your nonrevenue goals.**

   This list could include nonrevenue growth opportunities such as the launch of a blog or podcast, the release of a book, or the opening of a new location.

3. **Slot holiday promotions into the appropriate months.**

For many retail businesses, November and December are key sales times and thus require strategic marketing. Other businesses may have peak promotion at varying times, such as before a major conference or during a certain season.

4. **Slot annual promotions into the appropriate months.**

These promotions may include major sales, product releases, or events.

5. **Denote seasonality.**

Every business has slow and busy months, so note those months in your plan so that you can build appropriate promotion during those times.

6. **Slot nonrevenue goals into the appropriate months.**

Are you planning to release a new book or launch a new blog in March? You need space on the promotional calendar for these nonrevenue initiatives.

7. **Break your revenue goals into monthly allotments.**

Keep seasonality in mind (see Step 5).

8. **Add your standard revenue projections.**

Include promotional efforts, major events, standard rebilling contracts, and subscriptions.

9. **Subtract your expected revenue from the target revenue.**

After doing this, consider how you can fill in the remaining revenue needed. This step is where your marketing efforts come into play.

10. **Brainstorm additional promotional ideas that could generate the revenue you need to reach your goals.**

Will you need to add new products or services to promote to reach your target revenue? Can you find new ways to offer the existing products and services you already have?

11. **Spot-check and adjust.**

Ask yourself whether your calendar helps you meet your goals in a way that will be both effective and practical.

12. **List additional items that you need to meet your target.**

You may need to launch a new product or service, or to create a sales presentation, for example.

Creating a 30-day calendar

The next step is to get down into the nitty-gritty of what you're going to do for the next 30 days.

A promotional campaign should have three goals:

>> **Monetization:** Making money or making a sale

>> **Activation:** Moving your customer forward on the customer journey

>> **Segmentation:** Becoming more aware of customers' needs and desires so you can segment your list and deliver value

For your first 30 days, we recommend that you set one of these promotional goals for each week and reserve the fourth week for a wildcard campaign. A wildcard campaign gives you the chance to try something new, get creative, test new ideas, or try to replicate your most successful campaigns.

You can use a monthly planning worksheet (see Figure 11-4) so that you can easily track which promotions you're running and how they do. You might also plan a backup promotion for each campaign in case the primary campaign falls, so that you still reach revenue goals regardless of how the campaigns perform.

FIGURE 11-4:
A 30-day
promotional
planning
worksheet.

TIP

You can download your own monthly email planning worksheet at http://www. digitalmarketer.com/email-planning.

Creating a 90-day rolling calendar

When your 30-day promotional plan is up and rolling, you can plan a bit farther in advance with a 90-day rolling calendar. We call this calendar a *rolling calendar* because by repeating similar promotions every 90 days or so, you keep your customers informed and engaged without making the same offers with the same campaign goals over and over again.

TIP

Use a calendar application like Google Calendar or hang a dry-erase board with a 90-day calendar template on it in your office so that you and your team can routinely map out a schedule that meets your revenue targets without repeating the same promotions too often. When viewing your 90-day calendar, you might find that you have three monetization campaigns in April, but none in May. Moving a monetization campaign or two to May will make it more likely that you hit your revenue targets in May and reduce the number of monetization offers you send to your email list in April.

Creating Email Campaigns

How do you create email campaigns that move your customers along the customer journey in a way that creates long-term brand engagement? And how do you do so without spamming or annoying your customers the way so many brands can do? This section walks you through five types of email campaigns so that you know how to build email campaigns that will work for your business.

A campaign structure page (like the one in Figure 11-5) will help you keep track of each campaign and the purpose of each email in the campaign.

SAMPLE CAMPAIGN STRUCTURE
EXAMPLE BUSINESS: Mattress Store (Physical or e-commerce)

DAY #	EMAIL TYPE	SUBJECT LINE
1	Welcome	Welcome to the Mattress Store (20% off coupon)!
2	Best of #1	Is Facebook stealing your sleep?
3	Best of #2	This made me think of you

FIGURE 11-5: A sample campaign storyboard.

Indoctrination campaigns

An *indoctrination campaign* is a triggered campaign sent immediately following an initial subscription. This campaign is designed to teach new subscribers about your brand and convince them that they've made a good decision by joining your email list and, by extension, becoming a part of your community. See Figure 11-6 for an example of an indoctrination email.

FIGURE 11-6:
An example indoctrination email that welcomes a new subscriber.

Customers don't sign up for your email lists on a whim. Instead, they probably were introduced to your brand and then considered the value of your email list. Perhaps they were given the opportunity to get value in advance with a gated offer. (Learn more about gated offers in Chapter 3.) Or perhaps they were signed up as they made a purchase or engaged with your website. In all cases, an indoctrination campaign reaffirms positive action and shows your customers that they made the right choice.

The fact that customers made a positive choice to join your email list, however, doesn't mean that they're fully engaged with your brand. They don't know you well enough to be anticipating your every word. They may not recognize your name in their inbox and are still unsure about the value they can expect from you.

A carefully crafted indoctrination campaign can help move customers down the path of their customer journeys. (See Chapter 1 for more on the customer journey.) In the aggregate, when you add an indoctrination campaign, you see a positive effect on the open and click-through rates of the email you send to these subscribers in the future because they know, like, and trust you better.

Indoctrination campaigns generally run one to three emails and introduce customers to the brand on a deeper level. These campaigns help you put your best foot forward with new subscribers, introducing them to who you are and what you stand for.

Your indoctrination campaign should do the following things:

>> Welcome and introduce new subscribers to your brand.

>> Restate the benefits of being a subscriber.

>> Tell subscribers what to expect.

>> Tell subscribers what to do next.

>> Introduce subscribers to your brand voice or personality.

Engagement campaigns

An *engagement campaign* is an interest-based, triggered campaign sent immediately following a subscriber action. It's designed to make a relevant offer and potentially a sale to subscribers. The role of an engagement campaign is to turn subscribers into converts by prescribing the next logical step based on what you know those people are interested in.

Before you craft an engagement campaign, ask yourself two questions:

>> **What next step do you want your customer to take?** You may want her to make a purchase, opt in to a gated offer, or engage with your brand on your website.

>> **Do you believe that the customer is ready to take that next step?** If the customer isn't ready, you only annoy and alienate her if you push her to take that step.

WARNING

Sometimes it does hurt to ask — especially when you're asking too much too soon from a valuable customer.

Your engagement campaign should do the following things:

>> Turn subscribers into converts. A conversion might be buying a product or service, scheduling an appointment, or registering for a webinar.

>> Consider what the customer is interested in now and what will interest him next. Refer back to your customer journey and design your engagement campaigns to move the email subscriber to the next stage in that journey.

>> Reference the previous positive action.

>> Overcome or inoculate against known objections to converting.

>> Prescribe the next logical step.

>> Ask for an order or a next step.

Ascension campaigns

An *ascension campaign* is a triggered campaign sent immediately following a purchase to start the value loop designed to turn ordinary buyers into buyers who purchase from your brand again and again.

If a customer just bought a tent and four sleeping bags, for example, you could assume that she's looking to head out to the campground, and you could send her a coupon code for a camp stove. If a customer just bought a subscription to a social media training event, you could offer him follow-up training on email marketing.

An ascension campaign is a great way to move customers along the customer journey and build a long-term relationship with them. In an ascension campaign, you give customers what they want and then a bit more.

An ascension campaign should do the following things:

>> Overcome or inoculate against known objections.

>> Prescribe the next logical step.

>> Increase the average value of customers by selling more to them, more often.

>> Increase customer trust.

>> Make customers ascend to fans.

Segmentation campaigns

A *segmentation campaign* is a manual campaign sent to your entire database as a promotion designed to segment your subscribers by interest.

Consider a small publishing company that sells high-interest nonfiction books to teachers and librarians. That company is releasing a series of science books on gardening and plant growth. The books have similar content, but some target early learners, others middle-school students, and still others high-school students. The marketing department, being wise and astute in the best practices of email marketing, decides to send out a segmentation campaign. The department staff craft an email listing the books that are available, with clear guidance on what age level each book is appropriate for. Then the staff sends the email as a broadcast campaign to the company's entire mailing list. This campaign makes the company's entire list aware of the new product, and possibly more important, the resulting click data allows the company to segment the list by which subscribers are interested in early-learning content, which are interested in middle-school content, and which are interested in high-school content. The marketing department can create audience segments and send additional emails that meet those customers' exact interests. Figure 11-7 shows a segmentation email from Home Depot. The email lists six categories in which subscribers can get savings. When a subscriber selects one of these categories, the marketing team knows that this person responded to this email and clicked a particular product category. That person would then be segmented, and Home Depot would likely send follow-up emails on the product the subscriber selected.

FIGURE 11-7:
Example of a
segmentation
campaign email.

Reengagement campaigns

A *reengagement campaign* is a triggered campaign sent to any subscriber who has not opened or clicked an email in the past 30 to 60 days. This campaign is designed to reengage those subscribers with the brand. Perhaps subscribers got extremely busy and didn't check their email diligently. They may have gone through life changes and now have different interests. Or maybe they got frustrated with you and chose to disengage. A reengagement campaign can help those customers get back on the customer journey.

Figure 11-8 shows an effective reengagement email.

Nobody likes saying goodbye! We'd love to continue sending you the latest real estate tips and trends – no matter where your journey takes you.

Count me in!

If your bags are packed for good, that's okay, too. **Unsubscribe now.**

Unsubscribe from this email

FIGURE 11-8:
An example reengagement campaign.

REMEMBER

Email deliverability is greatly affected by disengaged users. Best practices in email list management require that customers who aren't engaged be reengaged or removed from the list. If you run a reengagement campaign and still don't get a response from some customers, you can unsubscribe those customers and protect your email list from deliverability issues.

Writing and Designing Effective Emails

If you want people to read your emails, you have to write and design emails that they want to read. But with thousands of companies writing and sending emails every day, you have to make your emails stand out.

Although email writing and design are art and not formula, this section lists a few tips to hone your copywriting and email design skills so that your messages stand out.

Harvesting proven email copy

Go into your own email account and check the last ten messages that you opened. Look at the copy and the design. Then ask yourself the following questions:

- >> Did the headline grab your attention?

- >> What hooks and leads did the copywriter use?

- >> What benefits of the product or service are mentioned?

- >> What proof or stories grabbed your attention?

- >> What was the call to action?

When you've read the emails that grabbed your attention, see whether you can use them as templates for emails that meet your own business goals. There's no need to reinvent the wheel if it's already been invented for you. (If you want to use the example emails that we include in this book and hone them to fit your marketing goals, feel free to do so.)

Answering four questions

To write great email copy, you have to figure out why a customer would engage with the promotion. Answer these four questions:

- >> **Why now?** Consider whether the promotion you have should offer new or on-sale items. Also consider whether it's seasonal or timely; that is, whether it's something that customers want or need now more than at another time.

- >> **Who cares?** Decide who in your target audience is most affected by having (or not having) what you're selling.

- >> **Why should they care?** You need to let customers know how their lives will be different if they have your product or service.

- >> **Can you prove it?** Provide case studies, testimonials, or news stories to prove that your customers' lives will be changed if they engage with your product or service.

Great email copy answers these questions in the body of the email in a way that clearly demonstrates to the customer the value of your promotion.

Knowing why people buy

People always buy things for a reason. By considering the reasons why people make purchases as you write email copy, you can hone in on what makes a customer click Buy. People generally buy things for four reasons:

- >> **Personal gain:** A product or service will help them reach personal goals or desires.

>> **Logic and research:** Customers have done their research, and this product seems like a logical fit to meet a particular need.

>> **Social proof or third-party influence:** Customers' friends have told them that the product or service is great, and they want to be part of it, or they see a large number of people doing something and want to do it, too. Nothing attracts a crowd like a crowd.

>> **Fear of missing out:** People have a genuine fear of missing an opportunity or of being the only person not to have something important.

Consider which of these motivations you think will drive your customers and then address that reason in your email copy.

Writing effective email subject lines

Because most people spend only three to four seconds deciding whether to open an email, the subject line is the most important piece of email copy you can write. A good subject line piques interest and entices a customer to open the email. Then your email body copy can do the rest to drive engagement.

Subject lines can be tough nuts to crack. One company has its marketing team write 25 subject lines for each email and then choose a favorite to use in the email campaign. This operation may be time consuming, but the company continually receives higher-than-average open rates for its industry and higher-than-average email engagement. You may not have the resources to write 25 full subject lines for each email, but it's a good idea to consider several options for each send, especially triggered sends that you'll use over time.

You can use three types of subject lines to give people different reasons to open an email. We discuss these types in the following sections.

Curiosity subject lines

Curiosity subject lines pique the interest of subscribers and encourage them to click to find out more. For example, Kate Spade, a clothing retailer, sent an email to its subscriber list with the subject line, *Ready for your close up?* That email contained an offer for Kate Spade's jewelry products and used a curious subject line to increase the number of people opening the email.

Benefit subject lines

Benefit subject lines clearly state the reason why subscribers should open the email and the benefits they receive for doing so. For example, OfficeVibe, a Software as a Service (Saas) company that helps managers measure the engagement and satisfaction of their employees, sent an email to their subscribers with the subject line, *38 Employee Engagement Ideas,* which clearly states the benefit the subscriber will get by opening the email. The opposite of a benefit subject line is a warning subject line. For example, OfficeVibe also sent an email to its subscribers with the subject line, *11 Statistics That Will Scare Every Manager.* This subject line type should be used sparingly, but, when appropriate, it can be very effective.

Scarcity subject lines

Scarcity subject lines cause subscribers to feel that they may miss out on something important if they don't open the email and engage with it. For example, Home Depot sent an email to its subscribers with the subject line, *Hurry! Labor Day Savings End Tonight* to encourage subscribers to take advantage of its Labor Day sale before it was over.

Writing body copy

Copywriting isn't a formula, but an art. It's also true that through some formulaic chunking, you can create email copy quickly and effectively.

This chunking method is based on the answers to the questions that we list in "Answering four questions," earlier in this chapter. By breaking your copy into four major chunks and allowing each chunk to answer one of the questions, you can ensure that your copy addresses the major points you're trying to cover.

Each chunk of copy should have one link. That way, by the time customers read the entire email, they've had all their questions answered and have been given multiple opportunities to find out more by clicking a link.

Here's how we recommend that you chunk your email:

>> **Introduction:** In this section, answer the question "Who cares?" by showing customers that they should care about this promotion and why.

>> **Body:** Next, help your reader to answer the question "Why should they care?" by explaining the proven benefits or results of the product or service.

>> **Close:** The close of your email is a great time to answer the question "Why now?" Tell customers, if it applies, that they have a limited time to engage with the promotion.

>> **P.S.:** A postscript is a fantastic place to answer the question "Can you prove it?" by sharing social proof such as a testimonial, positive review, or story of a customer whose life has been changed by the product or service.

REMEMBER

Include a link to a relevant place on your website in each chunk of the email. It's okay if multiple links go to the same location. Just make sure that customers are given ample opportunity to engage further.

Cuing the Click

You've written a killer subject line. You've chunked up your copy beautifully, and each chunk contains a relevant link. You have a product or service that you believe in. You're 99.4 percent of the way to your goal. But you still have one more thing to do: You have to cue the click by asking people very clearly to perform the action of clicking.

Here are a few methods that may be effective for you:

>> **Pose a benefit-driven question.** Example: "Would you like to learn to grow tomatoes indoors? Click <link> to find out."

>> **Connect proof with product.** Example: "Our customers are able to grow 20% more winter tomatoes using our Indoor Tomato Trellis! See how it works here: <link>"

>> **Show the "After."** Example: "When you have the Indoor Tomato Trellis, you'll enjoy ripe tomatoes picked from the vine even in the coldest winter months. Get the Indoor Tomato Trellis here: <link>"

For more on the "Before" and "After" of marketing, visit Chapter 1.

>> **Present a takeaway.** Example: "This is your last chance to get the Indoor Tomato Trellis at 35% off: <link>"

Getting More Clicks and Opens

When you go through your inbox, you probably pay close attention to only a few emails — maybe 10 percent.

What went wrong with the 90 percent of emails that you didn't engage with? Maybe they didn't have great copy or design, or you didn't like the sender's products or services. Maybe you don't have a trusted relationship with the senders, and those emails just got lost in the sea of emails in your inbox.

As we say earlier in "Writing effective email subject lines," you have about three to four seconds to grab your reader's attention, so a great subject line, perfect copy and design, and an awesome promotion aren't always enough. That may seem a bit unfair.

To get you over this final hump, here are some tips to give your emails an extra boost:

>> **Get the timing right.** Send your emails at times when others aren't sending email. Then your emails will stand out in people's inboxes and get a higher open rate. We've found that the best times to send emails are from 8:30 to 10 a.m., 2:30 to 3:30 p.m., and 8 p.m. to midnight.

>> **Call people by name.** Our research shows that emails with a first name in the subject line garner a 23 percent higher open rate. That's an amazing boost, but don't use this trick too often. It loses its effectiveness if overused.

>> **Be positive in the morning and negative at night.** We all wake up bright-eyed and excited to face the new day (okay, after we've had our coffee). Take advantage of that fact by sending positive email messages during the morning hours. In the evenings, negative messages are better accepted.

TIP

If you're going to send a negative message — perhaps about a declining market or an urgent need — make sure that you offer a solution to the problem as part of your email. No one likes to be made to feel hopeless.

>> **Be controversial or relevant.** Stand out in the inbox by bringing up controversial topics (even if you worry that some of your subscribers won't agree with you) or relevant content.

>> **Use odd or specific numbers.** Everyone has ten tips for doing just about everything. Try using different numbers: "6 ways to change your business tonight," "14 simple ideas to teach your child math," or "The $234,423 idea that changed everything," for example.

TIP

Never round up your numbers up. Doing that makes you sound like a liar. If you have only nine amazing ideas for holiday décor, say you have nine amazing ideas. Saying that you have ten and then delivering only nine makes you look dishonest.

>> **Keep your subject line short.** The best subject lines have six to ten words, or 25 characters. Short subject lines are easy to read and view on a smartphone while still piquing customer interest.

>> **Use a second subject line.** Most email providers have a second area of displayed content on every email. In many email systems, this area is referred to as the description, but if it's left blank, it defaults to the first line of copy. Instead of accepting the default, write a second, strong subject line and place it in the description section to tell your customers more about your email's content.

>> **Include symbols in the subject line.** Using a symbol in the subject line can increase opens by as much as 15 percent. This symbol can be professional, such as a copywriting symbol, or playful, like a snowman for a winter holiday promotion email.

TIP

We find loads of great symbols to use in subject lines at `http://emailstuff.org/glyph`. The site offers cool things like a clock to symbolize a sale that's about to end. Tick-tock.

>> **Press Play.** Instead of including a link, embed a still image of a video with a Play button superimposed on top. This technique can dramatically increase click-through rates in email campaigns.

>> **Ask customers for their thoughts.** This strategy results in the highest click-through rate of all campaign types we run, so we replicate it and get high click-through rates on emails again and again. This strategy involves asking a question and listing four to five answers, each with a link (see Figure 11-9). All the links go to the same place, where customers can find answers to the questions.

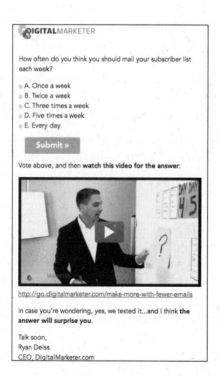

FIGURE 11-9:
An example of a "Your Thoughts?" email that engages the audience.

>> **Combine video and questions.** Video consistently yields high click-through rates and high customer engagement. Include a video and a "your thoughts" question in an email, and have subscribers watch the video to get the answer.

TIP

Many marketers worry that they don't have the charisma or budget to make highly professional video. Don't be afraid! Because email is about relationships, a simple conversational video can show your personality and voice to your subscribers, and allow you to connect with them in a new way.

>> **Add a countdown.** Phrases like "Four days until this sale is over forever!" and "You'll never get this deal again!" increase the urgency of the promotion. You can increase the urgency even more by adding a countdown clock or timer to show customers exactly how much time they have.

>> **Use animated GIFs.** Pretty or funny moving images in an inbox catch people's attention. If you have access to a designer who can make custom animated GIFs, have that person create some for you. If not, sites like Giphy (`http://giphy.com`) offer free GIFs that you can use to give your emails an extra edge.

Ensuring Email Deliverability

Everything we've talked about so far is moot if your emails aren't reaching your subscribers' inboxes. Did you know that 21 percent of emails worldwide never reach the desired recipients? A whole lot of work, effort, and brilliance are being wasted on emails that end up floating around in cyberspace.

How do you make sure that all your work isn't wasted? It comes down to one simple thing: You have to prove that you aren't a spammer and that you have no intention of being one.

Sadly, the Internet service providers responsible for determining whether you are sending spam consider bulk mailers to be guilty until proven innocent. They assume that emails are spam from the outset, and until you can show them that you don't act like a spammer, your email deliverability will be affected.

In the following sections, we provide some methods for improving deliverability. Most of these methods are very technical. If you're a tech wizard, go forth and set up your infrastructure to ensure deliverability. If you need help with technical stuff, find a local tech person or call your email service provider, and get some systems in place to ensure that your emails reach the people you want to reach.

Monitoring your reputation

To ensure deliverability, you have to keep track of how you're interacting with your list. Do the following things:

» Monitor the complaint rates and the volume of complaints you're receiving. Your email service provider should provide reporting capabilities on the number and rate of complaints your emails are receiving. See Chapter 16 for recommended email service providers.

» Respond to complaints in a timely manner.

» Make sure that you unsubscribe and stop sending email to anyone who unsubscribes. Your email service provider should provide a path to unsubscribe from every email and automatically remove those that unsubscribe from your email list.

» Keep your message volume steady. Don't send a million emails one month and then none for six months.

» Check your blacklist status on the major blacklist sites including Spamhaus (`https://www.spamhaus.org/`) and Spamcop (`https://www.spamcop.net/`). These major blacklist sites are referenced by mailbox providers like Google's Gmail to help them determine whether your email should be delivered to the inbox. Each blacklist has its own process for removal from its blacklist; you can find this information on its website.

Proving subscriber engagement

The best way to assure the Internet service providers (ISPs) that you're not a spammer is to prove that you engage your subscribers with every single email you send. If people are opening your emails, reading what you have to say, and then clicking relevant links, you aren't a spammer.

Subscriber engagement rates are based on the following factors:

» **Your open rate:** This rate isn't the number of emails that are opened, but the percentage.

» **Your lateral scroll rate:** This rate is how far recipients scroll down on your emails.

» **Your hard and soft bounce rate:** A bad email address is considered to be a hard bounce. A soft bounce can happen for many reasons, including a full inbox or accidental flagging as spam.

WARNING

TIP

If you continue to send emails to addresses that reject your mail, you look like a spammer.

Export your entire list, and send it to a company called BriteVerify (www.briteverify.com/). This company runs an analysis of your list and tells you which addresses are definitively good, which ones are questionable, and which are bad. If you expunge the questionable and bad emails from your list, you're practicing good list hygiene and increasing deliverability.

» **Unsubscription and complaint rates:** If you receive high numbers of unsubscriptions or complaints, examine your campaigns to see whether you're doing something to upset subscribers.

TOOLS THAT ENSURE EMAIL DELIVERABILITY

Several applications can help you ensure a high percentage of email deliverability. A few of our favorites are the following:

- **Mail Monitor** (http://mailmonitor.com): Mail Monitor breaks down delivery per IP address, message, and email service.

- **Return Path** (https://senderscore.org): If you have your own IP address, Return Path allows you to monitor your reputation and set up alerts. You get a baseline email deliverability score.

- **EmailReach** (www.emailreach.com): This service allows you to set up tracking on domain and IP blacklisting and scans these blacklists daily, notifying you if you've been added.

4

Measuring, Analyzing, and Optimizing Campaigns

IN THIS PART . . .

Assess the health and effectiveness of your marketing campaigns through data and analytics by using analytics suites such as Google Analytics.

Learn how to use split tests to optimize your digital marketing campaigns and website.

Chapter **12**

Crunching Numbers: Running a Data-Driven Business

F ew marketers disagree on the significance of collecting data. But for businesses to remain competitive, they must go beyond simply aggregating data to truly gain value from it. Simply knowing your averages is not enough. Companies need to analyze the data they gather in a process known as data analysis. True data analysis is data with a plan. Through data-collecting tools such as Google Analytics, you can track the return on investment (ROI) of traffic from your email campaigns, social media campaigns, paid ads, and more.

When you have the capability to track the ROI of your campaigns, you can cut the fat and double down on what's actually working. That way, you transform your business from one that spends time, money, and resources on strategies that just *seem* as though they'll work well to a business that makes smart, data-driven decisions and *knows* what strategies *do* work well.

In this chapter, we explore what data analysis is and what it can do for your company. We examine ways to make data useful using Google Analytics (which is free) so that you can create accurate, consumable reports that you can actually learn from as well as share with your team, client, or both.

Leveraging the Five Google Analytics Report Suites

Google Analytics is the most widely used website statistics service. After you've properly installed it on your site, Google Analytics gathers data on the traffic of your site, allowing you to make intelligent marketing and business decisions. This analytics suite can track visitors from search engines, social networks, and direct visits. Google Analytics has a basic service, which is free, as well as a premium version. To learn more about Google Analytics or how to install it on your site, visit the Google Analytics Help Center.

Within Google Analytics are five report suites that you can use to break down your data. You find these reports on the left side of the website:

>> **Real Time Suite:** Gives data and shows what is going on within your site that instant. For instance, you can see how many visitors are on your site, what pages they are on, and what their geographical location is in real time. Figure 12-1 shows some of the information displayed by the Real Time Overview report in Google Analytics.

FIGURE 12-1:
A look at a Real Time report in Google Analytics.

>> **Audience Suite:** This report centers on the people who are on your site and gives you insight into their characteristics, including their demographics, interests and behaviors, the electronic device or browser they use to access your site, and more.

>> **Acquisition Suite:** Use this report to discover how your users arrived at your site. For instance, you learn what website users were on before they came to

your site, or what keyword or keyword phrase they searched for to land on your website.

>> **Behavior Suite:** The Behavior Reports focus on what people do when they arrive at your site. This report suite displays information like what pages users visit, how long they stay on those pages, and how many people exit that page.

>> **Conversions Suite:** You run Conversion Reports to determine whether users are making purchases or completing the goals you've set up, such as subscribing to your newsletter or buying a product or service.

Each of these reporting suites contains multiple reports, and each of those reports can drill down into more and more detail. For example, you can view the Mobile Devices report in the Audience Report suite to see how visitor behavior differs when people visit your website from a desktop, mobile, and tablet. While you're in this same report, Google Analytics allows you to change the parameters to view behavior by service provider (AT&T versus Verizon) and operating system (iOS versus Android). If you want to get more granular, drill down by clicking one of the operating systems to view visitor behavior by the version of the operating system.

Understanding Where Your Traffic Is Coming From

Many different avenues can lead people to your site, ranging from ads to search queries to people bookmarking your page and then returning. Here are the common default sources of traffic as recorded by Google Analytics:

>> **Email:** Visits from those who have clicked the links in your email promotions and newsletter.

>> **Organic search:** Visits from people typing search queries into search engines such as Google or Bing.

>> **Direct:** Traffic from users who type the exact domain of your site, such as Pepsi.com, into their browser and navigate straight to your site. If someone bookmarks your page and then visits your site again via that bookmark, that visit also registers as direct traffic.

>> **Paid search:** Traffic from paid search is traffic you have purchased, such as pay-per-click ads from search engines.

>> **Referral:** Visitors from sites that link to your website, such as blogs and forums.

>> **Social:** Visits from social channels, such as Twitter or Facebook.

One of the most enlightening reports to view in Google Analytics is the Acquisition Overview report within the Acquisition Suite in Google Analytics. It is the first report you should view when evaluating the health and performance of a website. Figure 12-2 shows a pie chart from the Acquisition Overview report containing the various methods of traffic acquisition for a website.

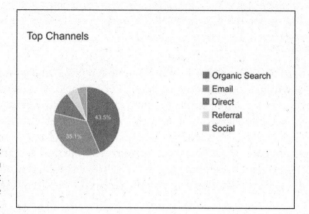

FIGURE 12-2:
The Acquisition Overview Report in Google Analytics.

Tracking the Origins of Site Visitors

Although analytics programs like Google Analytics track the origin of your site visitors using their default settings, you'll likely find that these default settings are too broad to ascertain meaningful data. To get more granular (and thus more useful) data, you can append UTM parameters to the links you share around the web. UTM stands for Urchin Tracking Module, and it is a tracking marker appended to a Uniform Resource Locator (URL). The UTM system allows users to tag hyperlinks in order to trace where visitors originated.

For example, if you want to track the number of leads generated by a single link shared with your Facebook fans, you can do that using Google Analytics and a link with UTM parameters. Simply put, you place a UTM at the end of a hyperlink so that you can figure out how people get to your site and what they do after they get there.

For every hyperlink you want to track, whether on your blog or your social media channels, that directs traffic to a landing page you own, consider adding UTM parameters. By adding this tracking code to the hyperlinks you share, you can track the origins of that visit.

A UTM consists of various parameters. Here are the UTM parameters that matter most:

- » Campaign source (utm_source)

- » Campaign medium (utm_medium)

- » Campaign content (utm_content)

- » Campaign name (utm_campaign)

We explain each of these parameters in the sections that follow.

Campaign source (utm_source)

Generally, the source of a UTM describes where your visitors come from. The source tells you the specific place where the referring link was shared, such as

- » An email promotion

- » A social network

- » A referring website

Common sources include

- » Facebook

- » Email newsletter

- » Twitter

- » Google

- » YouTube

The source enables you to know which email, search engine, or Facebook ad (or other source) a user came from. Knowing where traffic is coming from can be powerful because you gain insight into what your users are responding to.

Campaign medium (utm_medium)

This parameter identifies the medium or vehicle that the link was used on, such as email. Medium tells you how visitors arrived at your site. Some of the most common mediums include

- » Email

- » Pay per click (PPC)

» Banner-ads

» Direct (which tells you users directly typed in your site address)

Campaign content (utm_content)

Campaign content describes the specific ad, banner, or email used to share the link. It gives you additional details to use with A/B testing or content-targeted ads, as well as helps you determine what creative is working best at promoting an offer or distributing content.

TIP

Be as descriptive as possible with this parameter's naming structure so that you can easily remember what email or ad this UTM refers to.

Campaign name (utm_campaign)

This parameter serves as an identifier of a specific product or promotion campaign, such as a spring sale or another promotion you run. The campaign name's basic purpose is to highlight promotional offers or content distribution strategies so that you can easily compare performance across time and platform.

TIP

Campaign links should be consistent across all different sources and media for any given promotion to ensure that the campaign as a whole can easily be analyzed.

Dissecting a UTM

The previous sections go over the most important parameters that make up a UTM, and this one examines a UTM's structure. For instance, here's what a UTM looks like for a flash sale for one of DigitalMarketer's products, the Content Engine:

```
http://www.digitalmarketer.com/lp/the-content-engine?utm_source=house-
list-email-boradcast&utm_medium=email&utm_content=content-engine-flash-
mail-1&utm_campaign=content-engine-flash-sale-1-1-16
```

Your UTM might look something like the preceding. Following is breakdown of this URL with a UTM by section:

» **http://www.digitalmarketer.com/lp/the-content-engine:** The hyperlink.

» **?utm_source=house-list-email-broadcast:** The campaign source, which is the referring source of the traffic. In this case, it's an email to our "house" email list.

>> **&utm_medium=email:** Campaign medium, which is how the user was referred. In this case it was via email.

>> **&utm_content=content-engine-flash-mail-1:** Campaign content, which is the ad or campaign identifier you assign. In this case, this is the first email for the Content Engine flash sale promotion.

>> **&utm_campaign=content-engine-flash-sale-1-1-16:** Campaign name, which is the specific promotion or strategy. In this case, this campaign is the Content Engine flash sale beginning on January 1st, 2016.

Creating UTM parameters for your URLs

Google makes building UTM links super easy with a free, easy-to-use UTM builder called the Google Analytics URL Builder. Visit the page, follow the steps, and plug in your information to automatically generate a hyperlink with UTM parameters that you can then track with Google Analytics — that is, if you've properly set up a Google Analytics account. If you haven't already, visit Google Analytics Help Center. This resource contains further instructions about how you can use each of the different UTM parameters.

TIP

Creating properly attributed hyperlinks takes some time to get used to, but the data it provides is worth its weight in gold. To make consistency easy, create a unified document in which you track all the hyperlinks you use, which will make it easy to refer back to when you're analyzing later.

WARNING

UTM parameters are case sensitive, so if you use *abc* for your utm_campaign tags on some links and *ABC* for your utm_campaign tags on other links, they show up as separate campaigns in your Google Analytics.

Creating Goals to See Who's Taking Action

After you've created a UTM tag, as described in the preceding section, you can set up goals in Google Analytics. Goals provide a way to track the actions that groups of people take on your site by tallying specific behaviors. What makes goals really useful is not just the ability to track how many times an action was taken but also to see which groups of people took that action. Although Google Analytics does not allow you to track behavior back to personal identifiable information, such as the person's name or email address, it does allow you to track information such as the device they are using, where people are in the world, or the other pages they visited on your website. Thanks to the UTM parameters, you can actually see what individuals and groups of individuals do when they arrive on your site.

The most basic goal that you want to set in Google Analytics is an opt-in that generates a lead. When visitors fill out a form, they are often directed to a confirmation page. To measure the number of opt-ins you're receiving, you simply set up Google Analytics to measure how many people visit the confirmation page after visiting the opt-in page.

To set up a form fill in Google Analytics, follow these steps:

1. **Click the Admin section of Google Analytics.**

   The Admin menu appears.

2. **Click Goals under All Website Data.**

   The Goals dialog box appears.

3. **Click the + New Goal button to create a new goal.**

   The Goal Setup page appears.

4. **Scroll down and select the Sign Up Goal type; then click the Continue button.**

   The Goal Description page appears. Google offers a variety of goal templates that should fit your specific needs (although you can create custom ones as well). Because you want to track opt-ins, Sign Up should be perfect in this case.

5. **Name your goal and then, under the Type field, select Destination and press the Continue button.**

   The final setup page, called the Goal Details page, appears.

6. **Set up the specifics for your goal.**

   For Destination field, change your rule to Begins With and add your Thank You page's URL string — that's where people who opt-in end up. Using Begins With helps to ensure that all opt-ins are properly credited. The other way to ensure that you're tracking actual opt-ins and not just accidental Thank You page visitors is to create a funnel. This involves adding the URL string of the opt-in page as well (see Figure 12-3). To set up a funnel, you turn the Funnel option to ON and add a step with the page field, including the URL that precedes your destination page. Set this step to Required and you've added this rule! When you're done, verify your goal to make sure that you set it up correctly.

7. **Click Save.**

   You've built your first goal in Google Analytics!

Thank You Page URL String   Set "Required" to "Yes"

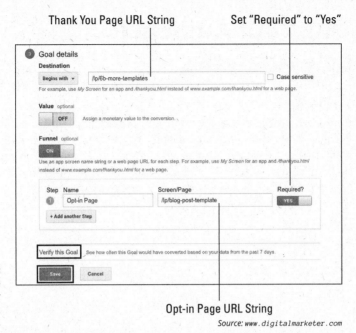

FIGURE 12-3:
Setting up the
specifics for
your goal.

Opt-in Page URL String

Source: www.digitalmarketer.com

TIP

For your URL strings, always use the text after your domain name, not the entire URL — Google already knows the root domain.

After a few days of collecting data for your goal in Google Analytics, you can review the collected data. The goal you set up with UTM parameters gives you insight into your customers. Goals are also a great way to see what channels, such as Facebook, email, and your blog, are driving the most visits. To take a peek at these insights, go to the Reporting section of Google Analytics and choose the Conversions Suite in the left menu. Then click the Goals drop-down menu and click the Overview tab. The Goal Overview report opens and shows how the goals you have set up are performing. This report shows aggregated data for all the goals you have set up. To review one specific goal, click the drop down located at the top of the page beneath "Goal Option" and select one individual goal. That goal report opens. This report will tell you total goal completions and the conversion rate for this goal.

With a little bit of know-how and a lot of proper attribution tagging, you can set up the Google Analytics campaign tracking to give you some great insights! You then have the foundation you need to properly track your success, allowing you to focus on what's working and eliminate what's not. This type of assessment is essential to do for any business so that you can make educated decisions as you grow.

Segmenting Your Audience with Google Analytics

The previous sections of this chapter give you the bare-bones knowledge you need to properly track success and determine what channels are driving that success, but how do you put all this knowledge to work? The answer is that you segment your audience, which we also discuss in Chapters 4 and 10. The powerful information you've gained from UTM parameters and creating goals in Google Analytics enables you to break down your audience into segments based on the following:

» Channel

» Traffic source

» Completed actions

» Conversions

In the context of analytics, a segment represents groups of visitors with shared characteristics or behaviors. Segmenting your audience in Google Analytics allows you to

» Figure out who finds your message appealing so that you can send more of this audience to this particular offer.

» Craft customized messaging to enhance ad copy and shape follow-up campaigns.

Segmenting might sound simple, but it provides one of the best ways to make the most of your budget, or to know where you should spend your time and energy to drive new customers. By segmenting your audience, you gain a better understanding of what's working and what's not so that you can plan accordingly. In the following section, we cover how to create useful segments, as well as how to drill down into these segments to better understand the people who are taking the actions you're looking for.

Creating audience segments

Using audience segments as a strategy shows you how to focus on the most valuable, highest-converting audiences. This allows you to figure out what makes them tick, so to speak. Before we dive into exactly what information you should be looking at, and how to pull it, we discuss how to create the segments you use to dig into your audience information.

Creating segments is fast and easy. You create a set of rules that include or exclude certain people, allowing you to narrow down your audience to look at a specific subset rather than all site visitors, such as people who opted in for a gated offer. After creating a segment, you can analyze how this subset of visitors behaved or who is in the subset, giving you valuable insight on what offers to make to this audience. Follow these steps to create your own segments.

1. **In Google Analytics, navigate to the Reporting section.**

   The report suites appear.

2. **Select the Audience suite and click the Overview tab within the Audience suite.**

   The Audience Overview report appears.

3. **Click the + Add Segment field along the top of the page.**

   The Segment menu appears.

4. **Click the New Segment button to create a new segment (see Figure 12-4).**

   The Segment menu opens, allowing you to set conditions for your segments to meet and exclusions you want your segment to ignore. For instance, you might set a condition for age or operating system.

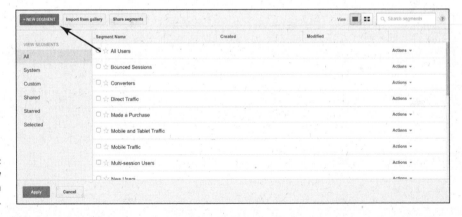

FIGURE 12-4:
Creating a New
Segment in
Google Analytics.

5. **Set conditions for your segment by selecting any of the following check boxes or filling in the field within in the following categories:**

   - **Demographics:** Segment your users by demographic information, such as age, gender, location, and other details. These are check boxes and form fields, depending on the option within the Demographics category.

- **Technology:** Segment your users' sessions by their web and mobile technologies, such as browser, device category, and screen resolution. These are check boxes and form fields, depending on the option within the Technology category.

- **Behavior:** Segment your users by how often they visit (called a session) and conduct transactions, such as sessions, session duration, and days since last session. These are form fields.

- **Date of first session:** Segment your users (create cohorts) by when they first visited your site. This is a form field.

- **Traffic sources:** Segment your users by how they found you, such as the keyword they used, the ad campaign, and the medium used. These are form fields.

- **Conditions:** Segment your users, their sessions, or both according to single or multisession conditions, such as time, goal conversions, and custom variables. This is a form field.

- **Sequences:** Segment your users, their sessions, or both according to sequential conditions, such as the steps they took to reach your site. This is a form field.

6. **After setting your conditions for your segment, name your segment by filling out the empty name field.**

7. **Click the Save button to successfully complete this segment.**

   Your new segment loads, and you can return to this segment at a later date when conducting future data research and analysis.

After your new segment loads, the data for your segment is displayed, allowing you to make assessments. For instance, it displays how many users make up the segment, as well as other stats. Figure 12-5 shows an example of a completed segment; this segment shows mobile users and consists of 122,263 users.

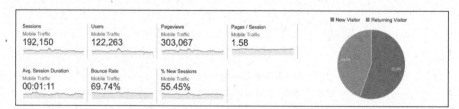

FIGURE 12-5:
A segment for mobile users.

As a general rule, you want to aim for a minimum of 3,000 people in your audience segment, which ensures that you have enough subgroups to have faith in your groupings. You can experiment with fewer, but the larger your segment category is, the more trustworthy your data will be, allowing you to make sound, educated business decisions.

TIP

Segments aren't limited to the Audience suite. You can create a segment for any of the following suites: Audience, Acquisition, Behavior, or Conversion. Choose the suite that best meets your needs to create this segment and select Overview within your chosen suite. Although the suite you choose may be different from Audience and thus the data it measures, the steps discussed in this section to set up a segment remain the same.

Honing In on Your Audience

After you segment your audiences, you can drill down further and gain more detail. Now is the time to run reports to figure out who's taking the action you want, such as opting in, and who's not, so that you can do more of what's working. Reports give you a better understanding of your audience, and understanding your audience leads to driving down ad costs, or figuring out better strategies for monetizing the leads you're getting!

You should look for two main types of data:

>> Demographic

>> Psychographic

Demographic data describes what people are like. Generally, this data includes statistical details like age and gender but can also include the type of device they're using as well as their location. Demographic information helps you understand exactly who you are speaking to and guides the targeting you use in your campaigns.

Psychographic data, in contrast, describes what people like. This data is all about interests, hobbies, and likes, and it speaks more to the personality of the audience. Psychographic information is most powerful when you use it to shape your messaging.

Figure 12-6 shows a breakdown of the data types and what they're best used for.

In the following sections, we build one report to look at demographic data and one to look at psychographic data. This way, you can easily run these reports for all kinds of audience segments.

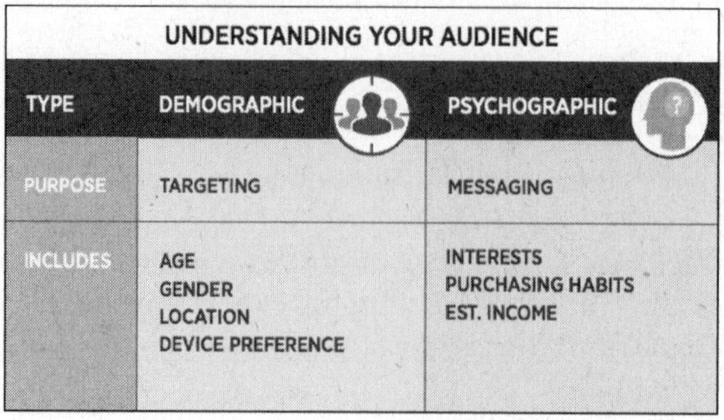

FIGURE 12-6:
The best uses for demographic and psychographic data.

*Source: https://analytics.google.com/analytics/web/?authuser=
1#report/visitors-overview/a54278530w87158541p110653994/%3F_.
useg%3Dbuiltin28/*

Drilling into demographics

Although the data that a report for demographic data shows is typically fairly cut and dried, it yields very interesting insights. You can quickly look at a demographics report on the Audience tab in Google Analytics; however, this report's key metric focuses on sessions (visits). To go beyond sessions and hone in on your users, you need to create a custom report.

To make a custom report for demographics, follow these steps:

1. **Go to the Customization section in Google Analytics and select the + New Custom Report button.**

   The Create Custom Report page opens. Create as many separate reports as you want to examine for demographics. At our company, we make four reports when drilling down into demographics: one each for age, gender, location, and device type.

2. **In the Report Content section of the Create Custom Report page, create Report Tabs.**

   Name the tab based on the demographic you are drilling down on. For example, if you are measuring age, name the Age. If you plan to measure multiple demographics in this report, as we suggest in Step 1, you can create a new Report Tab by clicking the + Add Report Tab button under the Report Content section. Name each tab for the demographic you are measuring.

3. **On the same page, set the Metric Groups dimension to Users by clicking the + Add Metric button and then selecting Users from the drop-down menu for every Report Tab you create.**

   The word *Users* will now be displayed in the Metric Groups dimension. Users is the constant among all your tabs.

4. **On the same page, in the Dimension Drilldowns dimension, set the demographic for each Report Tab you create by clicking the +Add Dimension button.**

   For Age, the Dimension Drilldown is Age; for Gender, it's Gender, and for Device, it's the Device Category. Your respective demographic now appears in the Dimension Drilldown dimension. Location is the only oddball; for the other demographics, you keep Type (located above the Metric Groups dimension) at the preselected Explorer Tab. For location, however, you set your Type to the Map Overlay tab, which will display the location data on a geographical map, and it replaces the need for a Dimension Drilldown.

   Figure 12-7 shows the setup for creating an Age report.

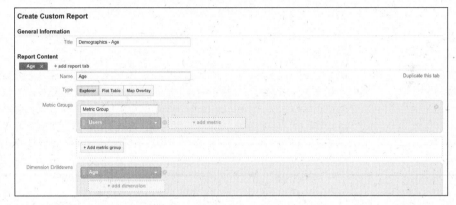

FIGURE 12-7:
Creating a custom report for age.

5. **Click the Save button when you're done.**

   The report you created loads, and you now have a ready-made demographics report to use repeatedly.

The following sections tell you what to look for in the demographics report so that you can gain insight into your campaign.

Age

First, examine the age of the people who are responding to your campaign. Who's opting in? Are there any surprises? For instance, are the age ranges that are opting in fitting the customer avatar you created (see Chapter 1 for details on creating a customer avatar)? If not, you probably need to reevaluate the ad copy for your campaign through the lens of that age range. This report allows you to create a more customized campaign, which can lead to an increase in opt-ins and a drop in cost per click (CPC).

Gender

Next, what is the gender of the users who opted in to your campaign? If opt-ins are more heavily weighted toward a particular gender, you'll likely see a benefit if you create a second version of the campaign that solely targets one gender, which leads to a boost in clicks and ad relevance while also dropping CPC.

Location

Location can be a powerful data set, especially if you're looking to break into a new geographic market or scale in other areas. For instance, you may find from a Location report that your campaign is doing particularly well in a certain city, state, or country that you hadn't previously considered. You can then make an informed decision about allocating more of your ad budget to target this location that you didn't previously consider, allowing you to take advantage of regional interests.

Device

With a Device report, you can see what device people opted in to your campaign with. Was it their mobile device, their tablet, or their desktop? Knowing the device people are using to opt in to your campaign helps you know how to design it. For instance, if your gated offer (see Chapters 3 and 4 for details on building gated offers) is doing particularly well with mobile users, then it is critical for this particular campaign to design your conversion funnel with mobile users in mind if you want to turn gated offer downloaders into purchasers.

Drilling into psychographics

The previous sections tell you how to dig into the cold, hard facts about your audience, and you can use that information to shape the targeting of the campaign during your optimization phase. But what about the messaging? What about your follow-up strategy? To figure out your best tactics here, we turn to psychographic data.

Again, you're going to create another custom report, this time looking at Affinity Categories and In-Market Segments. Although Affinity Categories look more at your users' likes and interests, In-Market Segments indicate what this audience wants to purchase (or may have just purchased). This process follows many of the same steps as when you created your custom demographic report:

1. **Go to Customization in Google Analytics and select + New Custom Report.**

   The Create Custom Report page opens.

2. **In the Report Content section of the Create Custom Report page, create Report Tabs: one for Affinity Categories and another for In-Market Segments.**

You add a tab by clicking the + Add Report Tab button under the Report Content section. Name one tab for your In-Market Segments and one for your Affinity Categories.

3. **On the same page, set the Metric Groups dimension to Users by clicking the + Add Metric button and then selecting Users from the drop-down menu for every Report Tab you create.**

   The word *Users* will now be displayed in the Metric Groups dimension. Users is the constant among all your tabs.

4. **On the same page, in the Dimension Drilldowns dimension, set the demographic for each Report Tab you create by clicking the +Add Dimension button.**

   The Dimension Drilldowns that you select are Affinity Category and In-Market Segment, respectively.

   Figure 12-8 shows what the setup looks like for creating an In-Market Segment report.

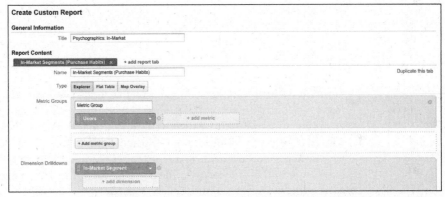

FIGURE 12-8:
Creating a custom report for In-Market.

Source: *https://analytics.google.com/analytics/web/?authuser=1#crbuilder/cr-builder/a54278530w87158541p90451453//CREATE/*

5. **Click the Save button when you're done.**

The report you created loads, and you now have a report that you can come back to repeatedly to study the interests of the users who have opted in.

Affinity Category report

Again, the Affinity Category report compiles what your users like and are interested in. This information allows you to create more customized campaigns by targeting specific interests. When looking at this data, setting the data view type to Comparison is best. (Click the Comparison View button, located on the right of the page.) This view highlights interests better than raw numbers do. Interests are listed from top likes to dislikes, as shown in Figures 12-9 and 12-10.

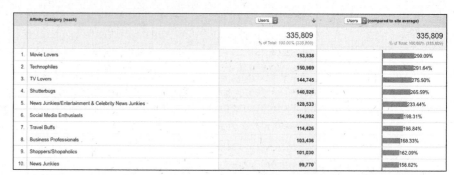

FIGURE 12-9:
An Affinity report that shows the top interests for this audience.

Source: https://analytics.google.com/analytics/web/?authuser=1#crbuilder/cr-builder/
a54278530w87158541p90451453//CREATE/

Affinity Category (reach)	Users	Users (compared to site average)
	335,809	335,809
	% of Total: 100.00% (335,809)	% of Total: 100.00% (335,809)
1. Movie Lovers	153,838	299.09%
2. Technophiles	150,969	291.64%
3. TV Lovers	144,745	275.50%
4. Shutterbugs	140,926	265.59%
5. News Junkies/Entertainment & Celebrity News Junkies	128,533	233.44%
6. Social Media Enthusiasts	114,992	198.31%
7. Travel Buffs	114,426	196.84%
8. Business Professionals	103,436	168.33%
9. Shoppers/Shopaholics	101,030	162.09%
10. News Junkies	99,770	158.82%

FIGURE 12-10:
An Affinity report that shows what this audience is least interested in.

96. Sports Fans/Rugby Enthusiasts	5,079	-86.82%
97. News Junkies/Women's Media Fans	2,961	-92.32%
98. Gamers/Sports Game Fans	2,708	-92.97%
99. Sports Fans/Skiing Enthusiasts	2,608	-93.23%
100. Gamers/Driving & Racing Game Fans	2,545	-93.40%
101. Music Lovers/Blues Fans	2,163	-94.39%
102. TV Lovers/Documentary & Nonfiction TV Fans	1,792	-95.35%
103. News Junkies/World News Junkies	1,711	-95.56%
104. Sports Fans/Swimming Enthusiasts	1,561	-95.95%
105. Sports Fans/Australian Football Fans	863	-97.76%
106. News Junkies/Men's Media Fans	611	-98.41%

Source: https://analytics.google.com

Through Affinity reports, you can start to hone your marketing message. For instance, the audience depicted in Figure 12-9 is clearly interested in movies, TV, and entertainment and celebrity news. This knowledge enables you to get specific with your ad copy as you optimize your campaign. For example, an ad that asks "How does your business's Social Media Score compare to Kim Kardashian's?" would likely be a huge hit with this audience. On the other hand, as the data shows in Figure 12-10, sports-themed ads would most likely flop. So if you went in blind and tried a sports theme with your next ad campaign, you'd probably have a failed ad on your hands.

TIP

When trying to think of specific messaging, drill down your categories into more specific niche categories, such as "TV Lovers/Game, Reality & Talk Show Fans" rather than simply "TV Lovers."

In-Market report

As we state earlier in the chapter, In-Market Segments give you some indication as to what your audience is in the market to purchase (or may have just purchased). This is extremely powerful information, allowing you to target your market based on products and services they search for. As with the Affinity report, when looking at this data, it's best to set the data view type to Comparison. This view highlights interest better than raw numbers do. Figure 12-11 shows a sample of an In-Market report.

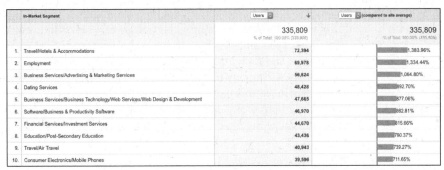

Source: https://analytics.google.com

FIGURE 12-11:
The data results
of an In-Market
report.

As shown in Figure 12-11, the audience who opted in to this campaign is also in the market for and researching employment, travel and hotel accommodations, and business and advertising services, just to name a few. Therefore, ads that used the language of travel or advertising services are set up for success.

You can also use In-Market reports to do some detective work to figure out your users' income range. Use your sleuthing powers to get a sense of whether this target market is interested in luxury goods to try to get a sense of whether prospects fall on the high end of the spectrum of income. To do this, look for high concentrations of interest in categories that indicate wealth, namely luxury items. Here are some general categories to use for this analysis:

>> Luxury Affinity Categories

>> Shoppers/Luxury Shoppers

>> Auto Enthusiasts/Performance & Luxury Vehicle Enthusiasts

>> Travel Buffs/Luxury Travelers

>> Luxury In-Market Audiences

>> Apparel & Accessories/Jewelry & Watches/Watches

>> Apparel & Accessories/Jewelry & Watches/Fine Jewelry

>> Autos & Vehicles/Motor Vehicles/Motor Vehicles by Brand/Audi

>> Autos & Vehicles/Motor Vehicles/Motor Vehicles by Brand/BMW

>> Autos & Vehicles/Motor Vehicles/Motor Vehicles by Type/Luxury Vehicles/
Luxury Vehicles (New)

>> Autos & Vehicles/Motor Vehicles/Motor Vehicles by Type/Sports Cars/Sports
Cars (New)

>> Autos & Vehicles/Motor Vehicles/Motor Vehicles by Brand/Porsche

This strategy gives you another technique to understand your users' income, and thus what products they may or may not be interested in. For example, if you ran this report and found that only about 3 percent of your audience for this campaign showed up within any of these segments, you could safely conclude that the people opting in for this particular gated offer aren't wealthy. Therefore, following up with a campaign for a particularly pricey item is likely to be less successful than one with more moderate, flash-sale–style offers.

Putting It All Together

Armed with the information from your custom reports, you can now take the demographics and psychographics data and combine it to get a better understanding of the audience who is opting in to this campaign and have a profile of your ideal candidate for this campaign. Instead of guessing, you now have proven data to use for optimizing and scaling your campaign, which in turn can lead to more opt-ins, improved ad relevancy, and lower CPC. This is the power of crunching numbers and running a data-driven business. Here's an example of what your customer avatar profile may look like after combining all the different data points that you've collected on your audience:

Gender: Woman

Age: Late 20s, early 30s

Preferred Device: Smartphone

Estimated Average Income: Under $100k Annually

Role at Work: Nonsupervisor

Likes and Interests: Movies, Celebrity & Entertainment News, Pop Music, Education, Career Consulting, Dating Services, Home Décor & Gardening Services

Dislikes: Sports, Horror Films, Board Games, Videogames, Automobile Accessories

Based on what has worked so far, you can then take this profile of your ideal candidate and create a more targeted campaign or scale it to other traffic platforms, but now your campaign can be even more specific. Armed with this information, you can attack the campaign from a new angle and speak more directly to your target audience. Imagine what your paid traffic team could do with this level of detail about whom they are targeting.

You can apply the data strategies covered in this chapter not only to people who opt in but also to purchasers or, with careful targeting, membership site users as well. In addition, you can use this strategy for any platform that drives sufficient traffic volume.

Chapter **13**

Optimizing Your Campaigns for Maximum ROI

magine that you've built a web page designed to sell a Caribbean cruise. At the top of this page, you show a headline that reads "Save on Caribbean Cruise Deals! Nobody Beats Our Prices!" Your business partner approaches you with a couple of new headline ideas that she thinks will improve the number of cruise bookings. What should you do — trust her gut and make the change? Or stick with the original?

The correct answer is to test it. As we discuss in Chapter 12, a data-driven business goes beyond making marketing decisions based on hunches and guesswork. To truly maximize your campaign's ROI (return on investment), you need to gather data and run tests to increase the impact. Otherwise, your actions are like throwing spaghetti at the wall and seeing what sticks — and they'll be just as efficient and impactful to your bottom line.

In this chapter, we examine the dedicated, repeatable process of campaign optimization. Although this process is easy to overcomplicate, we break it into understandable parts and give you the outline you need to run a successful optimization campaign — from the required tools to the final test analysis.

Understanding Split Testing

The cornerstone of optimizing a website is *split testing*, which means to conduct controlled, randomized experiments with the goal of improving a website metric, such as clicks, opt-ins, or sales. Split testing takes two different forms: *A/B testing,* a technique in which two versions of a page can be compared for performance, and *multivariate testing,* a testing method in which a combination of variables is tested at one time.

During a split test, you split incoming website traffic between the original (control) page and different variations of the page. You then look for improvements in the goals you're measuring (such as leads, sales, or engagement) to emerge so that you can determine which version performed best. You use split testing to test areas where you might be able to improve a measurable goal, such as your online checkout process. The test helps you try to determine what factors increase conversions, what factors deter conversions, and what can lead to an increase in orders.

Obtaining the tools you need to run split tests

To run split tests, you need effective tools. This section tells you about the technology you need to run split tests so that you can optimize your campaign for maximum results.

An analytics suite

To choose the right pages to test on your website, you rely heavily on your website analytics tool. This chapter focuses on Google Analytics, a website analytics solution made available by search engine giant Google. This tool measures website, app, digital, and offline data to gain customer insights. Google Analytics has two pricing tiers: free and premium. For most businesses, the free version of Google Analytics is more than sufficient. Pricing for the premium version of Google Analytics starts in the six figures annually; this tier offers higher data limits, more custom variables, a dedicated support team, as well as other features. For an introduction to working with Google Analytics, see Chapter 12 or visit `https://www.google.com/analytics/`.

Testing tech

Split tests require the technology that enables you to edit variations, split test variations, and track conversions. You can choose from among several services, including:

>> **Visual Website Optimizer:** An easy-to-use split testing tool. It allows you to run A/B and multivariate testing to optimize your website for increased conversion rates and sales. This paid tool has several pricing packages to choose from for individuals to large agencies. Visit `https://vwo.com/` to learn more.

>> **Unbounce:** Gives marketers the power to build, publish, and test landing pages. It also offers A/B testing. It has several pricing tiers to choose from for entrepreneurs and enterprise-level businesses alike. Find it at `http://unbounce.com/`.

>> **Optimizely:** One of the world's leading experimentation platforms for websites, mobile apps, and connected devices. Optimizely makes customer-experience optimization software for companies, which gives businesses the capability to conduct A/B and multivariate testing. The company offers three pricing tiers, and you can see them at `https://www.optimizely.com/`.

TIP

Make sure to integrate your testing tech tool with Google Analytics so that your Google Analytics reports reflect accurate data.

Test duration calculator

A *test duration calculator* is a simple calculator that determines how long you need to run your split test to get a reliable test result. You input data such as the existing conversion rate, the number of variations in the test, the amount of traffic your site gets, and more. The calculator then determines how many days to run this test to get a reliable result. Figure 13-1 shows the free test duration calculator offered by Visual Website Optimizer.

REMEMBER

Not every page on your website needs to be tested or requires optimization. In the next section, we discuss the ways for you to isolate the pages to test so that you can maximize your return on investment (ROI).

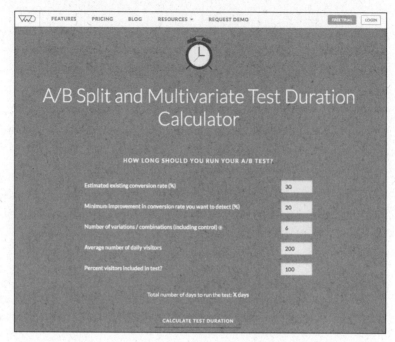

FIGURE 13-1:
A test duration calculator from Visual Website Optimizer.

Source: https://vwo.com/ab-split-test-duration/

Following the split test guidelines

When you're looking for pages to split test, use the following guidelines to determine how worthy a page is to test. First, here's what *not* to test:

» Your worst-performing pages (This sounds counter intuitive, but we explain why.)

» Pages that don't impact your longer-term business goals, for example, your 404 page

» Pages that don't get enough traffic to run a split test

So why shouldn't you test your worst-performing pages? When looking for pages to optimize, your job is to focus on *opportunity pages,* which are pages that will have the greatest impact on your goals. For instance, if you expect a 10 percent increase in conversions from your efforts, would you rather that lift be on a page converting at 50 percent or 5 percent? The one at 50 percent is an opportunity page.

Further, your worst-performing pages don't need a testing campaign; rather, they need an overhaul. The ship is sinking, and you don't have time to hypothesize over what to do next; you need to make a drastic change that likely doesn't need to be tested. Remember, in such a case, don't test; implement!

For the same reason that you don't want to test the worst-performing pages, you also don't need to test your nonconversion-oriented pages. These nonconverting pages include your About Us page or your "dead end" 404 page.

However, optimizing 404 pages has proven to be useful in marketing. Even on that page, you should include an offer, a call to action, or some additional steps to keep the user engaged. You don't need to test adding these elements to the page, however; just add content that meets your goals and then move on to more important pages that impact conversion. Amazon's 404 page, shown in Figure 13-2, directs people to the Amazon home page or suggests continuing to search.

Source: https://www.amazon.com/pizza

FIGURE 13-2:
404 pages, like Amazon's, should offer users a next step but they don't need to be split tested.

The final guideline you should follow when determining whether to split test a page is the page's traffic. Look at the number of visits and of conversions that your page gets over the potential test period. Notice where traffic falls off considerably.

You can easily identify your pages and their traffic numbers using Google Analytics. Examine the number of Unique Pageviews for pages under consideration for split testing. The best report to employ for this job in Google Analytics is in the Behavior suite, which we detail in Chapter 12. In Google Analytics, navigate to the Reporting section and then select the following: Behavior ⇨ Site Content ⇨ All Pages. The Pages report loads. From there, use the filter tool in Google Analytics to search for the specific pages you're considering for a split test.

After you gather the data from the Page report, you should contextualize the pages. You'll always see a massive drop-off in page views (the total number of pages viewed by a user; repeated views of a single page are counted) after your home page. However, your home page is so far away from your main converting action that it doesn't make sense to test. Now, if you see a massive drop from a product page to the checkout page, you know that something is wrong with your product page and that you need to optimize it, and that merits a split test.

By following the guidelines in this section, you can hone in on pages worthy of your time and resources for testing. When you find a page that you consider to be test worthy based on the guidelines, make sure to ask these four questions:

1. Does the page get enough unique visitors?

2. Does the page get enough raw conversions?

3. Does this page directly impact my goals? If indirect, how far away from the primary conversion action is the page?

4. What's the potential impact on your goal, such as for sales or leads?

Answering these four questions before you commit to testing a page accomplishes the following:

>> Qualifies that the page is worth using resources to test.

>> Gives you an idea of whether testing will actually be useful.

By determining which pages aren't worth split testing, you can find the pages that merit testing.

Selecting Page Elements to Optimize

After you find the page you want to optimize and run a split test on, what's your next step? What do you specifically test on that page? You have several factors to consider in determining the features you test on a page.

These elements will help you come up with the new versions, or variants, of your page to enter into the split test experiment. One way to start finding your variants is by using qualitative data, described next.

Considering qualitative data

Qualitative data is information that people can observe but not measure. In terms of digital marketing, qualitative data considers the users' behavior. Gathering qualitative data is relatively easy and inexpensive, and it's extremely helpful for picking the right elements to optimize on your page.

One of the most basic types of qualitative data involves click tracking, mouse movement, and scrolling. Much of this data gets reported in what is referred to as a heat map. A *heat map* is a visual representation of a user interacting on your site; it reveals where users focus on your site. Figure 13-3 shows a typical heat map.

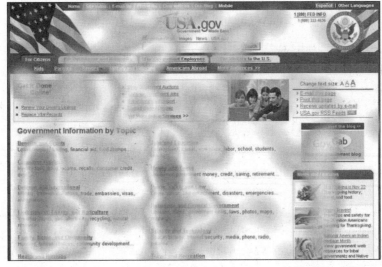

Source: http://webmaxformance.com/attention-scroll-click-heatmap-tracking-services

FIGURE 13-3:
A heat map
shows user
interaction with
your page.

Running a heat map on any page you're split testing is a good idea. Most good testing technology tools, such as Visual Website Optimizer, include heat map technology. Heat and scroll map reports can shed light on whether a call to action (CTA) is getting clicks, or whether people are consuming your content.

Here are other types of qualitative data and how to collect it:

>> **User surveys:** Use a tool such as TruConversion (https://www.truconversion.com/) to survey your site visitors and get qualitative data to analyze.

>> **Session recordings:** Also use TruConversion to record visitor sessions and analyze those recording to find elements to test on the page.

>> **Customer service questions:** Any team members who talk to customers are often a treasure trove of qualitative data.

Using qualitative tools

Qualitative data is incredibly important and severely underused. Some great tools are available, so start with one and move on to others when you run into user knowledge gaps. These tools can include:

>> **TruConversion** (https://www.truconversion.com/)**:** This suite of tools has heat maps, session recordings, user surveys, funnel analysis, and form-field analysis.

>> **Crazy Egg** (https://www.crazyegg.com/)**:** Focuses primarily on heat maps, tracking clicks, mouse movement, and scrolling.

>> **UsabilityHub** (https://usabilityhub.com/)**:** This site has five different styles of user tests:

- Preference test

- Five-second test

- Click test

- Question test

- Navflow test

TIP

UsabilityHub's five-second test, and ones like it, are extremely powerful. The five-second test measures people's first impressions of your site. If people can't figure out who you are and what they're supposed to do on your site within five seconds, you need to rethink your page.

Getting Ready to Test

After you determine what pages to test and select the appropriate variants, you're well on your way to implementing your test. You still have several other elements to keep in mind before you start your test, however. Pay attention to these components, described in the following sections, to create a strong split test.

Developing an optimization hypothesis

Your test needs a hypothesis. For your test to truly be meaningful and actionable, you need to come up with a plan, and you need to document statistics. Testing for the sake of testing or for a particular hunch only wastes your business's time and resources. A clear hypothesis puts a stop to ad hoc testing.

Create a hypothesis based on this format:

Because we observed [A] and feedback [B], we believe that changing [C] for visitors [D] will make [E] happen. We'll know this when we see [F] and obtain [G].

Following a basic hypothesis format like the preceding one sets your test's scope, the segment, and the success criteria. Without a hypothesis, you're guessing, and you don't want to base a campaign's success or failure on a guess.

Choosing the metrics to track

After you choose a page to split test and the variations you will be testing on the page, you need to determine the key performance indicators (KPIs) that you will use to evaluate your split test. KPIs are metrics that gauge crucial factors and help you to determine the success of a test. For instance, if you run a test that looks only at top funnel metrics, such as clicks, you don't get a full understanding of the actual impact. For this reason, you need to select your KPIs and know how they impact your business goals.

To help define your KPIs, make sure to have page-level goals as well as campaign-level goals for all your tests. Your split test goals might look like this:

>> **Page goal:** Leads generated

>> **Campaign goal:** Specific product purchased

Page and campaign goals give you the short view, that is, what happened on the page; and the long view, that is, how what happened on the page impacted your overall campaign. It is possible to see an improvement in the performance at the page level while experiencing a decrease in performance at the campaign level. In our preceding example, we may run a test that generates more leads at the page level but actually decreases the number of products purchased at the campaign level.

TIP

Keep a common thread throughout your KPIs and have them measure related metrics, such as add-to-cart rate and sales.

Calculating your test timeline

Every test needs a definitive stopping point. If you test into perpetuity, you ignore the possibility that no change occurs between variants. You need to create a clearly defined test time period before you start testing, and then stick to that time table.

Use your duration calculator, mentioned in the "Obtaining the tools you need to run split tests" section, earlier in this chapter, and round up to the next week. For example, if your duration calculator says that you would have meaningful results in ten days, run the test for fourteen. People behave differently on different days, and you must account for this variance in behavior. This little trick will help you gather more complete data.

Preparing to Launch

When you have your hypothesis, your variations, your KPIs, and your test schedule outlined, you're almost ready to begin your split test. Complete the following steps to take in preparation for your test and then you'll be ready to click the Start button in your testing tool!

Defining goals in Google Analytics

Just having Google Analytics on your site isn't enough; you need to establish your goals. (See Chapter 12 for how to set up goals in Google Analytics.) Setting custom events or e-commerce tracking works as well — you just need something to measure.

Having a measureable goal is important because when you have proper e-commerce or goal reporting in Google Analytics, the results of your testing are determined by objective numbers rather than subjective opinion. Having goals set up in Google Analytics is incredibly powerful and will start to show you the efficacy of your campaigns in a single platform.

Checking that your page renders correctly in all browsers

If a page isn't performing properly, it will corrupt the data. You may think that the variation you are testing has failed because your hypothesis was incorrect, but in truth, it might be a tech issue. For instance, if one of the pages you are testing is showing a broken image, the conversion lift (or failure) for that page is not caused by the changed variable but rather by the page's functionality, in which case your test will be for naught. Before you launch your test, double-check your page for bugs by using tools such as BrowserStack or preview options in Visual Website Optimizer.

Ensuring that you have no testing conflicts

You don't want your tests to overlap. Therefore, you should never run multiple tests on the same page at the same time; for instance, running a second, separate test on a page while another test is already being performed on the same page results in conflicting data.

You can run tests on different pages at the same time. However, when running tests on different pages at the same time, you need to make sure that traffic included in one test isn't included in the other.

Checking links

Just as you need to ensure that your page is functioning, you also have to make sure that your links actually work *and* go to the right page. A split test between a page with links and a page without properly functioning links is obviously a fatally flawed test that won't give you true results.

Keeping variation load times similar or identical

Keep your load time in mind when you optimize. If you have a variant with a better load time, that variant will likely beat out its competition, skewing your results. Use tools such as PageSpeed (`https://developers.google.com/speed/pagespeed/`) to analyze and ensure that your variant load times are as close as they can be.

Calling a Test

As we state earlier, you don't want a test to run indefinitely. You need to set a testing timeline and stick to it so that you can analyze the data and make informed decisions. Here's when you know you can call your test:

» **Your test timeline matches your schedule:** Make sure to actually run your test for the time you scheduled it for. Do not call a test early because it "looks good" and gives you favorable data. Likewise, don't string out a test longer because you didn't get the results you wanted. When you hit your scheduled end date, call the test.

» **You've "completed the week":** Unless otherwise specified by your test duration calculator, your test should run for a full seven days before calling it. In other words, a test that starts on a Tuesday must end on a future Tuesday to ensure that you've collected the minimum amount of data to make informed decisions.

Knowing How a Test Performed

For some tests, the data may overwhelmingly conclude that the variation you tested was a winner or a dud. But if you have trouble determining how a variation performed, follow these guidelines:

» **Your variation indicates it is successful and you should consider implementing it if**
  - Your lift is statistically significant.
  - You show at least 100 conversions, or more, per variation.

» **Your variation indicates it is a failure and you shouldn't consider implementing it if**
  - Your loss is statistically significant.
  - You show fewer than 100 conversions per variation.

» **Your variation comes out null if**
  - No statistically significant difference emerges.
  - The numbers have normalized.
  - The test ran for the entire test schedule.

Analyzing the Test

By now you either have a successful, a failed, or a null test result. After you've concluded the test, you can dig into the data to analyze what happened during the test period and determine your next steps. To analyze your split-testing data, follow these steps:

1. **Report all your findings.**

   Collect and put your testing data into words. You can use a test report sheet or PowerPoint deck for this. Considering breaking your report into the following sections:

   - **Slide 1:** Test title, URL, timeline, and metric(s) measured
   - **Slide 2:** Hypothesis
   - **Slide 3:** All the variants you tested
   - **Slide 4:** In-depth results
   - **Slide 5:** Results showcasing the winning variant, conversion lift, and confidence rate
   - **Slide 6:** Analysis
   - **Slide 7:** Other observations
   - **Slide 8:** Recommendations

2. **Report your conversion range.**

   The conversion range is the range between the lowest highest possible conversion rate. This range may be written in the form of a formula, as in 30% lift ± 3%, or you might say that you expect conversions to be between 27 and 33 percent. Be sure to report your conversion rate as a range. When you report a 40 percent conversion lift, but you really have a range of 35–43 percent, you're doing yourself a disservice by not properly setting expectations for your results or your recommendations.

   Don't let your boss or client think that the conversion rate is static. It isn't. Set proper expectations by reporting on your conversion rate as a range. Tools such as Visual Website Optimizer create this range for you.

3. **Look at each variant's heat map.**

   Observing each variant's heat map helps you find new things to optimize and test. Place these finding in the "Other Observations" section of your report.

4. **Analyze key segments in Google Analytics.**

   Here, you're determining whether the test indicates a higher or lower conversion rate for certain types of visitors.

5. **Implement the successful variation.**

Ideally, thanks to the results of your split testing, you know what works. Now you can put that knowledge to work. Use your data to make educated decisions about what changes you should make on the page.

6. **If the result of the split test was null, pick your preferred variation.**

At this point, if your test has declared no winner from either variation, you can choose which one you'd like to implement. Use this data to develop a new hypothesis and create a new test.

7. **Use your findings to create new hypotheses and plan future tests.**

Optimization is a process. Your latest findings should feed into your future work. Here is where you can learn from segments, heat maps, or the test proper to develop your next iteration or fuel a test on a new page.

8. **Share your findings.**

At the very least, you should send your report over to your boss or client, and to your colleagues who have a stake in the test. If you want to go above and beyond, you could even publish your findings as your own primary research. Case studies are valuable resources that can establish you as an authority in the market and also generate leads within your market. Turn to Chapters 3, 4, and 6 for more on the value of primary research and how to implement it.

5

The Part of Tens

Find out the ten most common digital marketing mistakes that limit your growth, along with tips to avoid them.

Discover the ten leading digital marketing skills to add to your resume, including job titles, job descriptions, and salary information.

Understand the ten types of tools you need to effectively execute your digital marketing campaigns, from building and hosting a website to using payment processors and managing your social media profiles.

Chapter **14**

The Ten Most Common Digital Marketing Mistakes

D igital marketing evolves rapidly, and you often find yourself trying out new tools and tactics daily. When you're constantly venturing into uncharted territory, you're bound to make mistakes. Don't sweat it; making mistakes is how you learn.

That said, not all mistakes are made equal. The mistakes listed in this chapter are more about your mindset than they are about a tactical error, such as sending out an email without testing the links. You'll inevitably make tactical mistakes in your marketing, and you'll bounce back. But making the mistakes described in this chapter limits your growth, and if you avoid them, you should see a significant positive effect on your results.

Focusing on Eyeballs Instead of Offers

This might shock you, but you don't have a website traffic problem. When you aren't making sales, the solution is not to get more eyeballs on the page. Eyeballs can be bought (as we soon discuss), but the messaging and offers that you deliver to those eyeballs are the biggest difference makers.

When things go wrong, and we mean really wrong, don't spend energy on optimizing the landing page for more Google traffic or scheduling more tweets about the offer. Instead, change what you're offering to meet the desires of your market. First, prove the offer; then, turn the traffic on. For more on crafting stellar offers, turn to Chapter 3.

Failing to Talk about Your Customers (and Their Problems)

People don't care about your product; rather, they care about how your product can make their life better. Stop talking about your product's features and instead describe how your product can transform the customer in a meaningful way.

Business is pretty simple. We get paid to move people from a "Before" state to a desired "After" state. In the Before state, customers are discontent in some way. They might be in pain, bored, frightened, or unhappy for any number of other reasons.

In the After state, life is better. They are free of pain, entertained, or unafraid of what previously plagued them. People don't buy products or services; they buy transformation. In other words, they buy access to the After state. A great offer genuinely moves a customer to a desired After state, and great marketing simply articulates the move from the Before state to the desired After state.

Most businesses that fail, particularly at startup or when entering new markets, do so because they fail to offer a desired After state (the offer is no good) or they fail to articulate the movement from Before to After (the marketing is no good).

Needless to say, getting clear on the desired outcome that your offer delivers is fundamental to the success of your marketing. Turn to Chapter 1 for more on the Before and After states, and see Chapter 3 for the process of creating offers.

Asking Prospects for Too Much, Too Soon

Imagine that a nice, good-looking, successful guy walks into a bar and immediately proposes marriage to the first single woman he sees. Although she may want to get married someday, and from a pure "feature set" perspective he's a good catch, that doesn't mean she's ready to commit to him. And it doesn't mean that she wants to commit to a marriage right now.

This idea seems super obvious when we put it in terms of human relationships, but for some reason, we often "propose marriage" (ask prospects for a major commitment) too early when marketing. Your business might be marketing Business to Consumer (B2C) or Business to Business (B2B), but every business is actually marketing Human to Human (H2H).

As a result, the offers you make to prospects and existing customers should progress in the same way that people develop normal, healthy human relationships. Human relationships go through a process, and the same is true of businesses and their customers. How can you structure the offers you make to prospects and new leads in a way that helps them progress through the relationship?

Being Unwilling to Pay for Traffic

There was a time when search engine optimization (SEO) and social media was easy, and free traffic from the likes of Google and Facebook was reliable and plentiful. Now, however, although search and social media marketing are still important, the days of free-and-easy traffic are over.

Today, reliable and high-quality website traffic is bought and sold like grain or gasoline. If you want a reliable source of gasoline, you go to the gas station and purchase it. Similarly, reliable website traffic is a commodity, and if you want to market at scale, you need to go to the traffic store and buy it. The web has no shortage of traffic stores (Google, Bing, Facebook, Pinterest, YouTube, and more) that are more than willing to sell you high-quality website traffic at a fair price. You can find out more about paid traffic in Chapter 10.

Being Product Centric

When most businesses are marketing, they focus on the product. However, the businesses that last don't define themselves by the product(s) they sell. Instead, they define themselves by the market they serve.

For example, in the 1920s, a French fashion designer and businesswoman published a picture of a simple black dress in *Vogue* magazine. Before this time, wearing black was reserved for periods of mourning. Since its introduction a century ago, however, the "little black dress" has become an enduring wardrobe staple for many women. The French fashion designer who published that picture in *Vogue* was none other than Coco Chanel, founder of the Chanel brand.

Although Chanel has sold many "little black dresses" in its time, the company has not defined itself by even this iconic product. Instead, Chanel sells everything from clothing and jewelry to fragrances and skin care products, all to women with a taste for fine fashion.

A product does not a business make. Identify who you're serving and advocate for that market by creating the products and services your customers want and need.

Tracking the Wrong Metrics

Digital marketing is trackable, almost to a fault. You can, for example, use Google Analytics (a free program) to determine the sales of persons visiting your website from Ohio, on Tuesdays, and when using an iPhone. Although that data might be absolutely relevant to your business, every business should be tracking two overarching metrics: Cost of Acquisition (COA) and Average Customer Value (ACV).

Cost of Acquisition is the amount of money you must spend to acquire a single customer. For example, imagine that you sell men's dress shirts and acquire new customers by using Facebook ads. Say that you determine that it costs $40 in ad spend to acquire each new customer. You've therefore determined that the Cost of Acquisition (COA) for this offer is $40.

Now, for this same shirt offer, you want to calculate the Average Customer Value, or ACV. You can calculate this in a number of ways, but our favorite metric is to calculate the immediate value of a new customer. In the example, each new shirt sale generates $20 in net profit (revenue minus expenses), and, on average, a new customer buys two shirts. So each new customer results in $40 in profit for the business. This is good news because it means that this business can generate new customers with this offer and marketing campaign at a break-even point. Any additional sales made to these newly generated customers result in additional profit for the business.

There is a time and place to dive deep into the numbers, but always remember that the amount it costs to acquire a customer and the average value a new customer brings to the business are the most important metrics to track. For more on data analysis and optimizing campaigns, turn to Chapters 12 and 13.

Building Assets on Other People's Land

Although networks like Facebook, Twitter, and YouTube give you access to billions of people, focusing 100 percent of your attention on creating audiences on these platforms is dangerous. These platforms can, and will, change their rules from time to time, and those changes may not be in your favor.

Instead, focus on building media assets that you own, particularly your email list. You should absolutely build connections on major networks like Facebook, Twitter, and YouTube, of course, but look to migrate those connections to an asset you have more control over. You can find out more about building email campaigns in Chapter 11.

Focusing on Your Content's Quantity Instead of Quality

The truth is that the Internet doesn't need another blog post, podcast, or YouTube video. Much has been written about the amount of content added to the web each day. It is, indeed, a staggering amount. Our social media feeds and email inboxes are crammed with content.

That said, the Internet does lack *remarkable* content, and if you can provide it, you will get traction from it. Instead of creating ten new blog posts over the next month, put ten times the effort into creating a single remarkable post. Then, prime the pump by forcing some eyeballs on your masterpiece by buying traffic to it, as discussed in Chapter 10.

Not Aligning Marketing Goals with Sales Goals

If you own or work for an organization with a sales and marketing department, you know that these two teams don't always see eye to eye. Marketing and sales fight with one another because they have different goals. Marketing thinks it's all about "awareness," whereas sales just cares about . . . well, sales. Marketing gets annoyed at sales for overpromising and under delivering, and sales gets annoyed at marketing because the leads aren't "sales ready" and there aren't enough of them.

The key to fixing this situation is to get marketing and sales on the same page. Literally.

Both departments need to understand that they serve different positions on the same team, and the goal isn't awareness, or sales, but rather happy, successful customers. To achieve this goal, marketing must generate awareness and leads, and sales must close those leads, but if the customer experience isn't amazing, everyone has failed.

Allowing "Shiny Objects" to Distract You

This mistake, more than any other, is responsible for the demise of businesses that market their businesses online. New channels, tools, and tactics spring up on a daily basis in this fast-moving industry, and your best bet is to ignore them. As we mention in Chapter 1, digital marketing is less about the "digital" and more about the "marketing."

Instead of becoming distracted by the new, concentrate on what has always worked. Focus on acquiring new customers with great offers and supporting those acquisition efforts with high-quality content and a sound traffic strategy. Focus on improving your email follow-up (Chapter 11) and the measurement (Chapter 12) and optimization of your campaigns (Chapter 13).

Whatever you do, don't delay. Start putting the fundamentals that you've learned in this book into practice and learn as you go. The beauty of marketing in a digital environment is that almost nothing you do is permanent. Virtually every campaign you create can be changed with a few clicks of the mouse. Let your competition focus on the "next big thing" while you focus on the fundamentals.

Chapter **15**

Ten Trending Digital Marketing Skills to Add to Your Resume

Forged in a world of constant innovation, evolving platforms, and cutting-edge strategies, digital marketing has the unique luxury of endurance in the job market. Maybe you're looking for a new career path that's not in danger of becoming obsolete. Maybe you're already working in digital marketing and wondering how your job will stand the test of time, or what your growth opportunity looks like over your career.

Arguably, careers in digital marketing, more than any other industry, are more concerned with your skill set than your job title. If you have skills (or at the very least, a major drive to learn), you'll never run short of assets to include on your resume. In this chapter, we focus on digital marketing skills and the possible jobs and salaries that go along with them.

Content Marketing

We can trace the origins of content marketing back to 1895, with a magazine published by John Deere called *The Furrow*. It served to educate farmers on how to increase profits, and threw in some nice pictures of the latest in farming machinery for good measure. It's still in publication today, which speaks to the staying power of this particular skill set.

Using content as a digital marketing strategy is a deep well of career development. Not only are skills needed to create and distribute engaging content across a variety of platforms, but that content must be designed to attract a specific target audience and drive people to take a measurable action (like buying a tractor, for example). The digital marketing space hosts a wide variety of content types: blog posts that serve to segment potential audiences; podcasts that educate and create brand awareness; social media updates; infographics; and even e-books that introduce people to your company and offers. It doesn't stop there, either. Content creators also create educational resources, surveys, and webinars that help prospects evaluate their choices. Content creators identify and broadcast customer stories and put together spec sheets that push prospects over the edge and help them decide to purchase.

Now imagine all those different pieces of content working together to guide someone from introduction to sale. These efforts all fall within the realm of content marketing, which amounts to strategically creating stellar resources that turn someone who has never heard of your company or products into a buyer and brand evangelist. If you can grab hold of content marketing as a skill set, you have a growing opportunity to apply yourself in any number of opportunities in the digital marketing space.

Brand journalist

Brand journalists, sometimes referred to as corporate reporters, specialize in producing a variety of multimedia that communicates brand value to a company's customers. Think of it as an in-house news operation — but that news is used as another way to generate leads and sales. For example, brand journalists often look for stories on how customers use a company's products and tell that story in engaging ways to convert leads into buyers.

A few personal attributes are specific to successful brand journalists. They are typically highly strategic in their approach, capitalizing on their ability to align content with the overall content strategy of the company. They must also be able to tell a variety of stories in new and engaging ways across a variety of platforms: blogs, video, podcasts, and the like. Because assignments are often deadline-driven, brand journalists tend to be highly organized. A typical brand journalist salary ranges from $50,000 to $70,000 per year.

Managing editor

Managing editor is another trending career option for the aspiring content marketer. As with brand journalists, managing editors handle the day-to-day storytelling of a company. Although managing editors aren't always the primary source of the content produced, they handle the scheduling, publication, and overall consistency of a company's content marketing efforts. You can often find them hunting down writers for blog posts or securing guests for podcast interviews.

This means that managing editors are highly organized. Projects, people, and deadlines: A managing editor has to juggle all three. Managing editors also need to possess a high degree of adaptability. Sometimes writers miss their deadlines or articles get nixed; a great managing editor has to be able to handle last-minute changes. Content marketers in this position also often deal with other content creators outside the organization, so clearly communicating a company's content goals to outside parties is a necessity. A managing editor can expect to make between $55,000 and $102,000 annually.

Content marketing manager

Content marketing managers serve as leaders of a company's content team and make sure that all of the content assets are in line with the overall marketing strategy. They are responsible for content management, design approval, developing resources, and audience development.

These content marketers are highly creative — they don't just focus on the science of content marketing but also put their creative minds to work in filling content gaps and repurposing successful content to new platforms. As leaders, they head up the company's content team, delegating and prioritizing tasks across multiple roles and positions. Because those tasks typically include a start and end date, experience in project management is also needed to succeed in this role. Content marketing managers typically earn from $72,000 to $133,000 a year.

Media Buying and Traffic Acquisition

Buying traffic is a vital part of a marketing strategy because paid traffic is a reliable and plentiful traffic source for your offers. Pretty important stuff. If you know how to make a business profitable, your skill set is highly desirable. Media buyers, in short, negotiate, purchase, and monitor advertisements, and in the digital marketing space, that means knowing how to generate the most leads and sales at the best possible price.

The skilled media buyer understands that paid traffic is a system that builds relationships before it sells. Familiarity with in-depth marketing research techniques assures that media buyers can place their ads on the right platform for the desired audience. These marketing professionals are also skilled with the following types of advertising: search, display, native, mobile, video, and third-party. They know how and when to use pixels in advertising campaigns and are adept at taking a variety of raw data and turning it into valuable metrics such as Average Customer Value, Cost per Acquisition, and more. Media buyers also know how to design ad campaigns that work in conjunction with a company's content marketing efforts.

Media buying is an important part of any traffic strategy, so companies invest a lot in this area of their business. A successful paid advertising strategy is the key to making the wheels of e-commerce turn.

The job of acquiring media can go by many names, including media buyer or digital media planner, but the job description is the same: develop a paid advertising strategy and successfully implement it across a variety of digital channels. Media buyers plan campaigns from start to finish and handle things like budgets and clients. They constantly look for new and better ways to get the most out of their campaign efforts.

Successful traffic acquisition specialists understand the nuances of changing digital advertising platforms, so they constantly keep up to date on the latest advertising channels and terms of service. Data drives their decisions — data pertaining to budget, ROI (return on investment), CPC (cost per click) and PPC (pay per click) — and a media buyer keeps an eye on them all. There is a definite strategy behind purchasing traffic, and acquisition specialists are intimately familiar with the structure and implementation of ad campaigns that align with specific business goals. Traffic acquisition specialists can expect an annual salary range of $49,000 to $75,000.

Search Marketing

Search engine optimization (SEO) isn't dead, but it has changed. Thanks to Google's Panda and Penguin algorithm updates, the old rules of SEO no longer apply. Today, to get ranked (and stay ranked), site owners need to emphasize user experience over traditional variables such as links and keyword density.

Marketers who specialize in SEO know how to create and implement search marketing campaigns that move the needle for their company. They understand that search should be optimized for mobile use, and they know how to optimize content for a wide variety of search engines, from Google and Bing to YouTube and Google Maps. They embrace the technical side of marketing and employ techniques that stay within the search engines' terms of service to increase return on investment through search strategies.

Your job title in this position might be SEO (sometimes also referred to as SEO Specialist). SEOs are responsible for driving global organic search strategy and improving visibility of web properties, increasing website traffic from target audiences, and driving qualified leads and sales. They know how to get eyes on content from blog posts to podcasts to YouTube videos, using methods that are consistent with the terms of service (TOS) of major search engines such as Google and Bing. They troubleshoot and track site performance, including in the areas of social sharing, page load speed, and other technical issues related to search marketing.

Successful marketers in this role possess a detail-oriented mind that they put to work identifying search traffic growth opportunities for content and products based on analytics. They are also researchers and constantly look into the latest in search engine compliance and guidelines so that they can adjust strategy as necessary. Data drives their decisions; SEOs also monitor and report on search metrics and demonstrate continuous improvement of the SEO strategy. SEOs can expect to make a yearly income between $38,000 and $60,000.

Social Media Marketing

Social media marketing is one of the most in-demand skill sets for organizations seeking to implement digital marketing strategies. Since skyrocketing to popularity in the early 2000s, social media has evolved into an unstoppable force that companies have harnessed to drive brand awareness and website traffic, generate leads and sales, and connect directly with their audience and community. Although social media powerhouses can rise and fall (sorry, Myspace), you'll be hard pressed to find any reasonable person who doesn't think that social media is here to stay, which means that social media marketing strategies are here to stay, too.

Competent social media marketers know the best way to position content, no matter the platform; that is, they know the right piece to put in front of the right audience. They are also typically in charge of curating short lists and using social media channels to network with other industry leaders who can move the needle for the company. As skilled listeners, social media managers route customer needs and pain points to the people who can create relevant content and products that meet those needs. They often create offer awareness, taking care that it doesn't feel intrusive or too much like a hyped sales pitch. Working to create a strong presence on the social web, social media managers dynamically connect with their audience and work to build a tribe around the brand.

Social media marketing is all about listening, networking, influencing, and yes, selling. It's about taking a company's content assets and making sure that the message is accessible, engaging, and translates across different social media channels.

Social media manager is a likely job title in this area, and people who fill this job are data-driven content curators who serve as a voice of the company on sites like Facebook, Twitter, LinkedIn, or wherever else the business has an online presence. They keep channels running smoothly by creating and scheduling content such as photos, videos, and graphics. They measure ROI by likes and follows, reach, engagement, leads gathered, and sales made.

Personal attributes of a great social media manager include an imaginative approach to content. A social media marketer creates a lot of content for multiple platforms, so the ability to adapt the same information to different content types is essential. The ability to write conversationally is equally important. You don't want all your messages to sound like advertising. Social media managers know how to mix it up. Their creative side is balanced by a healthy dose of analytics know-how. Successful social media marketers can look at raw data and calculate their next move. They can expect an annual salary between $30,000 and $76,312.

Community Management

Many companies are embracing community management as a way to make the customer relationship ascend beyond the level of buyer and seller. Online communities are places where people build relationships with each other around a strong common interest — namely, your brand, products, people, or mission. Thanks to the Internet, you can easily locate and connect with others who share similar interests, and community management is a growing skill set to create a healthy environment for those passionate people to connect with each other and facilitate, strengthen, and encourage those relationships.

Community management skills have deep roots in behavioral and social psychology, with emphasis on guiding and influencing group behavior and initiating relationship development. Professionals in this area of digital marketing understand that building community is a long game and return on investment can take months, if not years, of consistent hard work. The name of the game here is relationships — not only between customer and company but also customer and customer. Relationships take time to develop, and they need a safe space to do so. Online communities serve many different purposes, from increasing retention rates to reducing customer support tickets to identifying product and content gaps, but the end result is the same: increased brand loyalty and advocacy, higher customer satisfaction, and a direct line to the experiences of your customers.

A position in this area is community manager, a job that entails bridging the gap between company and customer. Whereas social media marketers work to make the brand attractive and engagement-worthy on various platforms, community managers build and nurture the human relationships hidden in social media communication. Social listening and moderating online "tribes" centered on the company and products are common responsibilities for this position. Community managers excel at advocating on behalf of the customer while also advocating for the brand.

So what personal attributes should you possess to be successful in this position? A community manager's first super power is empathy. The importance of being able to communicate empathy to the brand's community can't be emphasized enough. Social media can also be time consuming, so the community manager must effectively manage time and prioritize tasks. The community manager also needs to establish meaningful connections with community members and various members of the company's internal team to effectively advocate for customers. Community managers bring in $38,000 to $75,000 annually.

Video Marketing and Production

Video marketing is a niche of content marketing strategy, but make no mistake — nothing tells a story quite like a video, and companies know it. That's why video marketing is a specialized skill that will never go out of style, because nothing tells a story quite like *showing* a story. New features like YouTube Cards and Facebook Video make video more engaging and accessible than ever. Understanding the strategies around video marketing is a must for digital marketing efforts.

Video marketers know how to leverage interviews, testimonials, demos, and other storytelling styles to fit the needs of the target audience. They strategically examine available platforms and apps to ensure that the content is on the right channel. In addition, they know how to optimize video for search engines using keyword-enriched descriptions and tags, as well as possess a deep knowledge of video editing, production, and animation that enables them to tell stories in the most engaging way.

Video marketing is one of the most powerful digital marketing strategies that exist, and the technical, analytical, and creative know-how is in demand. Being able to leverage visual storytelling to strengthen emotional connections, engagement levels, and understand how all these aspects fit into a content marketing funnel is a valuable skill that companies actively seek.

Video production specialist

If you seek a job as a video production specialist, you can expect to be positioned on the technical side of video marketing. Production specialists direct, organize, and facilitate a company's video initiatives. Tasks include planning the content, filming, editing, mixing, compressing, and all other aspects of physically preparing the content and getting it out to the masses.

Production specialists must be able to take an idea and turn it into a compelling visual story. They often work under deadlines, so being able to effectively manage projects is a must. Great production specialists are also friendly, because a disarming personality can do wonders for nervous video subjects. Video production specialists tend to earn $49,000 to $73,000.

Video marketing manager

Similar to production specialists, video marketing managers often handle the technical side of content creation, with the added responsibility of communicating the content's unique value to the target audience. They concern themselves with things like publishing frequency, analytics, and determining exactly where the video content falls in the content marketing funnel.

Great video marketing managers are tactical, research oriented, and have knowledge on the cutting edge. They approach video content creation strategically so that they can understand where in the funnel their content will land. Video marketing also relies heavily on thorough research to ensure that the right message lands in front of the right audience. Constant attention to the latest in tools, techniques, platforms, and features ensures that video assets are always displayed the best possible way. Video marketing managers have an annual salary range of $42,000 to $80,000.

Web Design and Development

The website is often the first impression a prospect has of a business. The company website is, increasingly, where that important first impression of a brand occurs. A well-built, professionally designed website can generate leads and sales at a greater rate than a poorly designed website. With the ever-growing number of people accessing the web from mobile devices and tablets, a greater need exists for well-trained professional web designers and developers who understand how mobile technology has impacted web browsing.

Front-end developer

Front-end developers make sure that websites and other owned digital assets work smoothly for the end user. They analyze design elements of websites and recommend technical solutions to theorized project plans. They also analyze code and debug systems when things go south. Simply put, front-end developers create, maintain, and troubleshoot user-facing web pages so that your customers and clients have a great experience with your brand.

Technical prowess is a must for front-end developers. Along with a deep understanding of programming-language editors, front-end developers have to know the ins and outs of HTML, CSS, and JavaScript. Adaptability is also key here; these developers must be able to take on new versions of software and adjust accordingly. Possessing a good sense of project management is also helpful because front-end developers need the capability to implement requests and requirements while meeting schedule and quality goals. Front-end developers can make between $42,000 and $107,000 annually.

Back-end developer

Back-end developers program and maintain the structure of a company website and other digital assets; they are the behind-the-scenes builders of a company's website. These developers coordinate pages, forms, functions, and databases, and make sure that everything is running smoothly.

Back-end developers fluently speak server languages like PHP, Ruby, or Python. They are experts in JavaScript and frameworks such as WordPress or Drupal, and they have a basic knowledge of web server configurations. Because they are often the last link in the project chain, back-end developers must have creative minds and be ready to troubleshoot problems previously unforeseen in development. A back-end developer's salary range falls between $39,000 and $188,000 per year, a wide range to be sure. This range arises from the vast differences in responsibility between the junior level and seasoned back-end developer.

Email Marketing

Email marketing isn't anything new, which speaks to its staying power. Email is still the most profitable method of selling in digital marketing, which means the more skilled the marketer, the more future-proof the career. The skill set of an email marketer includes understanding the strategy behind email automation at each stage of the funnel, as well as knowing the importance of headlines and hooks. Successful email marketers can measure and analyze click-through rates, open rates, conversions, deliverability, engagement, trends, and anomalies. They can coordinate email schedules and campaign assets such as graphics and copy.

Direct-response copywriter

Can you write engaging, persuasive content that gets a reader to take an immediate action? Direct-response copywriters understand the methodology in getting prospects to take immediate action when they read through a marketing email, and they know how to create the irresistible headline that gets the email opened in the first place.

Copywriters possess strong powers of persuasion because email marketing copy is crafted to influence action. Successful copywriters are extremely familiar with their intended audience; they know what makes them tick (and just what to say to make them click). They are also accomplished storytellers and excel at using factual pieces to weave a compelling story. Direct-response copywriters earn between $40,000 and $85,000 a year.

Email marketing analyst

Responsible for email marketing campaigns from start to finish, marketing analysts (sometimes called email marketing specialists) do much of the day-to-day coordinating of campaigns, including promotion schedules, planning and implementation, and troubleshooting any roadblocks that arise along the way.

Email marketing analysts must be organized because they need to be able to manage multiple campaigns. Attention to detail is also a must. A sharp eye when reviewing email content is always appreciated. These analysts also look at lots of numbers and need to make methodical, informed, and data-driven decisions. As an email marketing analyst, you can expect to make between $61,000 and $85,000 per year.

Data Analysis

These marketers specialize in making data-driven decisions. They aren't big fans of making decisions based on hunches. The ability to determine the key metrics that a brand needs to track, as well as collect and analyze them, are part of this indispensable skill set in an industry that makes changes and adjustments based on what the numbers indicate.

Many marketers shy away from data analysis because the numbers can be daunting; so much needs to be reviewed and understood. Analysts specialize in not only diving into the metrics but also knowing what questions to ask in order to interpret the information correctly. They create accurate reports that are easy for employers, stakeholders, and clients to understand. These days, just knowing where to look for numbers isn't enough; you need to know what they mean.

Interpreting data correctly increases your company's ability to scale, gives detailed insights, and ensures that you're not relying on your "best guess."

Data analyst

Data analysts are responsible for aggregating and interpreting a variety of analytics for a company. They research new ways to collect data, analyze the information, and draw conclusions from the data. They identify new sources of data and develop or improve on methods of data collection, analysis, and reporting. Analysis usually involves identifying relationships and behavior patterns that can influence marketing decisions. They primarily work with data and reports generated by programs.

Data analysts are technically skilled with programs like Excel, Access, SharePoint, and SQL databases as well as company-specific data tools like CRMs, Google Analytics, e-commerce platforms, and more. Successful analysts have a keen eye for detail that can tie dips and peaks in metrics to specific events and initiatives of the company. A data analyst earns between $39,000 and $80,000 per year.

Data engineer

Data engineers (sometimes referred to as information engineers) specialize in collecting and analyzing raw data, with the added responsibility of constructing systems to track and display the data. They develop, construct, test, and maintain databases and data processing systems, in many cases applying their own algorithms and predictive models, and filtering information for their analysis. You'll find data engineers working with raw data to find actionable information and working to display that information in a format that is easy to understand.

Sound technical? That's because it is! Data engineers often collaborate with their company's IT team, but skills in scripting languages, creating custom software, and adapting to new technologies are highly desirable attributes for this position. A strong sense of order also serves the data engineer well; data engineers often work with unstructured data sets and unintegrated databases. A data engineer can expect to make between $62,000 and $125,000 annually.

Data scientist

Data scientists specialize in collecting and analyzing data from a variety of sources and data sets, as well as in forming hypotheses. They work to make sure that companies aren't making decisions based on incomplete data, and they identify the relationships and behavior patterns by comparing data sets from different channels.

Data scientists must possess an expert level of data complexity and have a sharp, analytical mind. This position also requires a high level of technical ability because data scientists must be comfortable navigating very large data sets using code. As a data scientist, you can expect an annual salary between $62,000 and $138,000.

Testing and Optimization

Marketers are social scientists. They are masters at trying something, looking at the results, deciding what those results mean, and then making changes as necessary. Savvy digital businesses focus on getting more out of what they already have, a discipline called conversion rate optimization (CRO). This fact explains why specializing in testing and optimization is an upward-trending career path for the industry.

As CRO grows in popularity, a strong need exists for marketers who understand what to test, how to test, and what the best way is to analyze the results. Optimization is the methodology of making websites and landing pages as fully functional and effective as possible, which means optimizing (and re-optimizing). You can see why this is an important skill that companies crave.

Skills in testing and optimization include the ability to research the best and latest in website optimization, as well as to know how to implement multivariate and A/B testing of features on landing pages, websites, and other web assets. Optimization specialists have a deep understanding of the cause-and-effect relationship of website conversions, and they understand what metrics to track at each stage of the marketing funnel. Testing and optimization specialists make sure that web pages convert and that prospects take the call to action. Businesses love it when conversions happen in higher numbers!

Competition is high in the realm of e-commerce, so making sure a website is top-notch is a high priority. One job in this area is that of website optimization specialist, who is responsible for making sure load times are speedy, implementing campaign optimization, and ensuring ease of usability across all of a company's web-based collateral.

Successful specialists have an innate curiosity about why things happen the way they do, and they have a sharp eye to locate the cause behind any number of occurrences in order to provide creative solutions. Optimization specialists also keep their eyes open for new and creative ways to improve conversion rates and increase website usability, so this specialist requires an innovative mind. A mid-level website optimization specialist will earn between $71,000 and $95,000 a year.

Chapter **16**

Ten Essential Tools for Digital Marketing Success

Using the right tool at the right time for the right job can make or break your digital marketing efforts. Because so much of what you do as a digital marketer takes place online and on a computer, you'll suffer no shortage of software and applications to choose from. The glut of tools at your disposal is both a blessing and a curse, however, because the choice can be overwhelming.

At DigitalMarketer, we test a lot of tools. We figure out what works and use them to grow our businesses. In this chapter, we walk you through the ten types of tools you need to run your digital marketing campaigns and, specifically, which tools work for each job.

Building a Website

In the early days of the Internet, you had to custom-code websites from scratch. Today, even the most nontechnical person can create and publish text, images, video, and audio to the web using a *content management system (CMS)*, which is a software application used to manage the digital content and design of your website. The most important choice you make when building your website is what CMS to use.

The best CMSs are

- **Intuitive:** Above all else, the CMS should be easy to use even for the nontechnical person.

- **Search-engine friendly:** The CMS should structure the website in a way that is easy for search engines to access.

- **Mobile friendly:** Your customers and prospects are increasingly accessing the web from mobile devices; your CMS should display your website in a mobile-friendly design.

- **Modular:** Your CMS should be capable of adding functionality, such as an event calendar or social sharing buttons.

- **Multiuser:** Look for a CMS that allows you to add users and control the level of permissions they have to make changes to your website.

- **Secure:** Although there are no security guarantees, your CMS should be as resistant to website hacks and malware as possible.

Following are some CRMs that we recommend.

WordPress.org

www.wordpress.org

This free, open source platform began as a blogging platform and has evolved into a full-blown CMS. It is extremely modular and search-engine friendly, and it allows for multiple users with various levels of permissions. The difference between WordPress.com and WordPress.org is that WordPress.org is a self-hosted platform, whereas WordPress.com is hosted on WordPress' servers. As a business owner, you want to use the self-hosted WordPress.org CMS so that you have complete ownership of your website. If you're looking for a low budget, flexible CMS, WordPress.org is a great choice.

Shopify

www.shopify.com

Whether you're selling physical products completely online or you're a brick-and-mortar retailer looking to sell your wares online, Shopify is worth your consideration. Shopify handles the design and layout of your store, but it also manages payments, shipping, inventory, and more.

Hosting a Website

A *web host* is a business that stores your website files and makes your website accessible on the Internet. Although you can set up a web server to deliver your website yourself, most companies want to use a web hosting company.

The best web hosts have the following characteristics:

>> **Significant uptime:** If your website goes offline, it costs you money. Your web host should have 99 percent uptime or greater.

>> **Support:** Look for a host that provides 24/7 customer support, both over the phone and with live chat.

>> **Speed:** Your customers and prospects expect your website to load quickly, and people will bounce if it takes too long. Your website host is a major factor in your page load speed.

>> **Security:** The last thing you want to deal with as a business owner or marketer is a hacked website. Your host should take the security of your website as seriously as you do.

>> **Redundancy:** Look for a host that backs up your website daily so that you don't have to worry about losing everything you've worked so hard to build.

We recommend the following website hosts.

WP Engine

wpengine.com

If you choose to use WordPress as your CMS, WP Engine is a great choice as your web host. This company is known for exceptional uptime, lightning-fast page load speeds, and unprecedented security.

Rackspace

www.rackspace.com

No matter what you're looking to deliver on the web, chances are Rackspace can handle it. Rackspace is a company with an excellent reputation in the industry and a long track record of quality.

Choosing Email Marketing Software

As we explain earlier in this book (see Chapter 11), email marketing is critical to the success of most digital marketing campaigns. Hundreds of email marketing tools are available to choose from, but a few stand out in the crowd.

The best email applications have the following characteristics:

» **Deliverability:** If your email never reaches prospects' Inbox, nothing else matters. Look for an email service provider with a sterling reputation so that your email avoids the Spam folder.

» **Automation:** If you want your email marketing to be working even when you're sleeping or on vacation, look for an email service provider with the capability to build automated email campaigns that are triggered by a customer or prospect's behavior.

» **Reporting:** You want to monitor the open and click rates on your emails, among other things. Look for an email service provider with a full reporting suite.

» **Mobile friendliness:** More and more of your email is being consumed from the small screen. Your email service provider should be able to deliver readable email to phones and devices.

Here are some email service providers that we recommend.

Maropost

www.maropost.com

Maropost provides enterprise-level email marketing software with the capability to handle complex email automation campaigns and advanced email segmentation.

AWeber

www.aweber.com

Despite its low cost, AWeber has a sterling reputation for deliverability, and the software integrates seamlessly with other popular tools like WordPress. If your budget is tight, AWeber is an outstanding choice.

Klaviyo

www.klaviyo.com

Klaviyo offers solid email marketing software for businesses that sell physical products. The software integrates with your shopping cart, payment platform, customer relationship management (CRM), and more.

Considering Customer Relationship Management (CRM) Software

As your business grows, you will likely need to add customer relationship management (CRM) software. In some cases, your CRM will replace your email software, but a CRM is much more than an email service provider. It can, in fact, be difficult to pin down the exact role of a CRM because that role varies widely from solution to solution. That said, all CRMs are designed to manage the relationships with your customers and prospects, as well as the data associated with that relationship.

The best CRMs have the following characteristics:

>> **Centralized data:** Do your homework on the CRMs you're considering and make sure that the software collects the data you need for your specific situation, and in a central location.

>> **Support and training:** The more features that come with your CRM, the more training and support you'll need. Choose a company that is known for its support and training.

>> **Reporting:** You gain power from collecting data about your customers and prospects only if you to make good decisions based on that data. Your CRM should have a robust and intuitive reporting suite.

Our recommended CRMs follow.

Infusionsoft

www.infusionsoft.com

With this CRM, you have the capability to manage products, record customers' and prospects' data, process payments, send emails, and more all from one system.

Salesforce

www.salesforce.com

Salesforce is a cloud-based CRM that offers solutions for every business, from small to enterprise level. Salesforce is known for its robust integration with thousands of applications, from QuickBooks to Evernote.

Adding a Payment Solution

The payment processor is arguably your most important tool because, well, it's how you process payments. The payment processor handles transactions from various channels, with the most critical ones being credit and debit cards.

The best payment processors are

>> **Secure:** Anyone involved with processing credit card information must comply with the security standards of the credit card industry. Make sure your payment processor takes payment card industry (PCI) compliance seriously.

>> **Intuitive:** Look for a payment processor that allows you to do things like set up order forms or integrate with your invoicing software.

>> **Capable of recurrent billing:** If you need to be able to accept recurring payments from your customers, make sure that your payment process can handle that type of billing.

We encourage you to try the following payment processors.

Stripe

`stripe.com`

Offering dependable, easy-to-configure payment processing with a rich feature set, Stripe handles recurrent billing and integrates with applications such as WordPress, Shopify, and FreshBooks.

Square

`squareup.com`

If you want customers to be able to swipe credit or debit cards in your store or on the go, consider Square. The Square app turns your smartphone or tablet into a credit card processing machine.

Using Landing Page Software

Landing page software tools contain templates to build effective landing pages, and some even come with split testing capabilities built right in. Turn to Chapter 7 for more on landing pages, and find out more about optimizing and split testing in Chapter 13.

The best landing-page software is

- » **Intuitive:** It sets up pages quickly.

- » **Responsive to mobile:** Your landing page must be mobile friendly or you risk losing opt-ins from mobile devices.

- » **Integrative:** Landing pages are designed to gather leads and offer products and services for sale. Look for a landing page software that automatically transfers new leads to your email software and works seamlessly with your payment processor.

Consider the following landing page builders.

Instapage

instapage.com

Instapage lets you build beautiful landing pages without touching a single line of code. It integrates with other tools such as AWeber (an email service provider), Infusionsoft and Salesforce (CRMs), GoToWebinar (a webinar delivery platform), and more.

Unbounce

unbounce.com

A more technical landing page tool with clean code, beautiful templates, and the capability to run A/B split tests from within the platform. Unbounce is definitely worth a shot if you love great design.

Sourcing and Editing Images

The web seems to become more visual with each passing day. With the rise of social platforms like Pinterest and Instagram, even text-based platforms like Twitter are embracing the power of the image. As a digital marketer, you'll likely find yourself needing to create images for everything from a Facebook ad to an email promotion. The gold standard of image-creation applications is Adobe Photoshop, and if you have the skill and inclination, you should absolutely use Photoshop. That said, you can choose from among a number of low-cost and easy-to-use applications for producing beautiful images that meet most marketer's needs.

The best image-creation applications are

>> **Cloud based:** Look for an image-editing software that you can easily access online.

>> **Intuitive:** For lightweight image editing, you want an application with a simple and easy-to-use interface.

>> **Low cost:** Images are critical to your digital marketing campaigns, but the tools you use to create them don't have to bust your budget.

Following are image-editing tools that we recommend.

Canva

www.canva.com

Canva is a cloud-based drag-and-drop design application that comes with millions of images, layouts, icons, shapes, and fonts to choose from.

SnagIt

www.techsmith.com/snagit.html

Capture any type of image on your computer screen and use SnagIt's dynamic editor to crop, resize, add callouts and text, and much more.

Pixlr Express

pixlr.com/express/

This application enables you to open an image and make changes to it by rotating, cropping, or resizing it in the cloud-based editor. Add effects, overlays, stickers, and more with this free image editor.

Managing Social Media

Thousands of applications allow you to monitor and publish to the social web. Prices vary based on the size of your organization and the features you need, but plenty of low-cost options for managing your social media presence without the big price tag are available.

The best social media applications are

>> **Cloud-based:** Look for a social media marketing application that lets you manage your social media from any device, including your mobile phone.

>> **Multiuser:** Most social media marketing campaigns require participation from more than one person in the business. Look for applications that allow you to easily add team members to your account.

>> **Reporting:** Social media channels such as Twitter and Facebook have their own reporting and analytics, but the right social media application adds more insight into what's working and what's not.

We recommend the following social media tools.

Hootsuite Pro

hootsuite.com

The best cloud-based, low-cost application for managing Twitter is Hootsuite. This tool also manages Facebook and LinkedIn, but you'll find it most useful for organizing your Twitter activity. You can use the free version, but Hootsuite Pro adds solid reporting and the capability to easily append UTM (urchin tracking module) parameters to links. (You can find out more about UTMs in Chapter 12.)

Edgar

meetedgar.com

Using the Edgar application, you can publish status updates to Facebook and Twitter automatically. Edgar breathes new life into your best content by consistently sharing it on autopilot.

Mention

mention.com

Find conversations about your brands, people, competitors, and more with this reasonably priced social-listening and reputation-management application.

Measuring Your Performance: Data and Analytics

Plenty of vendors claim to have the application that can end all your data and analytics problems. Luckily, most of the best tools have free solutions made available by Google. These tools are easy to use and provide the level of functionality that meets the needs of most businesses. (For more on analyzing your data, turn to Chapter 12.)

The best data tools are

>> **Easy to use:** The right report at the right time can make all the difference to your business. Look for analytics and data solutions that allow you to find what you need in an intuitive interface.

>> **Free:** Larger enterprises likely need to shell out big dollars for an analytics solution, but most businesses can get by with low- or no-cost solutions like Google Analytics.

>> **Robust:** Choose an analytics application that contains a wide range of available data. Although you may not use it all today, the data is being captured and will be available if you need it.

Try the following data analytics applications.

Google Analytics

www.google.com/analytics/

As described in Chapter 12, Google Analytics tracks and reports website traffic. We've tried the more expensive analytics solutions, and we keep coming back to good old Google Analytics.

Google Data Studio

datastudio.google.com/

Use this application to create stunningly beautiful and informative, interactive reports and graphs that you can share with others. Pull data from sources like Google Analytics, Google AdWords, and Google Docs.

Google Tag Manager

www.google.com/analytics/tag-manager/

Update website tags and add scripts to your website even if you aren't a code monkey. Google Tag Manager has a bit of a learning curve, but after you get the hang of it, you'll wonder how you ever lived without it.

Optimizing Your Marketing

There are some impressive tools on the market that will help you get more leads, sales, and engagement out of the traffic you already have. Most of these tools are reasonably priced and offer a free trial, so you can give them a whirl before putting any skin in the game. (For more on optimizing your marketing campaigns, turn to Chapter 13.)

The best optimizing applications are

>> **Supported:** Conversion optimization tools can be a bit intimidating. Look for a tool with a great reputation for support and plenty of training documentation that will help you get up and running.

>> **Multipurpose:** You want a tool that handles a number of different optimization activities, from recording visitor behavior to surveying to split testing.

The optimization applications that we recommend follow.

Visual Website Optimizer

vwo.com/

For intuitive set up and configuration of split and multivariate website tests we recommend Visual Website Optimizer. Its point-and-click interface and support documentation make it easy to get started testing.

TruConversion

truconversion.com

TruConversion is a multipurpose optimization tool that offers heat maps, session recordings, user surveys, and more in a single tool.

Index

customer service
  handling issues, 180–181
  questions, for qualitative data, 273
customer showcase post, 118–119
customers
  acquiring new, 26
  activating new, 26
  campaigns that generate new, 30–32
  converting prospects to, 157
  monetizing existing, 26
  onboarding with new, 26
  repeat, 55
  stories of, for bottom of funnel (BOFU)
    content marketing, 71
customizing content, 76

D

DadsDivorce.com, 67
data
  demographic, 259, 260–262
  psychographic, 259, 262–266
  in sales letters, 139
  types of, 259
data analysis
  about, 247
  Google Analytics report suites, 248–249
  segmenting your audience, 256–266
  sources of traffic, 249–250
  tracking origins of site visitors,
    250–253
  trending skills in, 298–300
  using, 266
  UTM parameters, 253–255
data analyst, 298
data engineer, 298
data points, monitoring, 85–87
data scientist, 298–299
debatable post, 117

deep-discount EPOs
  about, 38, 50
  checklist for, 53–54
  discovering your, 55
  "little victories," 53
  selling software, 52
  in social selling, 193
  splintering services, 52
  using a book, 51
  using a webinar, 51
  using physical premiums, 50–51
definition post, 107–108
deliverability, of emails, 241–243
delivering on your promise, in blog posts,
  101–102
demographic data, 9, 12–13, 259, 260–262
demonstrations, in sales letters, 139
demos, for bottom of funnel (BOFU) content
  marketing, 70–71
designing
  evaluating design in landing pages, 146
  gated offers, 40–50
  ungated offers, 39–40
developing brand advocates, as a stage in
  the customer journey, 22
device, as demographic data, 262
digital magazines/books, for top of funnel
  (TOFU) content marketing, 67
digital marketing, 25. *See also specific topics*
DigitalMarketer
  community, 20
  customer avatar for (website), 14
  customer journey road map (website), 23
  landing page for, 133
  promotional asset sheet, 224, 225
  "6 Trending Digital Marketing Skills to Put
    on a Resume" blog post, 76
  on traffic temperature, 196–198
  UTM, 252

Q

qualitative data, optimizing, 273–274

quality media, in blog posts, 99–100

Quality Score (Google), 201

quantity option, on product detail page, 134

question post, 118

questions

in emails, 240, 241

to prospects, 285

Quicken, 168

quizzes, generating leads with, 47

quote post, 110

R

Rackspace, 303

Radian6, 176, 179

rant post, 115

reaction post, 117

Real Time Suite (Google Analytics), 248

recurring billing, 58

reengagement campaigns, 233–234

referrals, as a source of traffic, 249

regulations, on social networking, 192

relational emails, 221–222

relevance

of blog posts, 99

of emails, 239

Remember icon, 3

repeat customer, 55

reports, free, generating leads with, 44

reputation, monitoring, 242

research

primary, 44, 67, 169–170

as a reason for purchases, 236

in sales letters, 139

research post, 106

resource list, generating leads with, 46

retargeting, 75. *See also* ad retargeting

retention, 161–162

return on investment (ROI). *See* optimizing

Return Path, 243

review post, 113

review sites, optimizing for, 166–167

reviews

gaining, 166–167

increasing, 164–165

on product detail page, 143–144

soliciting, 165

risk reversal, in sales letters, 141

robbierichards.com, 125

ROFU (top of funnel) content marketing, 65–68

ROI (return on investment). *See* optimizing

Rosetta Stone, 184

S

sales, building, 164

sales goals, *versus* marketing goals, 288

sales letters

on sales pages, 132–133, 135–141

writing, 135–141

sales material, generating leads with, 45

sales pages, 130, 132–144

Salesforce, 123, 306

SAQ post, 106

satire post, 111

satisfying searchers, 155–156

Save-A-Lot, 174, 175

scarcity headline, for blog posts, 94

scarcity subject lines, for emails, 237

scheduling content, 187–188

seamless, as a feature of marketing campaigns, 27–28

search engine, as a key player in search marketing, 148–149

search engine optimization (SEO), 100–101

search engine robots, optimizing for, 167–168

search marketing

about, 147

capturing leads through, 79

traffic temperature, 196–198

transactional emails, 221–222

TransferWise, 17

transitions, in blog posts, 98

trend post, 113

triggered emails, 223

TripAdvisor, 166

troubleshooting paid traffic campaigns, 215–218

TruConversion, 273, 274, 311

trust icons, evaluating in landing pages, 146

TurboTax, 71

12-Month Promotional Planning Worksheet (website), 225–226

Twitter

about, 173, 179

broadcasting content on, 186

building social media connections on, 18, 19

traffic platform, 203–204, 213

used by content creators, 89

U

ultimate guide post, 107

Unbounce, 269, 307

ungated content, for top of funnel (TOFU) content marketing, 66

ungated offer EPOs

about, 38

designing, 39–40

in social selling, 193

unsubscriptions, 222, 243

updates, to this book, 3

upsell offers, 56–57, 134

Upwork (website), 201

Urchin Tracking Module (UTM), 250–253

urgency headline, for blog posts, 94, 140–141

URL shorteners, 187

URLs

creating UTM parameters for, 253

errors with websites, 168

optimizing, 159

UsabilityHub, 274

useful content blog posts, 104–108

useful resources, for middle of funnel (MOFU) content marketing, 69

UTM parameters, 250–253

V

value. *See also* values and goals

lead with, 38

offering in advance, 38–39

providing, 192

you provide, 14–16

"value first" offers, 192–193

values and goals

of blog posts, 99

campaign, 275

as a component of customer avatar, 9, 11

defining in Google Analytics, 276

of digital marketing strategy, 26–27

marketing *versus* sales, 288

page, 275

vehicle, choosing for content marketing, 78

video marketing manager, 296

video marketing/production, trending skills in, 295–296

video podcasts

as blog posts, 120

for top of funnel (TOFU) content marketing, 67

video production specialist, 295–296

videos

in emails, 240, 241

on product detail page, 133

vidIQ (website), 161

About the Authors

Ryan Deiss (pronounced "Dice") is cofounder and CEO of DigitalMarketer.com, the leading provider of digital marketing training and certifications to small and mid-sized businesses. Ryan is also the founder and host of the Traffic & Conversion Summit, the largest digital marketing conversion conference in North America, and the creator of the "Customer Value Optimization" methodology.

Ryan's online business endeavors began at age 19, when he launched his first website from his freshman dorm room so that he could make some extra money to buy an engagement ring for his college sweetheart. It worked! Not only did the girl say "Yes," but this one, little website ballooned into more than 500 sites, and a hobby had grown into a real business.

Today, his digital media and e-commerce group, NativeCommerce.com, owns and operates hundreds of properties including DIYReady.com, MakeupTutorials.com, DIYProjects.com, SurvivalLife.com, and Sewing.com (just to name a few), and according to *Shark Tank* star Daymond John, "His companies practically own the Internet." He is also a bestselling author, and is considered one of the most dynamic speakers on modern digital marketing today.

Most important, Ryan is a proud dad of four wonderful kids, Jonathan, Joyce, Ruth, and Timothy, and husband to Emily . . . the girl who said "Yes" and inspired it all.

Russ Henneberry is the Editorial Director for DigitalMarketer. Prior to joining DigitalMarketer, Russ was on the content marketing team for Salesforce.com; he also helped to launch a blog for a well-known marketing SaaS, growing it from zero to 120,000 unique visitors per month in less than a year.

Russ got his start in search engine optimization and pay-per-click marketing, managing 20 developers and over 600 digital marketing projects for small to mid-sized businesses. It was at Salesforce that Russ began to master the art of content marketing at all stages of the sales and marketing funnel to create value for a company.

In his time at DigitalMarketer, front-end traffic to DigitalMarketer content has increased by 1,125 percent. The content marketing team, under Russ's management, generates thousands of leads and front-end sales per month by developing and executing a truly "full funnel" content marketing strategy. Connect with Russ on Twitter: @RussHenneberry.

Russ lives in St. Louis, Missouri, with his wonderful wife Sarah, his two amazing children, Thomas and Mary Grace, and an extremely enthusiastic dog named Buck.

Dedication

From Ryan: First, to the amazing team at DigitalMarketer. Thank you for letting me take credit for all your great ideas. This is truly your book. And also to Emily: Thank you for being my inspiration, both then and now.

From Russ: To my amazing wife, Sarah, who has always unquestionably loved, supported, and believed in me.

Acknowledgments

We are deeply grateful first and foremost to the entire DigitalMarketer team. This book is an aggregation of the incredible talent and expertise of Richard Lindner, Molly Pittman, Justin Rondeau, John Grimshaw, Lindsay Marder, Suzi Nelson, and Ezra Firestone. The graphics and images that help to illustrate the information in this book are the work of the very talented Britney Arkin and Taylor Nelson.

And to our editor, Susan Christophersen, for ensuring clarity in this book and sculpting the rough edges of our writing into something even the most persnickety composition teacher would be proud of.

Last, but certainly not least, to Matt Douglas, whose sheer will and determination brought this project across the finish line. This book simply would not exist without you.

Publisher's Acknowledgments

Acquisitions Editor: Amy Fandrei

Project Manager: Susan Christophersen

Copy Editors: Susan Christophersen,
Kathy Simpson

Technical Editor: Michelle Krasniak

Editorial Assistant: Serena Novosel

Sr. Editorial Assistant: Cherie Case

Production Editor: Siddique Shaik

Cover Image: Courtesy of Ryan Deiss

le & Mac

For Dummies,
Edition
1-118-72306-7

ne For Dummies,
Edition
1-118-69083-3

s All-in-One
Dummies, 4th Edition
1-118-82210-4

Mavericks
Dummies
1-118-69188-5

gging & Social Media

book For Dummies,
Edition
1-118-63312-0

al Media Engagement
Dummies
1-118-53019-1

dPress For Dummies,
Edition
1-118-79161-5

iness

k Investing
Dummies, 4th Edition
1-118-37678-2

sting For Dummies,
Edition
0-470-90545-6

Personal Finance
For Dummies, 7th Edition
978-1-118-11785-9

QuickBooks 2014
For Dummies
978-1-118-72005-9

Small Business Marketing
Kit For Dummies,
3rd Edition
978-1-118-31183-7

Careers

Job Interviews
For Dummies, 4th Edition
978-1-118-11290-8

Job Searching with Social
Media For Dummies,
2nd Edition
978-1-118-67856-5

Personal Branding
For Dummies
978-1-118-11792-7

Resumes For Dummies,
6th Edition
978-0-470-87361-8

Starting an Etsy Business
For Dummies, 2nd Edition
978-1-118-59024-9

Diet & Nutrition

Belly Fat Diet For Dummies
978-1-118-34585-6

Mediterranean Diet
For Dummies
978-1-118-71525-3

Nutrition For Dummies,
5th Edition
978-0-470-93231-5

Digital Photography

Digital SLR Photography
All-in-One For Dummies,
2nd Edition
978-1-118-59082-9

Digital SLR Video &
Filmmaking For Dummies
978-1-118-36598-4

Photoshop Elements 12
For Dummies
978-1-118-72714-0

Gardening

Herb Gardening
For Dummies, 2nd Edition
978-0-470-61778-6

Gardening with Free-Range
Chickens For Dummies
978-1-118-54754-0

Health

Boosting Your Immunity
For Dummies
978-1-118-40200-9

Diabetes For Dummies,
4th Edition
978-1-118-29447-5

Living Paleo For Dummies
978-1-118-29405-5

Big Data

Big Data For Dummies
978-1-118-50422-2

Data Visualization
For Dummies
978-1-118-50289-1

Hadoop For Dummies
978-1-118-60755-8

Language &
Foreign Language

500 Spanish Verbs
For Dummies
978-1-118-02382-2

English Grammar
For Dummies, 2nd Edition
978-0-470-54664-2

French All-in-One
For Dummies
978-1-118-22815-9

German Essentials
For Dummies
978-1-118-18422-6

Italian For Dummies,
2nd Edition
978-1-118-00465-4

Available in print and e-book formats.

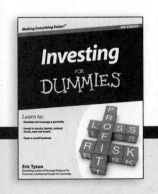

Available wherever books are sold. **For more information or to order direct visit www.dummies.com**

Math & Science

Algebra I For Dummies,
2nd Edition
978-0-470-55964-2

Anatomy and Physiology
For Dummies, 2nd Edition
978-0-470-92326-9

Astronomy For Dummies,
3rd Edition
978-1-118-37697-3

Biology For Dummies,
2nd Edition
978-0-470-59875-7

Chemistry For Dummies,
2nd Edition
978-1-118-00730-3

1001 Algebra II Practice
Problems For Dummies
978-1-118-44662-1

Microsoft Office

Excel 2013 For Dummies
978-1-118-51012-4

Office 2013 All-in-One
For Dummies
978-1-118-51636-2

PowerPoint 2013
For Dummies
978-1-118-50253-2

Word 2013 For Dummies
978-1-118-49123-2

Music

Blues Harmonica
For Dummies
978-1-118-25269-7

Guitar For Dummies,
3rd Edition
978-1-118-11554-1

iPod & iTunes
For Dummies, 10th Edition
978-1-118-50864-0

Programming

Beginning Programming
with C For Dummies
978-1-118-73763-7

Excel VBA Programming
For Dummies, 3rd Edition
978-1-118-49037-2

Java For Dummies,
6th Edition
978-1-118-40780-6

Religion & Inspiration

The Bible For Dummies
978-0-7645-5296-0

Buddhism For Dummies,
2nd Edition
978-1-118-02379-2

Catholicism For Dummies,
2nd Edition
978-1-118-07778-8

Self-Help & Relationships

Beating Sugar Addiction
For Dummies
978-1-118-54645-1

Meditation For Dummies,
3rd Edition
978-1-118-29144-3

Seniors

Laptops For Seniors
For Dummies, 3rd Edition
978-1-118-71105-7

Computers For Seniors
For Dummies, 3rd Edition
978-1-118-11553-4

iPad For Seniors
For Dummies, 6th Edition
978-1-118-72826-0

Social Security
For Dummies
978-1-118-20573-0

Smartphones & Tablets

Android Phones
For Dummies, 2nd Edition
978-1-118-72030-1

Nexus Tablets
For Dummies
978-1-118-77243-0

Samsung Galaxy S 4
For Dummies
978-1-118-64222-1

Samsung Galaxy Tabs
For Dummies
978-1-118-77294-2

Test Prep

ACT For Dummies,
5th Edition
978-1-118-01259-8

ASVAB For Dummies,
3rd Edition
978-0-470-63760-9

GRE For Dummies,
7th Edition
978-0-470-88921-3

Officer Candidate Tests
For Dummies
978-0-470-59876-4

Physician's Assistant Ex
For Dummies
978-1-118-11556-5

Series 7 Exam For Dum
978-0-470-09932-2

Windows 8

Windows 8.1 All-in-One
For Dummies
978-1-118-82087-2

Windows 8.1 For Dumm
978-1-118-82121-3

Windows 8.1 For Dumm
Book + DVD Bundle
978-1-118-82107-7

   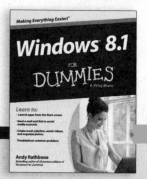

e **Available in print and e-book formats.**

Take Dummies with you everywhere you go!

Whether you are excited about e-books, want more from the web, must have your mobile apps, or are swept up in social media, Dummies makes everything easier.

For Dummies is the global leader in the reference category and one of the most trusted and highly regarded brands in the world. No longer just focused on books, customers now have access to the For Dummies content they need in the format they want. Let us help you develop a solution that will fit your brand and help you connect with your customers.

Advertising & Sponsorships

Connect with an engaged audience on a powerful multimedia site, and position your message alongside expert how-to content.

Targeted ads • Video • Email marketing • Microsites • Sweepstakes sponsorship

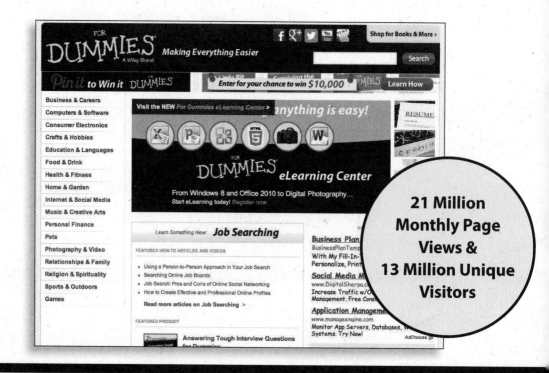

Custom Publishing

Reach a global audience in any language by creating a solution that will differentiate you from competitors, amplify your message, and encourage customers to make a buying decision.

Apps • Books • eBooks • Video • Audio • Webinars

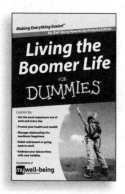

Brand Licensing & Content

Leverage the strength of the world's most popular reference brand to reach new audiences and channels of distribution.

For more information, visit www.Dummies.com/biz